THE HEART ASKS PLEASURE FIRST

KARUNA EZARA PARIKH

PICADOR INDIA

First published 2020 by Picador India
First published in paperback 2022 by Picador India
an imprint of Pan Macmillan Publishing India Private Limited
707 Kailash Building
26 K. G. Marg, New Delhi 110001
www.panmacmillan.co.in

Pan Macmillan, The Smithson, 6 Briset Street, London EC1M 5NR
Associated companies throughout the world
www.panmacmillan.com

ISBN 978-93-90742-82-0

3 5 7 9 8 6 4 2

Typeset in Aldine401 BT by R. Ajith Kumar, New Delhi
Printed and bound in India by Replika Press Pvt. Ltd.

Praise for *The Heart Asks Pleasure First*

LONGLISTED FOR THE AUTHER DEBUT AWARD
AND THE PFC–VOW AWARD FOR CREATIVE WRITING IN ENGLISH

'A remarkable debut, bravely tackling grand questions of history, love, loyalty and faith'

– Ranjana Sengupta, *Hindu*

'Poignant and riveting ... Parikh's writing also contains an element of the fantastical, a revelling in the possibilities of fiction that gives us a dirge layered with pain and ecstasy, and a memorable reminder of how life is made of deep, enduring human connections, asking painfully pertinent questions of politics, identity and the nature of love'

– Piya Srinivasan, *India Today*

'Prose that melts the heart and a plotline that tugs at every string of it'

– Shraddha Kamdar, *Femina*

'Love, longing, grit and grief flavour this fable ... fascinating'

– Priya Chadha, *Tribune*

'A moving debut ... evocative'

– *Times of India*

'A luminous, hypnotic novel, as much about the beauty of language as it is about the struggles of life'

– Ann Patchett, author of *The Dutch House* and *Bel Canto*

'A tender, elegant exploration of what it means to love as the world devolves into division and chaos. A wonderful debut'

– Prayaag Akbar, author of *Leila*

'*The Heart Asks Pleasure First* is about love across generations and boundaries, and friendships in the most unexpected places, about the many shades of faith, the danger and freedom of both belonging and unbelonging. With this wise and tender novel, Karuna Ezara Parikh will break, and heal, your own heart'

– Nilanjana Roy, author of *Wildings* and *The Hundred Names of Darkness*

'Enthralling and affecting, *The Heart Asks Pleasure First* blends folklore and facts, politics and poetry to create an intoxicating and immersive exploration of love and faith, of the forces that shape our world and relationships. This is prose that roams through the body and widens the senses. I will return to this book again and again as a talisman for dissenting hearts'

– Lisa Ray, author of *Close to the Bone*

'Evocative and transporting. Parikh is a poet and it shows ... This [book] is a fable for our time'

– Avni Doshi, author of *Burnt Sugar*

'Karuna Ezara Parikh's craft is first and foremost that of a poet, a gift she brings to prose through nimble, acrobatic, enchanting language … Poignant and powerful, her debut novel blurs the boundaries of landscape and love; with tenderness, it sews up a subcontinent divided … it left me mesmerized'

– Aanchal Malhotra, author of *Remnants of a Separation*

THE HEART ASKS PLEASURE FIRST

Karuna Ezara Parikh is a poet and writer, former television anchor and model known widely for her activism. Her writing has featured in publications including *Vogue*, *Wire*, *Outlook*, *Tehelka* and *Lonely Planet*. In 2015 she co-founded the sustainable company The Burlap People in Calcutta, where she lives with her husband and their dog. *The Heart Asks Pleasure First* is her first book, which was followed by a collection of poems, *Where Stories Gather*.

For my parents Kalpana and Rajen.
Thank you for the wings.

Prelude

There is a streetlamp outside the window and it glows amber, setting the room alight. It catches the hazel in one of his eyes every time the curtain flutters just enough to let the light touch half his face and she is newly convinced each time this happens that he has only one brown eye and the other is jet black. The curtain always rises towards the east, because the wind is blowing in from the west, but she cannot feel it, and she thinks of the rising curtain as heralding something new, like all things rising in the east do.

She faces him now and crossing her arms over her hips, holds the two ends of her T-shirt. It is grey and soft and he is acutely aware of the sound of the moths beating their wings just outside the open window at the streetlamp, as if the energy produced by their flapping is what keeps it burning. He is aware of the heaviness of his breath and the anxious whine of a police car siren in the distance.

Would they be caught? he wonders.

Then she turns to him and in one swift move her T-shirt is off and in her hands, held out like an offering, like surrender. The cloth has caught around her wrists and cuffed her. Her body is the colour of earth and she is moving towards him and he is tumbling towards a dream and, as the world settles into slumber, Aaftab is awakened for the first time in his life. He is aware of every single part of himself and he can feel and know each part individually all of a sudden. He is aware of how he is being betrayed by his body in pieces and how he no longer has any control over the sum of these parts, as his being is working out long division for the first time. He knows the only solution to regaining himself is to put his pieces back together again – the way his mother used to collect the champa flowers from below the tree in their garden back home in Pakistan, and until all the champa were not collected off the ground and placed in a bowl with water, she would not be at peace – and he knows in the warmth of this night, as he watches her nipples harden in a dash of icy moonlight, as he tumbles towards her mouth, as his broken parts collide first with one another and then with her, that Daya is that peace.

She is a bowl of water and he is nothing but fallen flowers waiting to be gathered, thirsting.

ACT ONE

1

Daya was born in a round house. Every room in this house was circular, like a cluster of lighthouses, one half of each room's circumference containing curved glass windows and the other side a slim rosewood door in a wall like a crescent moon. There were five rooms and each of these rosewood doors opened into one large central room, so that when viewed from above, the house looked like a child's version of a flower. At one point between two of the petals there was a pattern break for the front door, out of which led the driveway, like a stalk.

The roof of this double-storeyed building was tiled in white marble, and each day at noon you could see a woman in yellow emerge onto it. She would begin slowly to hang clothes up to dry on seemingly invisible strings. Viewed from a vantage point way up on some imaginary bough, she appeared to be a hummingbird, darting around a white flower. This woman was Kamla. She owned two sets of clothing and they were both yellow.

Her favourite part of the day was when at dusk the marble began to cool beneath her feet, and she would bring up the baby along with the radio and two wooden puppets from

Rajasthan that hung in the little girl's room above the crib which was in the shape of a flying horse, and white like one too. (Everyone knew only white horses could fly, Kamla most of all.) She would sit the child down and place the radio next to her. She would turn the knob slowly, and when the crackling gave way to the crispness of a radio station she would experience the same satisfaction she did when she managed to extract a stray strand of food from between two teeth, frown transforming into a smile. An ease would wash over her being and as the sun began to break and soften, she would hum along to the tunes of the stars, words slowly breaking loose until she was singing to the child. Then from behind the hanging bed sheets and towels, saris and trousers, she would begin to dance, bringing out the puppets in an elaborate show for her audience of one, on her flower-shaped stage under the setting sun.

Daya was born on a pale day in February. She had slipped silently into the world at 2 p.m. when the sky was wearing that shade of blue no one else can match. Her birth had no oddities save one. It was a soundless delivery. She came into this world so quiet it felt as if she arrived keeping secrets. She didn't cry at the universal misery of being born, and for the first three years of her life she made no sound other than the even intake and matching exhale of breath. No doctor could change this and her parents accepted with great love their future with a daughter the world might find a bit peculiar but they found absolutely perfect.

On her third birthday, it rained at 5 p.m. The downpour brought the guests rushing in from the garden to the living room where people milled around, ignoring the pale imprints of mud that appeared here and there on the floor. Shivering ladies sought shelter, chiffon saris clinging to their lovely bodies, their wrists inside single bracelets and glass bangles, their hair damp. The gentlemen stood at an open window smoking, and there were ayahs holding babies. The waiters from the catering company were called indoors and they hung about with nothing to do, awkwardly avoiding eye contact, boxy white uniforms soggy on their skinny shoulders. Eventually they were tipped and asked to depart. Standing at the long curved living room window, Daya's father Gyan could see them emerge from the front door on the ground floor, laughing, kicking puddles and lighting beedis. He saw them take out the notes he had just handed them and knew from their joy that he had over-tipped but he didn't care, happy as always being the benevolent fool. He blew cigarette smoke out the window, tuning out of the painful conversation of the men he was surrounded by. They were speaking of the state of the nation and whether the Prime Minister was the cause of it or whether she was doing everything she possibly could at the time to fix things. She would be dead by the end of the year and different things would matter and so many things would cease to matter.

He watched as rain gathered in evenly spaced drops beneath a leaf on the amaltas tree opposite the window, and how after some time, the weight of the drops caused them all to slide off the underbelly of the leaf and it would spring up a millimetre or two before the process began again. He wished the men who had collected around him like plump raindrops, rolling shoulders for space, would slide away, letting him spring upwards in respite.

'Want one?' A woman in a green sari as sheer as sea foam offered him a plate piled high with cucumber sandwiches. He declined and looked across to where his daughter was seated. She had been placed and forgotten upon an armchair covered in pale silk upholstery, block-printed with the orange silhouette of a tulip. In this garden of plush flowers sat Daya, entirely in white lace. She looked like a tiny, delicate French cream cake. The room rose to different volumes, snatches of conversation catching on Gyan's ear like thorns on his sweater when he walked down narrow, beloved paths in the hills, each one trying to hold him back for a moment until he could free himself. He saw Daya as if in a dream suddenly straighten her tiny dimpled legs and place them on the ground before her. He wanted to move towards her but something stopped him and he stood now in the centre of the circular living room, watching as his daughter slid off the armchair and her feet in their rubber-soled shoes made contact with the floor. She waited there for a moment, arms out daintily, like a girl on a tightrope, then extended her right hand towards the table before her, on which sat a black brick-shaped boom box. She pressed a button. Miraculously out of the speakers blurted the opening to Billy Joel's 'Uptown Girl'.

The room had begun to stop, and in the watching crowd's stillness her father finally felt like he could move, and he did, swiftly, towards her. He knelt before her and watched as she smiled and began stomping her small feet to the rhythm of the music. But most importantly – and the reason the room and Gyan's entire world had paused – Daya had opened her mouth and was forming words. On her third birthday, a blue Wednesday, Daya did what birds do – she bypassed speech for song. In the rosewood frame of the kitchen door, a kindred yellow bird smiled hardest of all.

~

When he heard Daya would arrive in February, Gyan had counted Joyce, Sarojini Naidu, Victor Hugo, Anthony Burgess, Steinbeck, Jibanananda Das, Bertolt Brecht, Marlowe, Anais Nin, Boris Pasternak, Auden, Meena Alexander and Leela Majumdar, Langston Hughes, his favourite Dickens, and his wife's beloved Faiz, as having been born in the same month. He had always found February the perfect month for poetry. 'It's less depressing than November but not as ridiculous as March!' he would say with his usual gusto. Though his hope for Daya to write was high, she wouldn't pen a single line, reading them instead by the thousands as she grew older. Into her room were installed shelves that ran in rows along the curved wall opposite the curved window, making the cocoon of a room one-half window and one-half shelves. They contained by the time she left for college approximately 2,400 books of which 2,181 were marked with her name, implying she had read them cover to cover.

Every few years, spurred on by his daughter's love of books, Gyan would begin to write a novel. Sometimes this passion lasted a few weeks, but mostly days into the project, business beckoned with its forceful crooked finger and he would file haphazardly the papers all scribbled and scrawled upon and forget once more his dream at his teak desk. He would always begin in utmost earnestness at that desk in the western part of the transporting studio on the ground floor of their house where he and Asha had created a haven for savoury pursuits of the soul. They called it Vaikuntha. They had there, for example, the best music system their money could buy, and had chosen deliberately not to place it in the living room upstairs where they entertained, but instead on the ground floor where either of them could come and play music while resting upon the impossibly sized mattress that lay at the centre. It was twenty feet by twenty feet, a huge custom-ordered fluffy white square which Daya's father had paid for with his dignity, the man at the mattress store staring him down as one would only a pervert. Indeed, the perversion of the music lover. Of the lover. It had all been Asha's idea of course and after the ordeal at the store, Gyan had insisted she deal with the mattress makers when they came. 'Alright then,' she had huffed robustly, disappointed by how brittle he seemed in that moment. He had never met a mattress maker before. Four of them arrived carrying foam and stuffing, spools and spools of thread and white cloth. Asha charmed them with chai and chatter, by the end of the day presenting Gyan with a mattress like an island, in the middle of their ocean of love.

On this floor of the house, there were no walls save the outline of the house. There were no doors save the front door. As a result, if you sliced off everything above this level of the house, you would find yourself looking down no longer on a flower with clearly marked petals, but instead a cloud, with five curved edges. Though she rarely went into that space, Daya had been conceived on that mattress – a cloud within a cloud.

~

When she was five, Daya was enrolled into a dance class. She went three times a week, after school, to an imposing old Soviet building in Delhi, a Russian 'cultural centre' offering chess and ballet lessons to children of the city. Daya and her best friend Milni were the only two Indian girls in a class full of expatriates. As they began the painful process of learning the language of dance, they also found themselves falling for it. French words, Russian technique. They fell in love with the music of *The Nutcracker* and the promise of tutus and the magnificence of a girl leaping across a stage into a lover's arms as if both were made of feather. Dance defined Daya. Long before she groped to create an identity for herself, dance became a part of her being, absorbed as a young girl by a life of discipline under the watchful gaze of her Russian teacher. She branched out to learning Bharatnatyam, which was offered for free at her school. She checked Astaire biographies out of the library. She listened like no twelve-year-old before her to Tchaikovsky and she did all of this with Milni, who was always by her side.

When they were thirteen, dance became something different. It became a way to indiscipline. The first time they went to a party, Daya had taken a beetroot from her kitchen and they had cut it open and watched its violent plum liquid pool out onto the chopping board. Then they had taken half a beet each and rubbed the gingery root onto their lips and their cheekbones, which had just recently emerged. They danced the entire night like the floor was on fire and their bodies were weightless. They had tumbled into Milni's bed later having learnt something new about dance. Milni's mother never understood why the girls' dresses came back from the laundry that week with what appeared to be carrot stubs in the pockets, and stains all over that weren't blood but looked like a massacre.

When Daya was fourteen she was asked to leave Milni in India and travel alone to Moscow for a three-week summer school dance programme for 'gifted dancers of other ethnicities'. The trip was planned for months and then took place just weeks after the Chechens took hostage 1,700 people in a hospital and her father wasn't happy. It was Asha who said, 'But she's not Russian,' and sent her off with sweaters that were useless in July. When she returned with her first pair of pointe shoes, Daya knew what she wanted. She wanted to keep dancing. Broken-hearted at not having been the one selected, Milni informed her in a letter left at Daya's school desk on her lavender 'My Little Pony' letter paper from when her father had visited Canada, that she would no longer be attending the dance classes after school. It was the last letter Milni ever wrote on those papers with the tiny rainbow in the corner. As she licked shut the envelope edged in glitter, Milni sealed into it alongside her farewell to dance, her childhood, too.

At seventeen Daya left for university – The Markova School of Dance, Cardiff, Wales, on the recommendation of her dance teacher – who had said she knew the Dean and would 'have a chat' which she did – so off Daya went, her aura a pale rosebud pink. She was curious and she was budding. '*Ladki khil gayi hai.*' The girl has blossomed. And so the nectar must travel, for a flower's purpose was never to simply please the eye.

Asha began to cry as Daya walked through the gate at the airport. 'Don't, Ma,' she said, because she could not feel pain. She could not feel anything in that moment but pure joy. But

Asha cried because she knew this child would not come home. A human would return but it would not smell the same as the one that had once emerged from her. The one she had made like clay from a riverbed into this magnificent adult creature with words and ideas of its own. She would not see *this human* again. All mothers know, the ones that return are changelings, and the universe keeps the actual children who leave, for itself.

2

Aaftab was standing by the library entrance watching the rain outside. He had no umbrella or raincoat and he couldn't understand how the Welsh weather went from one extreme to another sometimes in a matter of minutes. He hoped the clouds would clear soon. He was hungry and tired, and he hadn't looked at the book in his hand in over twenty minutes.

~

Behind each person's head just beneath their skull is a tiny dip where that last curved bone ends and the spine begins. In some parts of the world it was believed for a long time that when a person was born, this was the point through which the soul was placed in the body, after which it was stitched up and the seam to this pocket hidden beneath the hairline. It was never opened again until after a person died when the skull could be cracked for definite reincarnation. Otherwise the eye sockets, nostrils and mouth acted as convenient exit points. If you looked at the base of Aaftab's skull, you would find a scar two inches wide from when his father once beat his head so hard against a wall, a part of his soul had escaped.

Aaftab was born in Islamabad, the eldest of five siblings for whom he was made an example every single day. He had amber in his eyes and skin so smooth it sometimes felt to his father as if it asked to be scarred. His mother would line his lower lashes with kohl to ward off the evil eye and years later when he told Daya this as an adult, she said, 'What use was it? You tempt the good – how was evil to bypass you?' That was before the lines between good and evil erased themselves before their eyes. She also told him the word 'alcohol' came from 'kohl'. 'See. Intoxicating. Not the opposite.'

He was born with limbs that kept stretching out until he grew so tall his father could no longer hit his face with ease. He continued even then to play badminton with his siblings, hide-and-seek with the little ones, to roll their trousers up before he took them out to the garden.

At eighteen Aaftab had to admit to himself the truth – that he did not like his parents. He did not like that his father, so respected in this country where respect meant everything, could not find in his heart anything to love. He did not like that his mother who could shout such harsh words at her children, could not even whisper the wisdoms he wanted so much to believe she somewhere felt. He became, in his disappointment, unforgiving of them, and when he left Islamabad for university, to go study law in the foreign town his uncle had long ago settled in, he did it with gladness that he would no longer share their home. He had folded all six feet of himself into an airplane seat and when it had risen to the skies he had not prayed the way his mother had asked him to. Instead he had wished on the stars for things she would never know, and when he landed in that foreign land and unfolded his legs, he found he was three inches taller.

In Wales he lived, limbs all tangled, for the first few years in a hostel room the size of a walnut shell and then later in a two-bedroom house where the second room's resident kept changing until finally there was Wasim. It was a house across the road from a mosque. The mosque was the only reason Aaftab had been allowed to live there at all. His father had asked why he couldn't just stay with his uncle, Enayat taaya as Aaftab called him (he loved how it sounded when he said it fast – enayataya enayataya), the family success story who'd left Mirpur for Karachi, then caught a boat to Britain in the sixties, getting work as an engine room stoker. The fumes there followed by decades at a textile factory left his lungs weakened for the rest of his life, but in the eighties he'd bought his first house. Now he owned six and rented them out mainly to Muslim students in that town that seemed to billow around a university. Though Aaftab's father had moved to Islamabad and slowly become the big lawyer people had said he would, everyone, including himself, remained in awe of Enayat's achievements. 'Stay with him, you'll learn so much,' Aaftab was told. But he mentioned the proximity of the mosque, and his father relented.

Outside the tall windows of this house, on the curlicues of the streetlamp the white boys who played rugby in the park and walked that way home broke every time it was fixed, each night Aaftab could see a white owl come sit. The first time he saw it, it took his breath away. When it spread its wings to fly, he witnessed its true magnificence. He told Wasim about it one night as he crushed weed to roll into a joint. 'I know,' Wasim said. That's when he told Aaftab there were two of these birds. 'She has a mate, a grey fellow. He's larger – watch for him.'

~

London had arrived fast. Daya collected her bruised luggage from the rubber belt. Everything felt unfamiliar and she'd been aroused by it. Every pore on the surface of her skin felt open, yearning for this new air, this adventure she was pushed up against. She had climbed into a coach and watched from a drizzle-flecked window the London suburbia melt into Welsh countryside. The rows of houses became sparser until she saw a single cottage every few minutes.

She had not known exactly what Goth was. Never met someone who called themselves a hippie. She didn't quite understand yet where Ouagadougou was. Had never said out loud the word 'Scandinavia'. And yet, it was with ease that she adapted to her emancipation. To Cardiff, the small Welsh city full of Victorian and Edwardian arcades inside which were shops with cut-glass windows displaying everything from taxidermy bears to broken china mended with liquid gold. Even the name sounded strange like coal with a glint of diamond. Cardiff. Caerdydd. 'Ka-err-deed,' she mouthed, and wandered around its castle almost a thousand years old.

She moved into a house that was three storeys high, painted vanilla and placed behind a large oak tree. The way people grew trees next to houses, this house had been grown near the tree. It was planted as a sapling of a house in 1948 on a plot of land that had been chosen precisely because of and for this tree, a large oak which had been born of a family of trees in nearby Roath Park. Like the rebel of the family, the tree had jumped the prescribed twenty-foot distance all the other trees had maintained in a straight line from each other and made a diagonal swoop forty feet across the road from the park where it mothered and sheltered many years later the house that Daya came to live in.

The landlady Mrs Coombes once told Daya her husband had served in India, and she still called it 'that land of wonder'. She had in storage a piece of silk he had brought back for her, as strong as it was soft and fine. He had told her it contained in it all the colours of the peacock's tail. On checking, Daya informed her it was true. 'Have you ever seen one?' she asked and Daya told her how back home in India, hiding her house from the street was a row of eucalyptus trees, and how at dusk each day these trees reverberated with the cries of peacocks, a sound so sad it caused the sun to turn away from the earth. At a certain time of the year, just below the trees you could find whole feathers, up to three feet long, the colour and texture of Madras silk.

'Do you know the story of why the peacocks cry?' she would once ask Aaftab later, much later, almost when it was too late, their bodies twilit, facing each other like new leaves. He would shake his head. 'When God was handing out qualities to the animals all those years ago, they stood in line, transparent new souls, waiting to be filled in. The hippopotamus was meted out a handful from the bag of might and the cheetah was so proud to be given the largest share of stealth. The hummingbird took speed and both the elephant and the ant were granted size. The peacocks grew impatient because God had already invented the potential for the alphabet and had therefore asked them to appear in that order. Standing in front of the puma and behind the partridge, the peacocks decided to sneak behind God's great throne and steal all they could from the first open bag. This happened to be the Bag of Beauty. As they were making off with their bounty, God caught them and in his thunderous rage turned their feet so small they would forever be running. Then he made their wings so heavy they would never be able to fly long distances. Lastly, for such a large bird he chose the mouth of a sparrow so that it would never be able to eat to its heart's content. Thus the peacock, most beautiful amongst creatures, is destined to cry each evening.' And that was the sound of dusk in Daya's home, as if a reminder that beauty is the deepest trap, the shallowest bag.

For Mrs Coombes, India, *all of it*, was contained in four metres of peacock-toned silk. The India of her imagination was intact in this rippling length of cloth. And it's true the country could be compressed into such wonders. Into a certain shocking shade of pink that appears in only three places in the world – the bougainvillea of north India in the first week of spring, the powdered colour used on Holi in the second week of spring and the dresses of the sisters of the bride in red. You could see all the magnificence of what was once India in a square inch of a carpet from Kashmir. In the blanket-like perfection of a naan – soft inside, crisp on the periphery, flavoured with the buttery memory of childhood's winters.

The entire country could be held in a tiny piece of jewellery containing nine stones not always in this order – ruby, pearl, emerald, diamond, blue and yellow sapphire, red coral, hessonite and cat's eye, representing respectively – the sun, the moon, Mercury, Venus, Saturn and Jupiter, Mars and the ascending and descending lunar nodes. A piece of jewellery that combines these nine stones, with the ruby like the sun, always in the centre, can be used to balance a person's karmic energy but also to remind one of different aspirations – the other nine jewels or navratnas. Almost as old as the idea of karmic history were the courts of India, where the emperor chose nine extraordinary souls, gems of humans – nav ratans – to confer with and aid governance. The nine ministers of court were well versed in their fields, their actions nobler than noble, their stories living on.

Most famous of these enneads of the gifted were Mughal Emperor Akbar's chosen nine. Amongst them was the legendary Birbal, who spawned a hundred tales, told in classrooms and to grandchildren even today. Birbal was born a Hindu in a land ruled by a Muslim emperor. Ironically (and perhaps intelligently, for the vast majority of the population was still Hindu), he would become Akbar's unofficial chief religious advisor. Of the nine jewels of the Emperor's court, four were Hindu.

Birbal acted as Foreign Minister.

Raja Todar Mal was Minister of Finance.

Raja Man Singh served as Chief of the Mughal Empire's Army.

And the Cultural Minister was of course Tansen – creator of Hindustani music.

Hindustan. The Land of the River Indus.

India was all this. Here at this distance, from windswept Wales, Daya was beginning to see the layers and layers that had woven themselves together to create the fabric of her country. She could see now, they sometimes created something vibrant – a rainbow of deeply saturated colours, where violet was aubergine, and orange not just orange but saffron, say it – *zafran* – and red crimson, yellow was mustard, and blue … blue was indigo and indigo was ink, but sometimes the layers of colour were like a child's palette – if you didn't know how to mix them, they produced nothing but mud. Daya was for the first time viewing the world she came from as art, as a critic.

Like this she lived and dreamed and dissected in the attic of a house by a Welsh oak tree. A metal fire escape painted green exited the heavy foliage of ivy leaves that covered the back of the house, and next to it, a once-red ladder leaned perpetually against the wall, ending just beneath Daya's window. It gave anyone passing by the appearance that a thief had just made their way in, or a teenager their way out. From each step of the fire escape Mrs Coombes had hung on thin wires a different animal. A small plastic frog, a whale that had once been part of a key chain, a wooden bird once painted orange now washed clean of all colour and as naked as the day it was carved. A butterfly with moving wings. A mouse made of old coins. The animals weren't in proportion to each other, so the effect was that of a mad little safari making its way through a forest of ivy. And above it all Daya, legs dangling, some peculiar creature unto herself.

3

In her first month at university Daya saw an advertisement taped to the library window, requesting applicants. It was minimum wage, but it required limited interaction and she had heard working there meant they removed the limit on the number of books one could borrow at a time. At the job interview the head librarian had asked her a single question.

'What are you reading?'

'Chaucer.'

'Which one?'

'*Canterbury Tales*.'

'For the first time? How are you enjoying it?'

'For the fourth time. And not as much as the first time but definitely more than the last time!'

She had an email the next day saying:

> Can you start tomorrow at 9 a.m.?
> PS: The 14th time was my favourite.

The library was the oldest surviving building at the university, and remained 200 years later, miraculously and relatively undamaged. Other buildings had been ruined and rebuilt over time, but they could never find the space in which to house the books, in order to renovate, and the task seemed so daunting, each successive administration had respected the wisdom of the last, and left the library as it was.

From the start Daya loved the wooden floors, the tall central Greco-Roman-style pillars, going the entire thirty-six feet up. She loved that the building was essentially one huge box full of books, the expanse of wooden floor and then the endless space above filled with nothing but whispers. You could climb sets of steps along the walls that led you up to two different levels of balconies that simply ringed the inside of the building. You could walk the entire circumference with arms outstretched, hands touching books along one side and running along the balcony railing on the other. If you looked down you saw students strolling between shelves, sitting at desks, daydreaming and searching for the truth.

Daya loved that since the windows of the building had long been boarded up by the backs of bookshelves, all the natural light entered through the ceiling, which was a collage of painted skylights. At different times of the day the sun shone through different bits of skylight, causing patterns of stained glass to appear here and there as soft bits of rainbow, sometimes across an open notebook, at other times between two faces dipped in conversation so that someone watching from a distance might think they were in fact conversing through prisms. Daya had learnt quickly to tell the time by observing where the rainbows appeared. By the water cooler meant 9 a.m., by the bust of Churchill meant noon. It was 4 p.m. if they appeared by the books on semantics, and when they disappeared from the history of textiles, sundown. As the seasons shifted, so did the shadows. Only two things threw her. Rainy days and daylight saving.

She loved that there were seven private study alcoves on each side of the length of the library and on one side they were named after empires. Byzantine, Ottoman, Achaemenid, Macedonian, Mughal, Mongol, Roman. She wondered who had made the tactful decision to leave out the British Empire. On the other side of the library, almost as if in apology, the seven alcoves were named after British monarchs. William the Conqueror, Llywelyn the Great, Henry V, Henry VIII, Elizabeth I, James I, Victoria. Daya noticed that 'I'm sitting in the Queen Victoria alcove' did not sound as remarkable as 'Come find me in the Byzantine Empire'.

She loved that the building did not have wall-to-wall carpeting, instead boasting a grid of carpets and kilims from Afghanistan and Turkey, the gift of a student from Istanbul, who had once studied at the university. She loved that to reach the books on the higher shelves you had to climb wooden ladders that rolled around the periphery of the room. She loved most of all that on some days the head librarian would play, almost imperceptibly, Beethoven in the background, so soft it was simply the ghost of a tune, and no one was ever certain where it was coming from, but everyone was affected by the cinematic backdrop it lent the day and began unknowingly to move to match its rhythm.

~

The corridors of the dance school were long and straight like Miss Anna's spine. She was Russian, maybe fifty-something, maybe sixty-something – they couldn't really tell because she was timeless and therefore ageless, always in red like a Soviet flag. She filled in them dread and awe and adoration all at once. No one had ever called her beautiful and yet, she was undeniably ethereal. It felt like she would outlive them all. She terrified Daya at first, so it was with a great measure of bravery that Daya, a week into dancing under her, had stopped mid-pirouette and said, 'Miss Anna, it's Daya.' Anna, the only professor whose name they prefixed in those halls of educated equality that dashed titles and doctorates casually away, looked at her blankly. 'It's just … you keep saying Day-ah,' she continued timidly. 'It's Duh-ya.' Anna looked away like she had not heard her at all, clapped her hands twice and said, 'Fifty double tours, each side now, right and left!' but she never again mispronounced the word.

'Welcome!'Anna had bellowed on the first day from the front of the hall. Her English was accented and took Daya immediately back to her first day of ballet when she was five and had come home and asked Asha why the teacher sounded funny. 'Look around you,' Anna began. 'There are two hundred of you here today. You should know, by the day you graduate there will be less than fifty in this room.' It was true. The Markova School of Dance named after Prima Ballerina Alicia Markova who in 1960 famously played Radha to legendary Indian classical dancer Ram Gopal's Krishna, was rigorous and mean and those who did not manage to weather their way to blossoming beneath Professor Anna's death stare withered or perished each season. 'Dance is as old as the earth,' Anna said. She was immaculate with her dark hair pulled back into a severe bun, her mouth a line parallel to the floor. 'Everything dances! Wind and fire and water and soil.

How are you going to make dance different? How will you make it new? Tell me, how will you make it fresh for me and for yourself? In the next three years, I want only one thing, I want you to reinvent dance for me.'

Daya listened, eyes wide and mouth parted as if to sip on Anna's spirit which filled rooms the moment she walked into them. Daya who knew that she had perhaps not earned a spot at the school but been gifted it, thanks to her teacher putting in a call. Daya, who in India had been able to make rooms pause for her by using dance alone, knew from the start that she would have to work twice, thrice, ten times as hard in a country where so little paused for the likes of her. And she did. Daya had not had the same training as many of the students around her, and hadn't developed the arches required for the dance form. Her feet weren't flat, but she had been told repeatedy by her teacher growing up, how they were still too 'straight' and that she would have to work to create the curve. Daya worked till her body yielded and her bones bent. She worked harder than anyone else, long before they began and late after they all went home to bed.

She would practise in the park after the studios closed for the night, breaking the misty air into spirals, slicing it into shapes, cutting whole sections of the sky with her feet, sweeping past the moon in a jump. Early on she had tried practising her pointe work there but the ground, damp with dew and soft from earthworms at work, strained her ankles till she succumbed and saved that most difficult part for the studio's wooden floors. She would enter the park at sundown, walking there straight from the library or the dance school, past the pubs full of boisterous undergrads, she'd wander deep under spilling boughs and down tendrilled paths. Roath

Park was a hundred and thirty acres wide, dividing itself into a hundred acres of land and thirty acres of lake. Within it Daya felt entirely, arousingly alive. Alone and fearless in the night she would dance till the cold wind felt like summer breeze and the moonlight turned the grass into a stage. In those moments she was a gasp bound in muscle. She existed like water, perfect, but with the potential for ice and the threat of vapour.

~

Daya had been away from home two long years when she met him. She was sitting in the sunshine on a bench in Roath Park reading, when she noticed a boy on the bench next to her. He hadn't seen her. She was intrigued by the fact that he was wearing from head to toe a complete Pathani suit, like the ones worn in northernmost India. The baggy trousers fell in graceful folds around his legs, the long tunic spread across his thighs, falling over his knees like they were the rocky edge of a waterfall and his clothes a wide stream. He had his sleeves rolled up and on his head he wore a neat crochet skull cap, very white against his dark hair and almond skin. He was reading with concentration. He looked up and she thought he had seen her but she couldn't be certain. Then she saw he had simply raised his head to listen to the sound of the birds above him, and she relaxed. He reached into the pocket of his tunic and pulled out a pen to scribble something on the inside of the book's back cover, then sat back and once again began reading.

Inexplicably, Daya found she wanted to know what the last page of his book now said, the story forever altered by this peaceful boy just sitting under a tree on a park bench.

She stood and walked up to him and when she was standing right in front of him blocking the soft spring light from his page in a sudden eclipse, she said, ‘Hello.’ He glanced at her and blinked a few times. Somewhere the leaves on the trees in the east rustled.

‘Hello.’

‘I’m sorry, but can I ask what you wrote in that book?’ He closed it and she saw it was *Anna Karenina*.

Aaftab’s eyes began to adjust to the light, taking in the silhouette of the girl in front of him. She had short hair, a mop, some of it was in her eyes, and she was dressed in a pair of shorts that ended at her knees, a shirt one size too large and a deep moss green cable-knit men’s cardigan. He turned to the last page and handed her the book.

~

When Daya was born, her parents took the decision not to impose any single religion on their daughter and their home. It was not though a godless space but one with many gods, with every god. They celebrated both Diwali and Christmas, they had above their front door a carved wooden Jesus, and to the side of the entrance sat a Ganesha from Mamallapuram. The chubby Ganesha sat upon an elegant stone lotus – the flower a feat of the sculptor – which, because of its upward-curving petals, also served as a bowl in which Daya’s mother Asha, floated real lotuses torn from a nearby water body in which only buffaloes and their keepers – stray village boys – swam, both sets of bodies glistening in the noon sun. Initially, Asha had not wanted to buy the statue because Ganesha’s mount, his mouse Mushak, hadn’t been carved into the masterpiece. 'I just wish he was there – it would be complete, you know?' she had said to Gyan but he had convinced her of its superior sculpting, pointing out cleverly the naughty smile on the elephant god's face.

When they brought it home and set it beside their front door, Asha had said a small prayer, through which she had asked for Daya. After the prayer she had garlanded the statue with the jasmine she usually ribboned her hair with, and placed sweetmeats by the god's feet. The next day they were gone. For six days she continued to leave sweets at his feet. Each day they disappeared, leaving her bewildered. On the seventh day she opened the door to rush down to Vaikuntha where she could hear her husband calling her name for something, and that's when she saw it – a tiny brown mouse, no larger than her palm, sitting in the statue's lap, nibbling at the mithai he held firm in his tiny pronged paws. It was the first of many wishes the Elephant God would fulfil.

They had hanging on one wall of their living room a huge stretch of textile the colour of earth on which, painted in exquisite calligraphy, were two lines by Faiz.

Kahan hai manzil-e-rah-e-tammana hum bhi dekhenge,
Ye shab hum-par bhi guzregi ye farda hum bhi dekhenge:
Thahr, ai dil, jamal-e-ruh-e-zeba, hum bhi dekhenge.

There was no accompanying translation, but Asha would translate slowly if anyone asked.

'Where is the promised heaven at the end of this road of longing?

I too wish to see it.

This long night will pass me by too,

This promised tomorrow, I too will see it.

Wait, my heart, we too shall witness the soul's true beauty someday ...'

Faiz had died soon after Daya was born, and knowing her mother's deep love for his poems, friends had sent her the artwork. Ever since, Asha had begun to learn Urdu, so that she could read his poems in the original language, that language India had mostly lost at Partition when it was hidden in people's mouths and carried on trains across a border so young it didn't quite yet know where it stood. Daya could still recall her parents drinking with friends and Gyan raising a glass to the Faiz poem, speaking louder than usual, intoxicated, saying, 'But our souls ... must always be Sufi!' His friends would all knock back their drinks, eyes squeezed shut in response to the strength of the imported liqueur one of them had bought in black, and Asha would say, 'He's not Sufi, jaan!' Gyan would kiss her and say, 'His soul was!' And she would laugh and shout 'Remember! God is not religion! THIS is religion!' and put on some Rolling Stones or Kishore Kumar and they would all clap and begin to dance.

Irreverent Asha who one sunny day in a car had said to Gyan thoughtfully, 'Who invented the first luggage belt, you know, for airports?' He looked confused. 'And who invented the first hand-dryer? Or toaster? See, you don't know. But you would agree that they were all lazy people, right?' He laughed, 'Or maybe they were geniuses. At the very least they were efficient buggers.' Asha pushed her rose-tinted sunglasses up her nose, 'See, that's what I'm saying. Who invented religion? It must have been a lazy person. Or as you put it ... an efficient genius.'

For a long time, Daya hadn't understood what religion was. She knew who God was but she had so many images for him. For her. She understood the pantheon, and that Jesus belonged to Christianity and Allah to Islam, but she hadn't quite grasped the differences. In her house, they had never spoken of those differences, believing fiercely that you don't make the distinction. *We are all the same.* But wasn't it true that everyone was different? It was an argument her parents would have at times. You can teach children the purest fact of life, that everyone is the same. Humans eventually. Or, do you teach them that despite being different you must *treat* everyone the same because we are eventually the same? Bones, muscle, souls, blood, shame, hate, joy. In the first case, was a child not going to grow up and eventually be surprised by the differences she had never been shown? It was a fine line, and Daya had never understood it. Never understood she was one of the children who had been taught the simplicity of sameness, without the complications of difference. And because she had never identified with any one religion, Daya had no sense of the other, but what was a charming innocence about the world at age twelve, was edging towards ignorance at twenty.

~

'Aaftab,' he said, extending a hand.

'Daya,' she smiled.

He stood, reached into his pocket again and took out a single bent cigarette and a lighter. 'I was just about to leave when you walked up actually,' he said, pausing to light it, his head at an angle. He exhaled and in doing so seemed to gain some composure, the invisible thread that ran through his body from the top of his head straight down his throat, through his ribs, behind his navel and between his legs, pulling him upright again. She would learn over time how measured a young man he was, how outwardly calm.

'I've seen you before,' he said, one eye scrunched shut to avoid a wisp of smoke. 'At the library.'

'You're a student?' she asked.

'Was. Law. Graduated recently. And you?'

'Markova. Graduating next fall hopefully.'

'I've never met a dance student before.'

'Listen, did you keep your student card?' she said suddenly, frowning.

'What?'

'Your student ID.'

'No … why?'

'How were you in the library then?'

'I got the public pass,' he responded, bewildered.

'You paid for it?'

'Yes.'

'Well done. You might be the only person who ever did.' That grin. All her white teeth.

'I'm a lawyer. Thought I may as well start off an honest one.'

'Are you really?'

'Yes, usually.'

'No, I meant a lawyer.'

'That depends on whether you think someone becomes a lawyer when they graduate or when they start practising law.'

'So a non-practising lawyer?'

And months later she would ask, 'So are you Muslim or not?'

'Well that depends ...'

'Ah. *A non-practising Muslim.*'

'Something like that.'

'When do you start?'

'Next week actually. Right here in Cardiff city centre.'

'Is it your dream job?' she smiled.

He laughed a short, sharp laugh and she smiled wider, pleased that he understood her humour.

'The dreamiest.'

Now she laughed.

'The firm's alright. They seem like good people.'

'Good. Well, if you see me at the library again, come and say hi.' She said this with a breeze in her voice.

'I will.' He paused a moment, politely. They smiled again. Then he turned neatly on his foot and walked off down the path.

The next time he saw her she was outside the library staring at the sea bindweed creeper that grew up its northwestern side. They spoke about flowers, which he knew so little of but had grown to love, first from his mother, her only concession to softness, and then later from Wasim.

The next time she was in the coffeeshop. She was tired that day, a heatpack pressed against her aching muscles. They spoke more. He did not want to stop listening.

And then he found her once in the Ottoman Empire labelling new books with 'Library of the Arts' stickers. She told him he could keep her company. There was room for two chairs and no more. Aaftab and Daya sat there protected, transported, and when she was finally done labelling seventy new copies of *A Manual of Perennials*, he invited her home for tea.

~

Daya walked into his house and broke the still air with her scent, his living room suddenly transformed into a valley filled with lilies carried from some ancient empire into his home. He made her a cup of tea and they sat across each other at the small square dining table and spoke of other lives. She spoke with ease about her father, noticing that Aaftab did not mention his. He told her how he had been in love once, she admitted she had never. They exchanged views on the students' union, the new BBC series she hadn't seen (and never would) but had heard all about. He told her all his siblings' names and learnt that she had none. She told him how her feet bled so much some days they stained her pink satin ballet flats. He asked to see and she gently kicked one sneaker off, toe against heel, pulled off the sock and put her foot with its blackened toes, its crushed and bruised edges forward. In that moment, Aaftab was so overcome by the need to heal every scar upon and inside this girl, he did that evening something he had never done before. He reached out and placed one hand beneath, and the other on top of her waiting foot, and enclosed it in the closest thing to an embrace he could give a perfect stranger.

When she left it was late and the moon was rising cold over the slanted roofs. He stopped her outside the door, a light hand on her shoulder. 'Look,' he said. There under the broken streetlamp was the white owl. They watched her with a single breath held between them, until she flew off into the night. Daya turned to face him in the dark, 'The goddess Lakshmi travels on a white owl. When one sees the owl, they say the goddess must be nearby. And if the goddess is close, they say luck is on its way too.' They smiled as she walked off, towards her side of town, across Roath Park. Aaftab watched her, recalling how his father had once caught him reading a book about Hindu gods. He had snapped it shut too fast and it had caught Aaftab's finger. Staring out into the distance he had then said to his son, almost puzzled, 'What could there possibly be to respect about a religion that cannot agree on one god?' Fifteen years later, Aaftab knew the answer.

That it had goddesses.

4

Wasim had learnt English from the 'telly'. Hours – he had spent hours in front of it. He would watch the news in Urdu, then he would watch the same news in English. He would watch movies in English with Urdu subtitles on his crappy, second-hand laptop. Then he would watch movies in Urdu with English subtitles. This is how he learnt to play with languages.

His first language was Punjabi. The second Urdu. Now there was English. But his mother tongue was food.

Wasim was the youngest of four brothers, each larger, rougher and less academically inclined than him. He was the softest child his mother had birthed, with pale skin and green eyes. From the start he spoke in a language she knew she hadn't taught him. The language of their house was made up of quick sentences punctuated by smacks on the head and cricket balls bouncing off walls – when one hit too hard, it would leave a flaky crater, and chips of blue paint on the floor. His language was different. It referenced things like cardamom and chinchillas. He was the boy who knew the names of all the different mangoes.

'Alphonso, Bombai, Bathua, Mallika, Langra, Neelum,

Kesar, Dasehari, Fazli, Chausa, Sunderja, Vanraj, Malda, Kishen Bhog, Sukul, Gulabkhas, Pairi, Rajapuri, Baneshan, Banganapalli, Mundappa, Sarauli, Fernandin, Rumain, Mulgoa, Safeda, Olour, Totapuri, Jamadar, Himayuddin, Bangalora, Cherukurasam.'

'You forgot a few,' his brother said, looking at the photocopied paper Wasim had hidden from view to test himself, that his brother was using now to collect the warm shells of peanuts.

'I'll get them next time.'

'There are only Indian mangoes on this list.'

'I'll do the Pakistani ones next time.'

'Good. Do the American ones also.'

Of the mangoes grown in India he had only ever tasted the Chausa. Of the mangoes grown in Pakistan, he had only tasted the common Sindhri. Apart from the one time his family had sent him to Multan with his cousins. Fourteen of them in a van, and four more on the roof, they'd reached their destination covered in dust. But he didn't remember that; he remembered that in Multan he had eaten a mango so sweet and unique he wasn't sure at first if it was a mango at all. The peel was not yellow but plum-coloured, and breaking it open to see the yellow of the mango inside was like watching the sun bursting through rainclouds. He asked what it was called and the farmer who had given it to them replied, 'Shan-e-Khuda.' *The splendour of God.* The mud of Multan, so famous for making women's faces lighter, Wasim would always remember for making mangoes darker, sweeter.

His favourite of the mango names were:

Himayuddin, because when he first heard it he dreamt up a Mughal emperor who was also a botanist who adored aam so much he learnt how to cultivate the trees to grow gardens full of them, and then named his favourite variety after himself.

Totapuri, because Wasim envisioned a huge *bagh* of mango trees, a town made up of only these, avenues and avenues of them, and in the trees were thousands of wild green *totas* – parakeets living only off the flesh of the fruit, singing at dusk songs in praise of it.

And his absolute utmost favourite was:

Gulabkhas, because it made him imagine a mango that when cut open smelt and tasted of red roses. And inside, instead of the large central oval-shaped seed, deep within the mango pulp was a small single round seed, which when washed, revealed itself to be a rosebud, which when placed in water, blossomed and smelt exactly like mangoes.

Wasim crossed continents to become a doctor. His father had spent his entire life as the caretaker for a factory, diligently locking up behind the workers each day. His brothers drove trucks when they found work. But Wasim had been asked to change their fortunes. 'If anyone can it's you, and that way all you boys can have better wives,' his mother had said. He had never before leaving for Wales worn a pair of jeans. On the aeroplane he was unsure what to do. The lady sitting next to him filled out his forms. She shook her head the entire time and did not make eye contact with him when she gave them back to him. He said, 'Thank you,' and she said, 'You're welcome.' It was the first time he had spoken to a non-Pakistani in his life. His father had paid an agency 10,000 rupees to write an essay for him. He had paid the same agency to translate the acceptance letter into Urdu and help with a student visa. He used a bit more of the bank loan he'd taken to buy a pair of jeans. Leve's 051, said the label. He took a glass bottle from his mother's kitchen and filled it with earth from the courtyard of his home. He sought her blessings. He left to become a doctor, with an acceptance letter for a Physical Education degree.

~

'So your parents don't know it's a PE course?'

Aaftab and Wasim were at a doner kebab shop they didn't usually go to, watching India and Australia play cricket on TV. Wasim shook his head, eyes on the screen. They were conversing in Punjabi and the boy behind the counter could understand.

He watched as Aaftab questioned Wasim, then said in their shared language, 'I did the same thing. Told them I had a business degree but I actually came here on a visa for a Computer Science course. Now I make minimum class attendance and the rest of the time I work here. 'He tapped the counter in front of him.' Get cash pay, it works out.' The boys looked up from their table, surprised.

'Legal?' Aaftab asked.

The boy shrugged his shoulders. Aaftab knew the law. International students weren't allowed to work off-campus legally. He knew the boy knew this too.

'Your parents didn't ask about the degree?' Aaftab tried a different approach but a wedge had come between them. They were no longer the same coloured slice of the pie chart. They intersected on a Venn diagram and in the intersection lay their language and their nationality. But everything else about them occupied separate circles. Aaftab with his good English, his ability to pay the bill, his education, his lawyer father, his pen in breast pocket, his Islamabad home with a front garden, his lack of student loans, his leather-strapped watch on wrist. The boy behind the counter looked at him with a moment's contempt.

'My mother can't even read, mate.'

'Mine neither,' Wasim said quietly out of nowhere. A soft solidarity returned.

Wasim spoke now. 'So you only work here?'

'Mostly, but I also carry boxes for the 7/11 on Albany Road. The owner's Pakistani so he gives us work. You?'

'I work at the kebab shop on Albany. Can I come to the 7/11 tonight?'

'Yes, brother. But,' he glanced at Aaftab, 'don't tell too many people about it. Here's my number …'

A blond girl with her midriff bared walked in as Wasim took the tissue paper with the number on it. The boy turned to her and switching languages took the order in perfect, if accented, English.

At first Wasim had rented a small room in a house full of other students, most of them from Tunisia. The apartment was one of the many owned by Aaftab's uncle Enayat. The old man watched Wasim for a few months before finally picking up the phone to call Aaftab. 'Got a boy from Rawalpindi at the Moy Road place. Bit younger than you. Why don't you show him around? He looks a bit lonely in the middle of all those blackies.' Enayat taaya also owned a doner kebab shop on Albany Road between all the barbers slicing boys' scalps into zig-zags of hair, where Wasim soon began working illegally, for below minimum wage. A year later, finding himself easier in Wasim's company than anyone he had met in a long time, Aaftab asked him to move in. Wasim had hesitated.

'I'll pay the lion's share,' Aaftab said.

'Okay. But I'll take the smaller room.'

'And you can do the cooking, if it makes you feel better.'

'It does. That's a deal then.'

On the day Wasim brought his single clunky suitcase to the house Aaftab welcomed him with fresh mutton. After unpacking, Wasim, while washing the meat in the kitchen, had said, 'I never thought I would live with a lawyer – I was always told they were dishonest,' and Aaftab, smoking in the doorframe laughed and replied, 'Trust me, the cook and the crook a great pair shall make.'

~

On his first free weekend, months after moving to Britain, Wasim booked a train ticket. When he reached his destination he stepped out onto a station platform where on either side all he could see were fields. The station was not enclosed by wall or fence but by endless land on both sides. It reminded him of home. He was the only passenger there. He waited till the woman in the bright orange jacket went back to her little glass room, the door of which was stickered with wreaths and the words 'Department for the Environment, Transport, and the Regions'. When her back was finally turned he stepped off the platform straight onto the tracks the way he used to in Pakistan as a boy. He crossed them feeling the heat rise from the rails as he walked over to the fields that appeared deeper, the ones towards the left of the tracks. The tall grass closed behind him. When the orange-jacketed ticket collector looked up from her desk she could not understand where the boy in blue jeans had disappeared to. There were many ghosts in that part of the country and after a while she decided he'd probably been one but she was confused because she had never before heard of a ghost who wasn't white.

Wasim walked and walked until the land began to change and he reached what looked less like wild meadows and more like plantations. He recognized barley growing around him and he wandered straight into it. It was as high as his waist, and there in between the tall flaxen stalks he finally saw what he had come to see. Interrupting the evenness of the crop frequently were shocks of electric blue. Cornflowers. There they were growing in the wild.

The year before he came to this country, Wasim had been browsing the internet at a net café in Rawalpindi. He'd been waiting for his brother who was drinking chai with the owner of a truck company in the hope of getting some work as a driver. Each click reloaded the page and took about sixty seconds to do so. He'd been reading about regional trees, and then suddenly had seen an article about cornflowers. He clicked, he waited. It appeared finally and he began to scroll through it slowly. His initial surprise was that they had nothing to do with the corn plant itself, save that they grew in the same fields, but not even exclusively. He then read on in horror.

Of the 256 sites in the United Kingdom where cornflowers used to grow wild, only three remain active. The pretty blue flower has all but ceased growing naturally, due to the use of herbicides, and is now considered an endangered plant.

He had copied it into a diary and when he began learning English, it was the first complex sentence he had translated from the original Urdu he had read and written it down in. Out in the wild, the cornflower had all but gone silent.

He spent an entire afternoon lying back in that field praising Allah for making Britain a nation so small he could ride across it in a single day. For hours Wasim lay surrounded by the last of the original blue cornflowers of England. At the end of that day of bliss, he allowed himself to take one single flower from the field. He couldn't bear to remove more than one, yet another, from its natural habitat. He would not have taken even that one, he was not usually covetous, but he wanted never to forget that precise shade of blue, the shade a cornflower growing in captivity never could quite replicate. That shade he was certain his imagination could not recount later.

In the days following his short journey, he found ladybirds now and then. One he discovered in his hair in the morning while shaving, emerging like a tiny drop of blood near the top of his ear. Another appeared from his shirt cuff onto his wrist, climbed up his hand and flew off the tip of his finger. He first thought he'd been carrying them with him from the meadow, but when at lunch two bees came by and began to circle him, then a yellow butterfly accompanied him all afternoon, he understood. He had lain so long among the wildflowers, they now thought he was a meadow.

~

Daya was in her bed thinking about the first time Aaftab had invited her home. How he had taken her scarred foot gently into his hands and she had left it there for a second, before breaking into laughter and taking it back, shy. She was thinking of how he had told her he had once been in love.

On his first day at law school, across a sea of students

awaiting the future, Aaftab had seen Farida. She was dressed in a long black tunic over slim black trousers, low heels and a grey scarf that brought out the colour in her eyes. Her dark hair was cut shoulder-length. Two years later they were seated together upon a patch of green, the garden outside the law school. She was stringing together daisies. *Bellis perennis* – the flower of fairies, scattered over Britain like summer snowflakes. Women once drank potions made of it, to darken the silk of their hair and knowing this made him think of her hair beneath her hijab, and the times he had seen her before she had begun wearing it. She finished and handed to him absentmindedly the bracelet of blossoms she'd woven. There was a fraction of a moment when the tip of his ring finger collided with the edge of her thumbnail and he was starkly aware of the fact that they had never touched before. No two body parts. Even when they all huddled together outside lecture halls on November mornings he had kept his arm a few inches away from hers, his body tensed so as to not accidentally brush against hers.

He played briefly with the transient jewellery, then slipped it into the centre of one of his heavy law books. It always amazed him to open one of those books and turn a page, each one like tracing paper. Like a peepal leaf soaked in water all night, in the morning little more than a web of veins, threatening to crumble, so many light pages accumulating like leaves in a tree such weight in their finality. It reminded him of a riddle he had heard as a child. 'If you had a kilo of cotton and a kilo of lead, which would be heavier on a see-saw?' He had chosen the cotton, and the boy asking had run off laughing.

A few months later Farida had knocked on the door of

the tiny hostel room he still lived in then and he'd opened it, still in his pajamas. She asked to borrow some notes. He told her to come in. As she drank a glass of water, Aaftab noticed a strand of hair emerging from underneath her hijab. It had made its way out into the open, and fell alongside the crescent of her face, desperately tempting. He raised a hand to touch it. Farida didn't move, staring mid-sip into the glass of water where she could see reflected her wet mouth. 'Take it off?'Aaftab asked, pulling at the scarf gently. 'No, Aaftab, please, no?' She felt naked, stripped by those two fingers pulling on one errant lock. He had immediately removed his hand, ashamed. Then she had looked up at him and their eyes meeting, had timidly changed her mind. She put down with sudden resoluteness her glass and lifting both hands up, elbows in the air had unwrapped the scarf. She undid the knots and unswirled a cloth. She unpinned the pins and pulled at a last rubber band before the entire mass had fallen out, tousled over her shoulders. He had placed a hand at the slightly damp nape of her neck, his fingers inching into the black silk, and then before he could even touch it, he'd felt a need to smell it. So he bent and placed his nose behind her ear, taking in that scent which would forever remind him of what it first felt like to understand fully what it was to be a man. To understand beneath everything, how very soft a man really is.

Afterwards when she was leaving, he had handed her a book. 'The notes?' she asked. And he had opened those peepal leaf pages, that kilo of cotton, that weighty collection of butterfly wings, and reaching in had handed her the daisy chain.

Daya was wondering what a love like that felt like. She was

thinking of how they had seen a white owl outside his house and she had said casually, 'What do you call her?' Surprised when he had replied, 'Lucida.' Later she had looked it up.

Lucida – the brightest star in a constellation.

~

When Wasim had moved into Aaftab's apartment, replacing the student who was leaving for Pakistan, one of Aaftab's many temporary boarders, he was alarmed by boys dropping in at all hours asking for a bite to eat or a cricket match to watch. Aaftab would not respond to their requests in anything but the affirmative, and as a result, boys who barely knew him would knock on their door saying they were a friend of so-and-so's and could they please have a sweatshirt, ten quid, a glass of water, a bartan, battery cells, a place to stay the night.

'Why are there people you don't know knocking on our door in the middle of the night?' he asked Aaftab tiredly one morning.

'Because they need help.'

'No, Aaftab, they don't. You can't help every Pakistani boy you meet.'

Aaftab recalled how afraid and lost he had been when he first arrived in this land that had seemed so magical as a summer holiday destination as a child, and was now so hostile as a home. He remembered with painful accuracy how he had cringed when he needed to ask a shopkeeper for cigarettes. 'What? Oh you mean "won pack-it uv Maaarrll-buh-rohs"!' They would roll it off their tongues, gargling alphabets. But when he said it, it came out short and hard. 'Vun Mulbro pliss.' What frustrated him most of all was that *he spoke English*. He spoke English well. But it wasn't enough. People in line behind him would shake their heads at the shopkeeper sympathetically or look away. Once a boy had sniggered, and said under his breath to his girlfriend, 'Faaakin' Pakis.' So Aaftab had learned to listen and to roll his consonants. He learnt to greet shopkeepers with a 'Heya mate, you awright?' He asked for a 'packa Maarlbros, oh n this loaf-a-bread, thassit'. And he ended with 'You 'av a good weekend ... Say 'ello to the missus.' He didn't want that pain, the pain of not fitting into an entire system, for anyone else, and so he offered up a different eco-system.

But Wasim thought differently. 'No one helped me and no one helped you all those years ago. We looked, we learnt. We listened, Aaftab. And the idea was never to come here and make another Pakistan. The idea was to be part of Britain. British. Integrate. Why can't I keep my dignity without selling my soul?' Aaftab had simply slow-clapped, then smirked and said, 'Can't you see that's exactly what I'm offering them - integration. But at a pace that doesn't kill them. And with the kind of support system we never had.'

One night Wasim was woken by the bell and when he opened the door, found a boy sitting on the front step, shivering. His face was injured, as if he'd been in a fight. Wasim brought him in, gave him a sweater and his bedroom, then woke Aaftab up. They made tea and sat under Aaftab's duvet watching the tobacco as it crept up the white paper, an orange caterpillar burning a path slowly through the dark towards Aaftab's mouth. 'This has to stop,' Wasim began softly. 'I can't stop, they're too used to me saying yes,' Aaftab responded weakly in a hoarse whisper. 'We have a boy here tonight who claims he was hit by one of the white boys from the Cleanse Britain gang. He says he was coming home after work and this group leaving the pub attacked him without any provocation. I don't know if he's telling the truth, but whether he is or not, Aaftab, he should not think your house is the place to come to.'

'Our house,' Aaftab said.

'Whatever. It's just not safe.'

Our house. Wasim took things into his own hands. He stopped opening the door past midnight, he stopped buying biscuit packs by the dozen, or leaving a couple of pounds out on the living room table for anyone who may need bus money. He stopped saying yes just because they were from Pakistan. And peace prevailed. For some time at least. When it all hit later, Wasim would wonder for a moment if this way had not been easier. If closing their doors had not opened them to everything that would later unfold.

5

It wasn't until he had seen her at the park that day, sitting on the bench by his that he realized his mind had absorbed her into it from his frequent visits to the library. Daya who always turned up in her T-shirts with tiny holes in them, in her sneakers and long shorts like a teenage boy, her hair a mop falling always over one eye, so short at the back it looked at certain angles like it had been shaved, her delicate scalp almost visible. Later when they became friends, he would ask her how she kept it groomed for ballet.

'How do you see a thing while dancing?'

'I dance with my eyes closed, that's how.'

'No, but really …'

Sheepishly she showed him her collection of headbands. After she had walked up to him at the park she had become within minutes the most fascinating person he had ever met and now he wanted to discover her endlessly.

Aaftab would appear at the library, energized and cheery, and at other times wave haggardly across the room, then bury his head in a book she could tell he wasn't reading. She found herself looking out for him, and she always stopped to say hello but he hadn't invited her home again after that first time. A few weeks passed in which Daya, engrossed in a new tap dance module, did not see him as much, and when she saw him next, learnt he had begun his new job. His friends had congratulated him on the position with the sort of gusto only a first job receives, and he replied to each one of them with the same joke, 'I speak Punjabi, Urdu and English. I think a British immigration firm could use me.'

'Congratulations! Will I see you at the library anymore?' Daya asked lightly, the night he had appeared again, searching for a book for work.

'A lot less I reckon, but I'll still use it for research. And yes, I do have my pass, ma'am!' They laughed.

'Honestly the hours are so long, the only person I really see is Wasim.'

'Ah your friend! Tell me about him.''He's lovely,' he said. He looked different now, she thought, grown up, in his charcoal suit and blue scarf. She looked out to the sky where rain was gathering to pour from the cold cups of clouds and asked, 'What does he like to do?' The question so refined, without her realizing it, he thought. *What does he like to do?* Not what is he like? Not what does he do?

Like a poem, he recalled, by his favourite poet al-Khayal. 'Everything you choose to do, is everything you choose to be. Choose wisely.' Her profile inside the dark hood of her sweatshirt distracted him. For a moment she looked like she had loosely wrapped a dupatta around her head.

'He likes to cook. And he likes to find out things. Things like how to grow chilli plants and facts about … birds and stuff.'

'Birds?' she asked, slightly sceptical.

'Yes. Like this morning when he was leaving for work he

said to me, "Do you know the difference between white eggs and brown ones?" So I said I didn't, no. And he says, "White chickens lay white ones and brown chickens lay brown ones."'

'Is that true?' she asked, delight and disbelief on her face.

'Oh, he never lies.'

He wanted for Wasim and Daya to meet. There were so few bits of his life that Wasim wasn't a part of that it felt strange not to tell him, and yet he hadn't. It was an interruption to their routine, he knew this. To their world. But the day came when these worlds joined like Daya was a single dew drop meeting a tiny trickle that eventually would make its way to a stream that became the river of Aaftab's slow-flowing life. And later, precisely as it is with life, Aaftab would try to remember if he had had any role in it at all or if it had been – that dreadful and beautiful thing – inevitable.

~

It was a cool Tuesday and Daya was more tired than she had been in months. She too spent less and less time at the library, now in her third and final year. She had asked for a cut in the number of hours she worked. She exited the dance school and caught the last of the sun's rays, throwing a last embrace over a darkened sky. She was bathed in sweat, and her muscles hurt more than usual. She walked slowly, taking a longer route, past the library. She missed her now-shortened hours and the calm and order that came with working there. She missed whittling books from shelves when someone needed one, and an entire world ordered by the alphabet. She missed bumping into Aaftab. As an only child Daya had always been so private, finding comfort in being alone, and she was awkward with the awareness of how swiftly she had felt at home in his company.

She entered the library but didn't see him at any of his usual spots. She walked past the empires (neither of them ever sat with the monarchs) but didn't find him in any. She had found that morning on her way to school a feather with exactly one black half and one white, and had wanted to give it to him for his friend Wasim. In her disappointment at not finding him, a voice inside asked if the feather had not been an excuse, and she left hurriedly, cheeks hot from embarrassment. As she made her way home a storm broke and drenched her already damp body. She walked through it slowly, mesmerized by the way her movement broke the lines of rain. She skipped dinner from sheer exhaustion and woke the next day, her body a furnace. With difficulty she dragged herself to her tiny kitchen and drank water, her mouth to the tap. She collapsed again. When she woke once more from sleep that was more delirium than rest, for the first time, she dialled a previously unused number from her phone. She called Aaftab. She called Aaftab, because sick in bed shivering under blankets, sweating then sleeping then waking with her skin on fire, finally admitting to herself she was deep down in her shy bones so very lonely, and that more than anything, she wanted something that felt like home.

He picked up on the first ring. 'I'll be right over in a taxi, get ready, I'll bring you to mine,' he said. At his house he gave her a thick towel and a clean set of pajamas and told her to take a hot shower. When she emerged from the steaming bathroom as if through clouds, he gave her a sweater, a cup of ginger tea and two paracetamols. 'I don't fall sick very much,' she said weakly. Lilies were coming to bloom on her cheeks, pale and dewy. She drifted into sleep and dreamt they were amongst mountains, violet-coloured and steep. When she woke he handed her a plate of Indian food. 'Pakistani food,' he corrected her with a smile. 'Did you make this?' She wanted to tell him how it had transported her to her mother's round kitchen, to Kamla's loving warmth.

Naan, roti, daal, chaawal. Mandi ki bhindi, koftey, ghee.

Everything she wanted to say sounded too sentimental, so she complimented Wasim's culinary skills lightly – 'really nice food' – and lay back down, drifting once more, vaguely aware of Aaftab's cool, dry hand touching her forehead to check for fever.

~

Wasim came home with groceries and found Aaftab in the kitchen in the dark smoking a cigarette.

'*Theek thaak?*'

'*Theek thaak* ...'

Aaftab did not know how to broach the topic so he didn't.

He put out the cigarette and walked to his room where Wasim followed. Daya swathed in blankets began to stir and her sickness filled the room with heat and the tinny scent of medicine evaporating off a body. 'Who's that?' Wasim asked and Aaftab suddenly self-conscious turned to open the windows and started to say, 'A friend of mine,' when he heard Wasim say 'Assalamaleikum.' He froze. When he managed to turn around it felt like hours had passed. Later he would understand that it had simply been the longest second of his life. He saw Wasim with his hand extended towards Daya, and Daya slowly untangling her arm from beneath the blanket and attempting to shake his. Before she could open her mouth to respond Wasim dropped her hand, and turning to Aaftab, his eyes wide lagoons in his sandy face, returned in that moment to the first language he had ever known. 'Aaftab! *Ae kuri eh!*'

Aaftab.

It's a girl.

It was as if she had just been given life.

Outside of college Aaftab had never been seen with a girl. Outside of college Wasim had never seen him speak to one. Not an unrelated one. Not in this country. Except one time, they had never had a woman enter their home. But here in his bed, wearing his pajamas, on his pillow was unmistakably a woman. Wasim was aghast. 'What have you done? They'll skin you,' he told Aaftab in Punjabi. Aaftab shrugged his shoulders and began, to everyone's collective surprise, including his, to laugh. Wasim continued to look at him, open-mouthed. From the bed Daya giggled softly. Wasim did not know then how things change or what makes humans act. How he would put his own hide on the line for Daya when the time came. How she was waiting in the wings of his life to play his best friend. How at centre stage she would become his sister.

For weeks afterwards whenever Daya dropped by, Aaftab would turn to Wasim and say, 'This is Daya, she's a girl by the way,' and the three of them would laugh anew.

It was a Saturday morning when she finally felt well enough to leave. Daya emerged in the doorway of Wasim's room where Aaftab and Wasim were still asleep, rearranging themselves for the week to allow her the comfort of Aaftab's room during her illness, praying no one would drop by after Friday prayers at the mosque. She nudged Wasim gently awake and setting her backpack on the ground handed him a feather, one half black, one half white. 'Aaftab said you like birds, so this is for you. Thank you for letting me stay.' He showed her out and they both decided to let Aaftab, exhausted from a long week, sleep. '*Jaldi waapas aana*,' he said. 'Soon,' she promised. And true to her word, Daya came back.

~

The boys were sitting on the steps of the fire escape. Breaking through the leaves of the ivy that cloaked Daya's house were wisteria flowers, planted at some point and then forgotten by everyone except the sun. Lilac-tipped and light as air they dipped and danced and Wasim delighted in watching them. Daya was inside her room with the windows open, playing music and talking to the boys over it. She was boiling water in a kettle to make tea. The first time she had invited them over, she had swept in a great hurry her clutter beneath her bed and served them tea in two mismatched mugs, one taken by accident from the library cafe when she had wandered out still sipping from it. Wasim had asked her what tea she had made. 'Umm, Tetley?' she had replied. For a long time, Wasim had thought she'd said 'kettley', because it was made in a kettle and not boiled in a pan the 'proper' way. When Aaftab had discovered this and called Daya to tell her through howls of laughter, she had said, 'Well, I guess it's Kettley now, isn't it?'

'Forevermore,' he had replied solemnly.

She handed them two cups of Kettley tea and changed the track on the CD. 'Do you always listen to English songs?' Aaftab asked curiously. 'Mostly, yes.' She knew she had replied in defence, immediately made self-conscious by his question. 'Can I see your CDs?' Daya kept her thick collection of music in a big black leather wallet that unzipped to reveal pages of

CDs in clear plastic envelopes. Like a book made of glass. She handed it to him and he began turning the pages slowly. 'I don't know any of these,' he said finally.

'Of course you don't, they're all goras,' Wasim snorted. 'Let me have a look.'

'And you'll know them?' Aaftab said indignantly even as he handed him the book.

'All the names … why are they all one describing word and one … noun?' Wasim looked at Daya to see if he had used the word correctly. She nodded, 'One adjective and one noun? What do you mean?' Wasim traced titles with his finger. 'See: *velvet* revolver. *Smashing* pumpkin. Green day, blind melon, deep purple, dusty springfield …' She cut him off with a smile, 'Dusty is just her name.'

'Why?'

'Because her parents gave her that name?'

'Why would they do that?'

Aaftab who had been quiet for a long time reached out to touch the wisteria and said, 'How could you have lived your whole life in India, and not at some point have loved Lata?' He stood up to climb in through the window and pulled out from his jacket pocket a CD without a cover. It caught the light and glinted for a second like a charm in his hand. 'I made you something,' he said, and placed it gently in the bed of the music system. There was an infinite silence in the moment between her music and his, in which they heard a woodlark singing, as if it knew this was its moment to have all that silence to itself, to paint on that aural canvas whatever it wished … to be the language-less song connecting two worlds. And then a gentle crackling filled the air and a gentleman's voice wafted through the room and both Aaftab and Wasim began singing softly …

Daya was overcome with an urge to cry, assaulted by some lost memory of her parents, young and beautiful, dancing in the rain, and singing along to this voice. 'Who is it?' she asked shakily. 'Mohammed Rafi. I figured it's an easier start than Lata,' Aaftab replied. Wasim smiled at her barely concealed emotion and added, 'But we'll get you to listen to Lata soon.' Daya smiled back, her throat hot with emotion. 'Never.'

~

As a child, Daya had longed for a sibling. For a mirror. She had been from the beginning a lonely girl, unable to easily make friends, often tongue-tied. She was convinced for some reason that she would have a little brother soon. She had plotted for one, and those plans finally failing, had begun creating endless playmates for herself. A sparrow she inexplicably named Sheetal. A lizard called Khartoum, named by Asha for the tile-like pattern on his back. A butterfly called Butterfly for whom she made a grave in her colouring book once he died. Gyan and Asha decided at this point to help out and thereafter came Kazi the crocodile. A lime-coloured stuffed toy the size of an actual baby crocodile, Daya loved him so much and spoke to him so many hours of the day, at one point Asha was convinced he actually came to life at night. 'How else can she have so much faith in … their conversations?' she asked Gyan.

Then came Shanti the Stegosaurus. A rubber dinosaur not at all the size of a real-life one, whom Daya insisted on carrying everywhere with her. Shanti was lost at an elegant restaurant during an epic battle between Daya and her father when he tried to prise her fingers off the prehistoric creature in favour of a bread roll. When a screaming Daya finally did let go, Shanti flew acrobatically across the table, bypassed Asha's head and landed in a dish of crème brulee two tables to their left to an applause of absolute silence.

And finally there was Barfi. Barfi was the puppy her parents rescued for her off the streets when she was eight. He was white with a fawn patch on his nose and tufts of fluff around his paws and behind his ears. They told Daya the dog was hers so long as she learnt how to take care of him. Apart from that she could do whatever she wished but she could not allow Barfi on the bed. They bought a cushion-bottomed basket of woven straw for him and placed it at the foot of Daya's small bed. The next morning when Gyan came to wake his daughter for school, he found his honest eight-year-old asleep in the basket, a white puppy nestled in her hair.

In Barfi, Daya finally found the brother she had been looking for. He grew into a large, handsome dog with almond eyes and was so protective of Daya even her parents avoided entering her room if she was still asleep. He made exceptions for Milni, Daya's only other friend. More than Milni, more than her parents, more than Kamla or her flower-shaped house full of Burma teak furniture or the city in which she grew up in itself, Daya missed Barfi.

~

Wasim was overjoyed that true to her word Daya had come back after her illness. She came to play cricket with them on Sundays and she came to eat the food he cooked. She came back again and again because they became her gentle caretakers and because she had not realized she was hungry for friendship, for her mother tongue, for familiar curses with which to fill her mouth and familiar reactions to echo in other people's. She wanted to hear Wasim's discoveries about the world and Aaftab's ideas about how to fix it. And every single time she saw his tall frame across the library, so tall he never asked her for help with the ladder, her heart told her what she hadn't asked it.

~

The next time Aaftab came over, he was alone. 'Come up the fire escape!' she shouted down as she saw him walk up the road, a box of pizza in his arms. Daya was falling slowly in love with the way the light caught the high cheekbones of Aaftab's face. With the way his jaw clenched when he concentrated. The way his hands drummed on the surface of tables, the tops of his knees. She wanted to eat small pieces of his brain to taste how his thoughts had made him this human being. This young man. If love was measured by the number of minutes you could spend with a person without tiring of them, Daya loved Aaftab. Every human being she had met in this world, even Wasim with his endless questions and observations, had tired her. But Aaftab with his long silences, his awkward modesty but deep self-confidence, his voice with its gravel from too many cigarettes, his long limbs and way with dogs, she never, ever tired of.

He entered her room through the window and they ate pizza together on her bed, the sun streaming in and lighting up the wisteria stem she had cut and placed in an old wine bottle filled with water now instead of Merlot. The pizza was halal, Daya noticed, the word printed in red ink across the box. Happy Halal Pizzeria. 'Wasim had to work today,' Aaftab said. It sounded unconvincing to his own ears. He knew less and less how to behave when alone with Daya. Her large eyes under her mop of hair looked into him, asking questions he did not have the answers to. He knew he should spend less time with her, but there was no one he wanted to see more. He adored the bruises on her knees as they peeped from those long, boys' shorts she wore. Her scuffed sneakers. Muddy laces hiding scarred feet hiding narrow fan of bone that had led her step by step to him.

He noticed a photograph on her bedside table. It was of Daya looking slightly younger, with another girl many inches taller than her. They were dressed for an occasion, both in white gowns, Daya's simpler, with matching white flowers in their hair. Her hair was open and waist-length, the flowers a halo around her head. Aaftab reached out and touched the image in its frame made of seashells.

'That's my best friend Milni,' Daya said, answering what Aaftab hadn't asked. Aaftab wondered for a second if Milni knew about him.

'When did you cut it?' he said, his finger now tracing the length of her glossy hair.

'Just before I came here.'

'So much of it,' his voice was unable to disguise the sorrow. 'Why?'

'Because I wanted to feel free.'

He thought of freedom, the very idea of it, as a Western one. In his country, and in Daya's, they had fought all those years for it … *the struggle for freedom*, and yet he agreed here with his father – they were bigger slaves to the West than ever before. It was so American, he thought, the idea of freedom. Free spirit, free speech, free love. 'Free Hugs' – he had seen a boy wearing a cardboard sign bearing these words, standing outside the library one day, and girls and men alike had been walking up, giggling and embracing him. He heard it had been a gimmick and the boy would now run for university student president. His campaign line? 'I can't believe I'm not butter!'

'There's no such thing as a free lunch,' his father always said.

There's no such thing as a free country, Aaftab always thought. Every nation's borders a noose around it.

There's no such thing as a free person, he wanted to say to Daya now.

'And do you?' he asked instead.

'Do I what?'

'Do you feel free?'

'I suppose so … yes.'

'Daya, the freedom fighter!' he teased.

She paused, then said, 'But I want new things now.'

'Like what?'

'I guess I want more. I want to feel safe.'

'Aren't they opposite things?' he asked.

She thought about it for a moment before replying.

'Only if freedom scares you.'

What he did not say in reply was,

And what if I want to be held captive?

6

The year that Daya met Aaftab, she met a different man who would alter her life almost as much. She'd rushed into the building on the first day of her final year at university. 'You're late,' Anna announced in her very no-nonsense way. Daya took her place, cross-legged on the wooden floor of the dance studio and prepared to listen to the modules and plans for the year. At the end Anna asked her to wait as the other students filed out. 'There's been a problem with the dance partners, Daya. We've had a dropout but we've also had …' she shuffled through her papers, '… Colin?' she announced to the flock of students. 'Colin Orwell?' A tall boy broke away from the group and drifted towards them like a stray fish from a school. 'A transfer. You are to be partners. Daya, meet Colin. And Colin, this is Daya. Colin just moved here from Northampton. I need you both to go to the medical room and weigh yourselves but from what I can tell, you'll make a wonderful pair.'

Colin was made of dark sinews and long lashes, and Daya noticed how his palms were pink, like an inversion of the rest of him.

He asked her where she was from and spontaneously she

told him her secret name for her city – 'Lalabad' – and all the reasons she called it that. City of red sandstone, red dust, red heat, built of blood. A city constructed on dreams that had forsaken other dreams … a la la land. And of course because it was a city filled with lalas. Rolling their bellies, scratching their crotches, lighting their matches and making their deals. Lalabad. Home. And he told her the truth.

Colin was not from Northampton. He was from Johannesburg. When he was born, his mother wanted to go live in the bantustan and his father who felt anger and sorrow at abandoning those in the slums around the city and didn't believe the rumours of it being any better in the bantustan said no. 'What will you do over there? Will you dance without your dress for white men who come to play?' And so they stayed, living in squalor in the slums until eventually he was made to disappear. 'But he was invisible long before that already,' Colin said. And his mother was brought to England by a white woman who missed fresh cream and lawn tennis and the life she had left behind for a husband making his wealth in the country's burgeoning casino business. So, she went back to that life and took with her a slice of Africa, to wash her sheets and cook her bobotie pie when the strawberries and scones would not suffice, when she missed the taste of a country she could not forget despite the distance. 'Basically,' Colin said, and he said that word a lot, 'I grew up the son of a housemaid in Northampton.' Two women – one black and one white – had fled two invisible husbands, one black and one white, with two children, one black and one white, and had come across to sunny England where, as far as Colin's eyes could see, everything was grey.

When they arrived, the white woman stared long at her

daughter and said, 'I'm renaming her. She will be called Lesedi.' Light. It was meant to bind that little girl forever in some way to the land of her birth. And the black woman said, 'Tell me a name. A name that will let him leave it all behind.' The white lady thought. 'Take my husband's,' she finally said. And so he became Colin Orwell. 'And what was it before?' Daya asked. 'That … I will not say.' As her country had awoken to life and freedom, his had entered into a nightmare-laced sleep and eight long decades after even America had declared slavery dead, white men who could no longer say what they wished on land long ago stolen and made their own, said it loud on African soil. And in their own homes, upon their own land, it became illegal for South Africans to live within their own skin. In a cold country across a cold sea, to stay in his body and escape it at the same time, Colin began to dance.

Daya loved his accent which he one day admitted to her was not real.

'What do you mean?' she asked, confused.

'Daya, I moved here as a child. I don't speak like bloody Mandela, I speak like a Chav.'

'But … you don't.'

'It's *put on*, Daya!'

'You're putting on a South African accent?'

'Basically,' he said and then laughed with his body.

She loved his laughter which had never left him, his grace and his big pink hands that lifted her high. Whenever she asked him to tell her more about himself he replied with a grin, his ever-so-slightly bucked teeth emerging, 'More dance, less talk, Daya.' Daya who had learnt to dance ballet in the diplomatic centre of her beloved Lalabad, and Colin who had learnt in the rain-soaked streets of a country he never claimed as his own, to forget the one he could not leave behind. Somehow, they had found themselves thrown together here in Wales, in a school with so many white faces that later Colin would say they'd had to find each other if only to survive the blizzard.

~

Soon after they were married at a small Hindu temple in his ancestral village a few hours' drive northeast of Lalabad, Daya's father Gyan decided he would not take the path that had been set out for him. He would not join the 'family business' producing blankets for the wealthy and for the snow-white people they were exported to. Instead he set aside six months during which time he and his new wife would learn the craft, working, to the initial embarrassment of his father, on the factory floor with the tailors and craftspeople, rather than behind the glass screen that divided that space from the more comfortable air-conditioned offices the rest of the family occupied. The young couple called these offices the 'box seats' and joked with the family that they would earn their way there. 'Some people are better at viewing, some must do the doing,' Gyan, then just twenty-six, had said with a laugh.

After the first six months they travelled for another six, using a small portion of the money they had received as wedding gifts. They travelled to some of the softest and then the roughest areas surrounding Lalabad and spoke in that time to countless women, widows, young and old. From this they built their workforce. As their first wedding anniversary arrived, they set up a small workshop just across the city borders where they began teaching the women who could travel there all that they had learnt. They went door to door collecting forgotten and discarded fabrics, then soaked them in tubs of dye made from flowers. 'Toss them in the nectar!' Asha would shout out when it was time to dye the cloth. Over the years Asha had experimented with marigolds and sunflowers, onion skin for lavender, dandelion and the roots and peels of carrots. She had used walnuts and of course roses, thousands of roses. Her favourite though was hibiscus. Once the fabric had been coloured and dried in the sun, they would cut it up into patches. From these patches they created blankets in patterns of stars. By their second anniversary they had twelve women working for them, a workshop in a village that had a pond and three bad-tempered geese, an organic vegetable garden and a name. Thus The Stardust Sleepers was born.

~

They had met at college. Asha in those days, always in saris, her waist-length hair tangled at her hips. She wore underneath her saris white tennis shoes. She was nimble in that outfit, playing badminton, eating golgappas, attending protest marches and theatre practice. It was an all-girls' college but they held an annual carnival (The Acacia Inter-College Carnival, named for no apparent reason after a plant) to which the city's male college-goers flocked with unequalled pomp in their step each year. And that is where Gyan first saw her in the early winter of 1970, at the far end of the football field on which no woman had ever kicked a ball. She was in charge of announcements, climbing on to the short wooden stage erected the night before, cluttered with blue and white balloons and adorned with a handful of limp pink and yellow streamers. Her voice floated through, her enunciation so perfect already at nineteen, husky above the screech of the microphone. She had on a chiffon sari in mauve and realized only after she'd left the house that the outfit wasn't quite right. The blouse with its dreadful puffed sleeves, the brown lipstick – all saved for a special occasion and now clashing with the tennis shoes. To his gathered friends' amusement Gyan said, 'My god, it's Aphrodite!' It is safe to say before Gyan fell in love with Asha, he fell in love with the way she won a battle with a screeching microphone while dressed in an utterly atrocious ensemble and – he found out later – wanting desperately to pee.

He approached her with the certainty of rejection and it made him confident. 'You look ravishing … what a sari,' he said without a trace of sarcasm, and she looked him bang in the eye through the metal frame of her spactacles and said, 'I look like two-day-old dog turd.' And that was that.

He took her out later that month on their first 'alone outing'. They went to the talkies, the dark-cushioned romance of the cinema, the fizzy excitement of the soda, the sweaty-fingered anticipation, the fans stuck sideways into walls, where they would whir away come summer. They argued over which cinema. He kept insisting on Sheila and she said it was just too far for her and she would never make it back home on time. 'It's my favourite. Besides, the screen is bigger.' And then Chanakyarama opened and they both agreed on it, though Asha did so reluctantly, unlured by the lure of the brand new, boastful 70mm. 'I mean, it's *slightly* closer to home but I'm still going to be late getting back, you know.' They watched

Cromwell, which Asha found terrifically boring and Gyan wished he hadn't chosen. After the film was over, he asked how come she wasn't wearing her glasses. She looked at him like he was an idiot, then without breaking the gaze took his cigarette from him, sucked on it and as she exhaled revealed, 'They're not real. And even if they had been, a blind person could tell you this film was the pits.' He looked disappointed and after a long pause said, 'Not real?' in a voice so thoroughly betrayed she rolled her eyes but then said with emphasis, 'They're the only inauthentic thing about me, okay?' She was in jeans with extraordinarily wide flares which she claimed she had stitched herself. He had his heart in his mouth the entire time, leaving his chest behind his sleeveless cardigan from London, hollow. When he dropped her home she said, 'This your daddy's car, rich boy?' and for the first time in his entire life he had felt ashamed at the ease of his wealth. The next morning, he decided he would do whatever it took, to have her respect him. But he hadn't counted on her loving him.

~

How had they ended up in a house full of circles? In a house the shape of a flower? Everyone presumed they had bought the house with the considerable inheritance Gyan had received. The truth as always was more layered. They had bought the house with a small part of Gyan's inheritance, yes, but the house people saw was not the one they had once found. They had chanced upon it some years after they had married, in the old part of the city, the realized fantasy of an erstwhile landlord or warlord. It seemed abandoned but for the trees surrounding the property – a beautiful laburnum, a few neems, eucalyptus almost hiding the house from the road, creepers up its sides and bougainvillea bushes everywhere. Someone was caring for these plants, watering them and pruning them into ingenious natural shapes and cascades. But who?

'Nobody knows it, madam,' the honest broker announced a week later when they had sought him out through the number scrawled on a tin board held to the gate with rusted wire on one side and a ribbon from his daughter's hair on the other. 'Locally, you see, everybody is saying ghosts are coming.' Asha's eyes lit up. She smelt a bargain and she was not afraid of ghosts. It was theirs by the end of the month. A huge, two-storey, flower-shaped house. 'The lower floor as you can see, madam, is a hall of some variety. For functions in the old days. Locally they are saying a funeral parlour maybe,' the broker went on disapprovingly, worried for the safety of the young couple, discouraging them with all he could. If anything happened, it would all come back to him of course. And yet, he could not afford not to sell it. After questioning his conscience, he gave it to them at a price that he felt was fair in the face of any disasters, ghosts included. Asha was beside herself with happiness.

Over the next few months she spent day upon day reviving the house. It was an art deco relic, built with love sometime in the 1930s. It was eccentric even by European standards and she wondered about the original owners, but nobody in the neighbourhood could tell her anything about them. Finally the local dhobi explained, 'All the old tenants moved from this area of the city.'

'Where to?' she asked.

'Pakistan mostly.'

And so they learnt to live with ghosts, slowly colouring

in their flower. The floors had been stripped bare long ago, of whatever tile or marble they once had, so Asha covered the entire place with stone in warm colours – Jaisalmer, pink Jodhpur marble, polished sandstone. She tended to the plants that the ghosts had once watered and she bought curtains in fabrics that let in the light and kept out the heat and she painted the walls in shades of soft teal and marmalade and grey and when she tried to hang paintings on them, Asha, adorerer of art, finally realized there was perhaps something she did not like about her dream house. Because she discovered the only problem with a round house was that frames are generally made flat. When faced with this singular issue, Asha did not simply find a solution, she created something beautiful out of it. She explained to Gyan and they agreed to hang only textiles on their walls. 'I mean, we have no other choice,' she said. When they heard, friends of theirs – originally exchange students – from Pakistan sent them the Faiz poem painted on cloth, the long Urdu calligraphy fixed in place but gently bobbing, like anchored boats. 'It's exquisite!' Asha had gushed to them and they had written back: 'The work of an Indian poet, by a Pakistani calligrapher, on Bangladeshi jute … we call it One Nine Four Six.'

7

It was an oddly sultry night for Caerdydd. They were returning from a rare evening of drinking, walking home under a clear sky full of stars, both of them with their necks craned backwards, to appreciate the hedonistic beauty of the night. Aaftab was telling her how he felt the stars all held hands, so that when one of them shifted, all of them shifted alongside, inching like sleepy children safe across the dark field of the night sky. Tonight he was drunk and every star looked like two.

The first time Aaftab had tried whisky it had been with apple juice. 'You'll like it,' he'd been told. He loved it. And then one day he was at a law school party where they'd run out of apple juice. 'Have it with a splash of water,' one of the boys suggested. His mouth had exploded into the colours of the sun.

Daya drank wine. Wine with hand-drawn labels and ancient names, cranberry undercurrents and fig notes. Smooth red wine with layers of velvet, or crisp white, with an edge of stardust. Sometimes they drank together. It wasn't often, but sometimes she convinced them to come out with her. It wasn't interesting for them, they said. Wasim, sober, would stand around stiffly, shocked by the things he saw at bars, including the sight of Aaftab drinking. Aaftab would be wary, wondering always if they might be seen, recognized, always aware that the world was full of spies. His taaya's friends or tenants, his father's business associates, all their sons. They knew him as the pious law student from Pakistan. As a college student he had learnt to drink with white friends, but these days as an occupant of the adult world, he was cautious. That night he'd been different though. Wasim had refused to come out at all, so the two of them had gone together to a nightclub housed in the intact shell of a seventeenth-century cathedral. In the day it stood out, a dark spire surrounded by the nondescript staples of the high street – shoe shops, a Gap, an H&M. At night though, one could imagine what Caerdydd had once been, with this structure at its grand little centre. Alone with Daya in there, Aaftab had been lighter somehow.

They stopped walking. She watched him. The angle from which she saw him, his tall frame against the sky, head tilted back, it seemed as if he could drink the stars, if only he opened his mouth. He turned to face her and in the dim light she saw his face in full. That face so soft and so grave all at once. His eyes so beautiful with the lashes splayed, the crooked lips she had sometimes stared at while he spoke to her about important things. He was saying something now in fact about how he wasn't going to drink ever again but his mouth was so wild and plush and distracting in the strict lines of the cage of his jaw and cheekbone, under the gaze of the lamplight, she suddenly saw no option but to kiss it.

Her body's wants steadily eclipsed her heart's knowledge. There was a single repeated request gnawing at her, and it asked only that she be taken and ruined with love. That her aimless lonesome ache be put to rest, and that all that was healing may be wasted upon her. When they separated, he looked devastated. His mouth still parted, he stood, the foot between them now a forest. She cut through it. 'I'm so sorry.'

'No, don't be,' he replied.

'Is there nowhere we can be alone? There's so much I've wanted to say.'

He said nothing in reply.

'Just this once?' she asked.

They went to a small hotel he passed each day on his way home. It was full. 'Can't we just go to your house?' he asked.

'I've never brought a boy home before. My landlady …'

The truth was yes, she had never brought a boy home before, but it wasn't Mrs Coombes who would mind; in fact she had often asked Daya why she was 'so single for a pretty young thing'. It was Daya. Daya who was so used to being alone. And how does one go back to being without? So they went to a second hotel. 'We do have one room,' the man at the reception desk said. 'And it will be forty-two pounds.' He was overcharging them, and they knew this. Aaftab looked at her, hazy-eyed. It felt like the umbilical cord connecting him to all of reality and righteousness was about to be cut. 'Give us a moment?' he asked the concierge. 'Daya,' he took her aside. 'If we do this, it goes to the grave with us.' He stood before her so big, so tired, so serious and beautiful, the only thing she wanted any longer was to feel him collapse upon her. 'To the grave,' she whispered.

Come to bed, lay on me,
eat me up and pierce me through.
Write on me like letter paper,
then rip me up in two.

The curtain fluttered. He had one brown eye and one black. The moths beat their wings against an amber light. A police car sounded in the distance.

Would they be caught?

He undressed her. Wrist by wrist, sleeve by sleeve, cloth by cloth. Flesh by muscle by blood by bone.

She was a bowl of water and he was nothing but fallen flowers waiting to be gathered, thirsting.

… and she was heartbroken, by the absolute magnificence of it.

~

They woke to Wasim calling. 'I'll be there in twenty minutes?' Daya heard Aaftab say. Her parched mouth wanted to drink from his lips but morning had brought with it the slipperiness of reality. It is not fantasy that is evasive. We are certain of our dreams. But real life is a mirage at the best of times. 'You're leaving?' she asked him. Lying there in a once-smooth sea of sheets that their love had churned up into mountains, she began to break and did not have to say why. He took her in his arms and her back curved, revealing its long bones that perhaps he did not even realize he had begun to love. He noticed how the inches of his forearm were more than those in the width of her waist. He could smell the night still clinging to her and understood she was not ready yet to face the day, so he held her until his embrace carried her over that hard threshold.

'Why didn't you ever say anything?' she finally asked.

'What would I say, Daya? And more importantly, to what end?' And then softening, 'I won't put myself, or you, through that.' From perfect fantasy, gently back into the unevenness of reality. He padded for her that fall, protecting her from the pain that was like leaving the womb, like reentering the earth's atmosphere from outer space. Most things that try to do that – to re-enter the earth's atmosphere – fail. They explode or then disintegrate. This is how shooting stars are made. This is in fact all they are – meteors rushing too fast into a space they do not understand. So fast they burn the very air they touch. And all we see is the afterglow. He kissed the back of her head as she said goodbye to the proximity of stars.

They left together, and on departing she noticed the room number was the same as that of the house she had grown up in. 502. It made no sense as the small hotel had only twenty rooms. She asked them downstairs. 'Oh, the numbers begin at 501 and go up to 520, the owner finds it more glamorous,' the boy at the desk said, rolling his eyes.

From the very start, like coming home.

They walked out onto the streets cautiously, him more than her. The world was a blur and all the dangers that could be, became so present in their potential. From inside a glass bubble they had descended to a world of shards. Unbeknownst to them it had begun to rain in the early hours of the morning and a rough, sudden storm had followed. Trees now lay in massacre across streets, a car crushed underneath one. Water pooled and a sign for a pub had capsized after falling obscenely down the side of a building. They looked around startled, blinking in the bright white light of day.

Inside they had heard nothing. Held safe, they were the eye of the storm in a room rocked only by the reverberations of the endless echoes of their sighs and moans, and then the silence of their satisfaction. Surrounded by the debris of their choices and limitations, they said goodbye, and walked in opposite directions home.

Weeks before, she had asked Aaftab, 'What happened finally, with you and Farida?'

'My father said no.'

'Why?'

'Because he hadn't chosen her.'

'But she was Muslim?'

'Yes.'

'Pakistani Muslim?'

'Yes. Well … born and raised in Britain.'

'So British-Pakistani Muslim.'

'Yes, Daya.'

'So then?'

'Like I said. He had not been the one to pick her. He would not have picked her.'

'Why?'

'Because of those very reasons.'

Now she wrapped up her dreams.

Now she folded them into a paper plane.

Now she aimed for the wastepaper basket.

8

After the night of the storm they were not alone for many weeks. They tried to resume a life of banter, of book-loaning and cooking, of debate and argument but she faded from their lives by just one shade, like a shirt left a moment too long in the brilliance of the sun. He grew silent, she more absent. In the midst of it, Wasim did not notice a thing, as he struggled with his own disasters and regrets. Wasim was too full of urgent dreams.

He moved as if he had just experienced his first growth spurt and hadn't developed yet an idea of how to manage his suddenly extended frame or lengthened limbs. Wasim was born in the old part of Rawalpindi in a house painted azure, just like the one his mother had grown up in. She insisted it stay that colour because it reminded her of her own mother's house in Afghanistan, where the walls were covered in blue pigment made of crushed lapis lazuli, mined from the land. It had been years since she had been back, and she was an old woman now, but the house was still bright in her mind, and though he had never seen it, and never would, Wasim understood.

She had taught him to cook as a boy. The youngest of four,

he was her daughter. He remembered his childhood as viewed from behind her dupatta, the whole world veiled in sheer pink or pale blue, dotted with flowers. When he was five she started him on the easier tasks. He would shell peas, rinse grapes, mix the flour and knead it into dough with tiny hands. When he learnt how to use the sharp knife she taught him how to slice onions. She showed him the wonder of them – deep violet on the outside, shy lavender just underneath, white at the centre, translucent and crisp. Then she showed him how they would make him cry and she laughed and laughed when he did. He loved her, and she was the absolute centre of his world. He loved the way she sprinkled fresh coriander on everything after she was done cooking and before it emerged magically on the floor of the big room in their house, where she would ask him to lay out a piece of cloth and call his brothers to eat. And he loved how when they were done eating, clearing the space and rolling their mattresses out to sleep, she would come place her hands on his cheeks and tell him Allah was watching over them.

When he first arrived in that cold country he did not understand how to live each day. He had grown up being told there were two kinds of places on earth. Dar al-Islam and Dar al-Harb. The first were of course the houses or lands of Islam. Also known as Dar al-Salam, or the Lands of Peace, these were the places on earth where Muslims lived, under Islamic rule. The second were the lands of *harb*. These were the places on earth where Muslims lived, under governments other than Islamic ones. *Harb.* The Arabic word for war. And by this idea, all the lands where Muslims lived that were not under Islamic law and rule, were automatically, Lands of War.

Harb, he read on the internet, '... also a common name for boys born to Muslim homes.'

He had read shortly before coming across the world that it was his duty as a Muslim to turn war to peace. *Harb* to *salam*. How? He had turned a page, reading by candlelight the book he had borrowed from a friend who said it was imperative to read it before leaving for the West. 'Jihad.' Is that why they were warring lands? Because jihad was inevitable in these lands? This word troubled him, and he understood enough about the world now to know there was no way to explain to people any longer what he had grown up calling jihad. Jihad for him was his soul struggle with truth, with honesty, with goodness and chastity. His everyday battles that he sometimes won – small things like showing a child in the neighbourhood how a butterfly bursts from the cocoon, wet and silver with God's spit, even if it made him late meeting his brother. Things like choosing to better himself when he wanted instead to be playing cricket or visiting the cinema. His jihad was so personal, and the word had become so public.

He asked Aaftab what to do and as always, Aaftab had thought all these things before him, and had the answer. 'You must continue your jihad the way it's always been. If this is a land of harb, you spread al-salam. You take war, and you turn it to peace. And you do this softly. I'll tell you one thing though: the easiest way to start is to banish the word jihad. Over here, it means only one thing. They do not understand a jihad of love. They only understand this: that you have the potential to blow your own balls up just to hurt other people.'

So in place of jihad, Wasim learnt other words. He learnt the word 'orange'. What he called oranges sounded nothing like 'orange'. *Malta*. Orange. Now he learnt Malta was a place, and orange was both a fruit and a colour. So was peach. 'Peach,' he said, the end of the word sounding just like the flesh of the fruit. He remembered that the word 'banana' was a fruit and did not mean 'to make' the way it did back home.

This is how he got through each day. By learning the language to speak peace to those around him. He made lists.

Words that sound exactly like what they are:

Meander
Zest
Drowsy
Sparrow
Box
Plump
Fragrant
Soothe
Feather
Wet

Words that sound nothing like what they are:

Word
Chair
Enthusiastic (Wasim hated this word)
Bored
Incense
Book
Mountain

He made series of words, linking them to remember them better.

Scalloped, scallop, gallop, jalopy, happy.

Autonomy, astronomy, gastronomy. (Also remembered as the '*apne sitaare khaana*' series.)

He learnt he had been saying English prepositions wrong his entire life.

Sit *at* a table, not on it.

His birthday was *in* September, not on it.

Go out *at* night and *in* the day – those were tough to remember.

Wasim's English for anyone who could comprehend or give time to it, was an absolute marvel. It was often all that he had learnt squeezed into one single sentence and it would take years before he understood he could use less to convey more. When Daya met him she complained to Aaftab that he sometimes used everything to convey nothing, and Aaftab laughed and said, 'That's because you aren't listening properly. You're looking for English, but he's speaking a different language. He's a boy from Rawalpindi. He uses everything he has to tell you everything he's got. Listen for it.'

When Wasim read about a Pakistani couple eloping in Swansea, he said, 'Two birds in a bush have flown the nest.'

When he exited the shower with his hair fluffy around his head, he would say, 'God helps those who help themselves be clean and godly.'

And when Aaftab waited on something for work he would say, 'A watched pot never boils, the same as a watched kettle.'

'I have realized if you look at language, it gives you great clues to the world,' Wasim told Daya triumphantly.

'Really?'

'Yes, really. See, there are no victors, only victims, so there are no doctors, only dictums.'

And Daya watching the news where a man and a woman discussed female infanticide in China, said, 'There are no sisters, only systems.'

'Yes. See!' Wasim beamed at her.

'I don't think it works that way, Was.'

'But you just proved it yourself!'

It's true, she thought. If you listened carefully, there was wisdom in Wasim's apparent drivel.

He'd been searching for a text on English manners when he saw the thickly bound book with the strange name in deep-set gold lettering. He slid it out, the spine creaking like an old man's, and stared at it. *The Book of Saint Albans*. The leather was crimson and the letters had been embossed like cuts into skin. Skin that bled gold blood. Thinking it to be some sort of religious text Wasim had opened it. The pages were all but crumbling inside and he found beneath the relatively new leather jacket a body wrinkled by the ages, and the original title of the book. *The Boke of Seynt Albans, 1486*. He had checked it out for two weeks and taken it home immediately. On returning it almost a month later, happily paying the two-pound fine, he was told by an overwrought senior librarian that the book was not actually for loan, and somehow owing to a mistake in the system he had been allowed to take it home. He would be the last person to ever take it out of the library, or touch it with ungloved hands.

The book was divided into three sections: Hawking, Hunting and Heraldry. None of the English in the book was anything he could understand. It was a whole other language unto itself. Baffled, he skimmed through the medieval gentleman's manual, until he found under the chapter

'Hunting', a list titled *The Company of Bestys and Fowlys* and unearthed to his absolute delight and marvel, the magic chest at the bottom of the stuffy mansion that is the English language. Collective nouns.

He found out it was a parliament of owls. And just like that, it began to make sense to him. Of course it was an unkindness of ravens. A charm of finches. An exaltation of larks, but obviously, look at them! He found a more modern book for them and expanded his list. He laughed so much at some – a rascal of boys and an impatience of wives. Not a bunch of bananas but a hand of them. Five yellow fingers attached to a spiny wrist. Others broke his heart … a worship of writers, a host of angels.

When he discovered a dazzle of zebras they almost begged him to stop because he insisted for some time on including that word in everything. 'Daya!' he would greet her. 'You're looking dazzling today just like a magnificent zebra!'

Or 'The sky is dazzlingly bright!'

'That girl has a dazzling laugh.'

For a few weeks he was constantly bedazzled.

Language is finally what made him love a country and its people. Learning the language was his jihad, it brought him peace to understand how to say things. To express and spread his ideas. To understand how to hear things anew. He wished he could speak every language in the world so that he could fall in love with every people, so that no one sounded like the enemy to him. So that every land he entered felt like Dar al-Salam, a land of peace.

When he thought Wasim was ready, Aaftab decided to bring to him the diamonds of any language. He gave him a book of poetry – though Wasim would inform him of course that it was actually *a garland of poems* – and in a sudden act of weakness, he bought for Daya the same book, the same garland. It was a slim, dusty compilation of Mirza Ghalib poems containing three versions of each poem. The original in Urdu, then a transliteration in English or Roman Urdu, and finally an actual English translation. 'My favourite poet is actually Jamal al-Khayal, but I couldn't find a translation. I'll try and translate him for you at some point,' he said as he gave her the book.

~

Jamal al-Khayal was born to a Christian nun and a Muslim soldier on the run, neither of whom swore allegiance to their habit any longer. Jamal was raised communist and fed ideas of freedom the way some children are given candy, and others tales of hate. He would live his life on the run too, and towards the end of it when a reporter managed to track him down and interview him, he said he had made his peace with a life of constant movement. 'I was born when my parents were fleeing the world. If anything, my life has been a testament to them.' Nobody knew what his real name was but by the time he was sixteen, he was called Jamal al-Khayal – beauty of thought. Some called it the beauty of imagination, but that made him sad. He didn't like that and once joked that it made it seem like his thoughts would remain fantasies. 'These are no imagined things,' he would protest. 'This war between the heart and the heartless is real!'

By the time he was eighteen, he was known across the land as al-Khayali. Thinking had become so sparse by then, he was simply The One with the Thoughts. His rousing speeches, his wayward ideas, his fantastic approach to God and politics made students flock to see him. The elderly came too, eager to see this youth everyone spoke of with such reverence. 'I do not believe in God's word,' he said cheekily. 'I believe in the printed word … alas, there were no presses in the time of Muhammad.'

At nineteen, he opened a printing press inside an abandoned church. 'When the missionaries came to this country they brought with them presses to print Bibles to distribute to us – the unwashed, faithless masses. Today we are opening a press inside a church, to distribute intellect to those with faith. People think I have done this as redemption. I have not. I have done this because the rent was cheap.' Laughter in the crowd as the light caught the twinkle in his eye. 'No, this is not redemption. Even I cannot grant such a thing. This is balance. The universe decides these things over time. It sees everything from the start of time to the end of it. And it knows how to keep balance in the story. If you watch for the signs, you will see this balance in each one of our lives and across history.'

Later they would come burn the building, killing two birds with one matchstick. Down with communism. Down with Christianity. And what of all the other unnamed players who were charred. Down with poetry. To hell with words. With common sense. 'Education, science, reason, law,' he would say and crowds would roar. Whoever came to see him, however large the gathering, they all reported back one curious thing. Al-Khayal never spoke louder than a whisper and he did not use a microphone. And yet each person there could hear him above the din, as if he were speaking straight into the shell of their ear, calling forth the tumult of the ocean. The softer he got the louder the roar from his listeners, the greater the impact. Maybe it was why towards the end, he chose to go almost entirely silent, saying what he had to through the written word alone, infusing it with echoes.

His poems were his prayers, he often said. And they would appear everywhere – under bridges and inside wells. Behind toilet doors when toilets had doors. On the walls of mosque gardens, scratched out in tiny letters by some student with a compass. When the words became too big, too blasphemous, they were made to disappear, like goats allowed to graze until they destroyed a carefully manicured garden if allowed to stray. Inevitably, they would always reappear.

In thought and in ink, raise your voices, your pens,
hold your heads above your fears,
they are mightier than one man in power
they are sharper than all his swords.

Everyone presumed Aaftab was a lawyer because of his father. They were wrong. Aaftab was a lawyer because of al-Khayal.

~

'Thank you for the book,' Daya said as they made tea together in the kitchen and Wasim pored over his copy of Ghalib in English in the living room. Then bashfully, aware she was asking for something, she added, 'Translate the al-Khayal for me soon, this is the second time you've mentioned him.'

'I will.'

Later that day Wasim left for his dreaded Sunday afternoon shift and they were finally alone. As soon as the door closed Daya turned to him. 'I can't do this.' He looked away. Despite everything he wanted to believe in, the rules of Islam were imprinted upon some deep inner layer of Aaftab through ceaseless recitation sessions after school each day, and repeated beatings by his father's hands till the sermons and scars became permanent. Till he could no longer forget. He knew that his father somehow believed that when he woke from one of those beatings, it would be with a respect for religion in his body. And yet as his knowledge of Islam had stretched, his respect for it had shrunk. How could Islam forbid intoxicants? Forbid love? Forbid everything that made a life rich with wonder? Art and music and women and wine ... Now he stood at a crossing. Daya before him, pillars behind.

The first pillar: an oath promising to be faithful to Islam. *Lā ilāha illā -llāh, muḥammadur rasūlu -llāh.* The first Kalima. If she uttered these words, Daya knew she would become a Muslim instantly. Once upon a time Aaftab knew all six Kalimas by heart. Now he could recite two, maybe three, the long years at university erasing what he called the 'unjust' ones he had endured. And yet, he understood deep down, one could forget exact words, but not their feelings. 'I testify that there is no God but Allah, and Muhammad is the messenger of Allah.' Sixteen words, and she would be Muslim. She would be entirely a part of him. The part of him he couldn't be rid of.

The other pillars: prayer, charity, fasting and Hajj.

He prayed. Not as much as he should but he did.

He gave away his money. Not one-fortieth of it as prescribed but he certainly took care of those in need.

He fasted during Ramzaan. Thirty long days that made no sense to him.

And Hajj? Sadly, he was far from planning a trip to

Mecca. He could still hear his father's voice, from when he was younger. 'Your mother and I finally have time to go,' so grateful, so blessed. 'Someday, you must go too.'

'Maybe not yet, Abbu,' he had said then.

Maybe not ever, he thought now as Daya's skin flashed before his eyes, blazing, her body taut beneath his as it unfurled for him.

Non-practising Muslim. Practising Muslim. Instead of saying I practise, was it okay, he wondered, to say 'I am practising'? I am practising how to be a Muslim. Maybe someday I'll get there. Maybe someday I'll even see Mecca.

Before he'd left the house Wasim had looked up from the Ghalib book and read out loud a line about believers, and asked, 'Do you know what a group of Muslims is called?'

Aaftab smiled, 'Yes, I do actually.'

'Tell Daya,' Wasim winked at her.

'A pilgrimage.'

~

'I can't do this any longer, did you hear me?' Daya repeated. She walked up to Aaftab and placed her hand on his arm. He did not have the heart to move it away. 'If you touch me, it makes it harder for me,' he said weakly. She dropped her hand. 'Does Wasim know?'

'No one knows. No one will ever know.'

'Why? Because I embarrass you?'

'No, but the way you look at me breaks my heart.'

They stood so still before each other and when he could no longer resist her sadness he placed her in the cavern of his chest and arms though he already knew that later he would have to unlock his bedroom door holding horror in his heart for what he had done again.

But in the shell of his ear, al-Khayal's whisper echoed:

The more walls you bring down, friend,
the safer you will become.

~

Asha was lying on her stomach in Daya's bedroom, her chin resting on the edge of the bed, her arms dangling off it, a book on the floor. 'Asha?' Gyan walked in. 'What are you doing here?'

'Reading.'

'No, I can see that, but why here?'

She rolled over onto her back and stared at the ceiling where they had painstakingly helped Daya trace out the constellations as a little girl and stick on small glow-in-the-dark stars.

'I miss her.'

He sat down. She'd been reading Daya's favourite book from when she was a child, *I Only Have to Close My Eyes*. He picked it up off the floor and pretended to read a verse out loud from it but changed the words as he went along.

'I only have to close my eyes and I can immediately see,

You want to bake me chocolate pies and serve them to me on thaalis of steel.'

She laughed.

'Gyan,' she placed a hand on his knee, pushing herself up.

'Do you think we were there enough?'

'What do you mean?'

'You know, all those years when we were setting up the business and travelling. And even now … we haven't even visited her once.'

'It's been the busiest few years we've ever had, Asha. And she said she understood. In fact, she urged us not to come.'

'But that's just kids, they always say, "No, it's cool."'

'Let her be, baby. If anything, we were probably overbearing. That's what only children grow up to say anyway. We'll go for her graduation.'

'I'm just worried, that's all. She doesn't even call that much anymore.' She ran her fingers down his arm and noticed the hair there had just begun to grey. He sighed and pulled her cheek.

'You know what I'm worried about? I'm worried you've become an old lady who's lost her mind.'

She looked at him, hurt. He started to laugh and then they were both laughing and couldn't stop. They laughed so hard tears rolled down Asha's face and he was breathless and then just as they stopped Gyan giggled and it set them off all over again. He pulled her close to kiss her, 'Come here, you crazy old lady.' She let one hand wander beneath. Breaking away from the kiss she said, 'Tell me, old man, do *you* still have all *your* parts working?'

'Oh they're worse than your mind,' he whispered into her neck and she squealed. 'What about Kamla?' she whispered insistently.

'It's Sunday, she's gone to watch the new Shah Rukh film.'

'Okay, but not here!'

'Yes, here,' he said, and rose to lock the door out of habit.

Later Asha lay with her head in the dip between his shoulder and collarbone. Years ago they'd been walking through Shalimar Bagh in Srinagar and had spotted two trees, distinctly different species, one with white bark and the other with brown, entwined like lovers. The trees had not simply met in the middle or wound a branch around one another. They had become one single tree. Every crevice and curve of one, filled over the years by the other. 'Let's grow like them?' she had said to Gyan, and they had. Now when she lay on his shoulder, it was as though the groove there had been hollowed out by the spade of her cheekbone and nobody but her would ever fit there again.

'You know what you have to do when you miss her?' he asked.

'What?'

'You only have to close your eyes and you will clearly see your little girl is all grown up and loves life more than she loves you or me.'

'You should just write your book,' she mumbled into his chest, where too the hair had begun to grey.

'Old lady's lost her mind,' he mumbled back.

~

Lying two feet of bedsheet away from Daya, Aaftab noticed everything. The elegance of her frequently injured dancer's feet crossed at the ankles. The way her mouth had fallen open softly as she slept for a few minutes, exhausted from their love-making, from crying, from the exhilaration of calling her body to pleasure. He took note of all her perceived imperfections, her ideas of herself about which he was gathering knowledge by listening to her. Though they found themselves inexplicably more and more in rooms with locked doors, alone he found himself labelling each piece of information and planting it carefully in his forest of memories, like seeds of her that would grow into fantasies that he could later hold on to and walk through and call 'his'. *His Daya*. His Daya laughed louder than other people's Dayas. His Daya had breasts so magnificent under her big shirts no one could tell. His Daya was not always shy.

As they had finished making love in the gossamer twilight, his body still shielding hers, she had made a light, insignificant joke and as he'd begun to laugh, she had drawn her head back for a moment to gaze upon the scars that interrupted the topaz skin on his back. She touched one. 'Stretch marks,' he smiled and explained … from when his anger had tried to leave his flesh as a teenager and God had stitched him up over and over again. 'I thought …' she began and glanced at her hand. He kissed her forehead then her fingers and said, 'No, you didn't do that, your nails are too short.' But what she had really thought was: Was this done to you? And what he did not say was: You didn't do that, but someone else did. *And it was not an act of passion, but one of violence*. He could still hear the hiss of the belt through the air, before it touched his flesh, the sound that came before often more terrifying than the wound that came after. The lie had floated in the room quietly before dissolving into a mist of kisses, but for that one moment Daya had wondered if as much as she ached to heal him, there was perhaps no way to, and that the river between their worlds was actually an ocean. One she could not cross bank to bank but would have to maneouvre shore to shore – a much longer distance than she had negotiated.

She stirred and saw him watching her. 'Give me the rest of the year?' she said.

'What?' he asked, sitting up.

Give me time.

'And then what?'

'And then we part.'

'From a single night, you want an entire season?' he joked.

'What I want is a lifetime, and what I'm asking is a pittance in comparison.'

She was smiling everywhere but inside her eyes. He lay down next to her again in the slow, departing sunlight, his entire body one shade lighter than hers. His entire life, one shade darker.

And if I could I would give you all my seasons.

She had known from the moment she had seen him that he was trouble. His shoulders where he held all his confidence. His beautiful uneven mouth from which words fell like raindrops and she had heard when he was angry, a storm. She knew within moments of the second time they had met, that this was a man she could love, and knowing this, she felt her entire being take a step towards him. And seeing her, and seeing how magnetic he found her, he like any sensible man told his entire being to take a step away from her. And because everyone apart from her usually obeyed him, it did. But now, it fought back.

Many days into their courtship of which no record was meant to remain, she found the courage to ask for what she knew she deserved.

'Daya,' he started. 'The reason I resist you is not because I do not want you. It's because I *cannot* want you. And I do not want to keep taking from your body what I cannot give your heart.'

'But what about *your* heart?' she asked the questions he always wished she wouldn't.

'My heart is used to not getting what it wants.'

She nodded, understanding the unsaid weight of his past.

She had never liked the words, 'I love you.' They had always seemed to her the ultimate cliché, the commonest quote. She wanted to say other things like I adore you. I like you *so much*. I would like to grow old with you. I want you and only you. I worship you. You are my temple.

Sorry, my mosque.

But now she succumbed. 'I love you,' she said quickly, kissing his cheek, rising to throw on her sweatshirt and track pants over a body still salty with love. She opened the door swiftly, backpack already on one shoulder. At the front door she paused and only half turning her head, said, '... and at least I know you want.' He said nothing as she walked out. He did not reply until she was halfway down the street. Then he whispered, 'I love you too,' and the empty house mocked his empty life.

~

The thing no one could quite comprehend about al-Khayal, but that Aaftab knew and connected with deeply, intrinsically, was his anger. People called the poet sad, wise, gifted, even depressed. They called him insane, hilarious. No one called him enraged. But Aaftab knew, because behind the calm of his words, Aaftab always saw the glint of something steelier.

Al-Khayal was angry at religion. He had grown up hearing the echo of his mother's voice say, 'What were we to do? While the Hindus and Muslims fought their righteous wars, what could we do? And my skin, too dark for England, that country I, a Christian, was told to go to.'

There was a story he told about his life sometimes, and a rare recording of it still exists today in the Quaid-e-Azam Library in the Bagh-e-Jinnah in Lahore. As a child travelling endlessly with his parents, al-Khayal remembered a day when they had stopped along a highway crowded with young men. He understood later, as an adult, that it had in all likelihood been Afghanistan where his father had communist connections. They stopped by the side of a road where many other trucks were gathered. This was unusual as people did not stop here; they journeyed on. A woman stood to one side, weeping. Jamal remembered leaving the car, holding the edge of his father's kameez. They joined the long row of men standing with arms crossed and heads shaking. The road descended to the east into a pit of nothingness, white dust, empty … but then he looked again and saw it was not so. There in the dust, something terrible. Something awful. He blinked again and again, he did not want this dust in his eyes. The woman's crying had turned to a wail and began to sound like the azan and Jamal found himself kneeling, praying and finally vomiting.

Before him, in a pit off the side of an ordinary highway were the mangled bodies of a mass murder. Skeletons, without anything to hold them in human shape. Without flesh or features they had tumbled into one another. Bone on bone they lay collapsed.

He had two odd thoughts then, one which he would never in his life remember and one which he would never again forget.

The first: How in God's name did they rebuild the dinosaurs?

The second: Bones have no religion.

Without the markers, what religion is a person? Without the thread around wrist or arm or chest. Without the hats, crocheted and close-fitting, or broad and black, the cloth wound around a face, sheer and delicate covering only the head, or dark and heavy covering the entire being, shortpant showing ankles, turbans, bangles, bindis, braids, crosses, collars, materials, colours. Without language in our mouths and skin on our bones, the body is still marked in various ways, sliced or tattooed to reveal something one can see even when as naked as the day we are born. But without our skin, beneath it all, he thought, 'Our bones have no religion.' And further, further inside and under … under skin and blood and bones, what there lies? You know the word. *Soul.* Does that wispy thing that possesses the power to move between worlds possess a religion? Jamal thought of how the endgame of every single religion on earth was the salvation of the soul, and yet, looking at that vast pit, he knew the greatest secret of the laughing universe. *That bones and souls have no religion.*

In that moment, he became Jamal al-Khayal.

On his deathbed he was alone save a devotee who treated him much to his annoyance like a saint. He had finished his writing for the evening. By then al-Khayal had turned his old theoretical phrase – my poems are my prayers – literal, and every time he heard the call to prayer from the mosque, he would rise and rinsing his hands in a basin in the corner of his tiny room, sit down at the small writing desk by the window looking out to endless greenery. Over there, five times a day, seated cross-legged on his prayer mat on the floor, wrists resting on the table before him, he would write. It was in fact in this time that he had begun to write love poems and everyone said they were to an invisible lover. That day, at the hour of the maghrib prayer, he glanced up between verses. The mustard field before him was so vibrant, so green, it distracted him from his words and he stared into it, transfixed. In the field he suddenly caught a glint. He frowned, and a moment later the bullet found that same frown.

As he went to that final godless frontier, his life's work left him and he recalled for the first time that initial odd thought and whispered it to a room empty except for his lackey who now sat stricken by his fallen saint. Not one person would believe him later when he told them the last words the great al-Khayal had uttered, were: 'Show me then, how in God's name did they rebuild the dinosaurs?'

9

Daya had wanted to study Islam as the enemy, as the thing keeping him away from her. Instead, she fell in love with it. She fell in love with the poetry and the piety and the ideas of immense purity. She fell in love with calligraphy and male modesty. With the sound of Arabic words and the white and green mosque opposite the boys' house. She fell in love with the saints and the Sufis, the architecture and tales of Arabia. She wanted to enter and witness the veiled world that was forbidden to her.

Mecca – that glorious city she would never see. Faith at its most fervent. What Wasim prayed to five times a day. What millions of Muslims made their way to, to perform Hajj, the once-in-a-lifetime opportunity. Pillar Five. She had heard from Wasim with whom she spoke frequently of religion how non-Muslims had been there. 'Some have gone … illegally of course.' They had swept themselves in, shrouded in swirling white, blending into the masses of Muslims as they prayed, calling themselves names like Abdullah, in place of Richard. And Aaftab, between eating grapes, 'It's the largest mosque in the world.'

'How large?'

'You can stuff four million people in there.'

'More than the population of Wales,' Wasim offered.

'Rock in Rio times three,' Aaftab said.

'Los Angeles,' Wasim replied.

'It's not laas, it's Los, like loss,' Aaftab corrected him.

'It's still almost four million!'

'How on earth can you two keep at this fact-checking nonsense?'

Wasim grinned, 'While other boys are chasing women, we look things up.'

And they laughed but Aaftab was very quiet after.

Daya who had never had to think about religion before, began to recall the rare times it had been of consequence in her home, and not simply prevalent in the odd alchemy of it her parents had adopted. She drew on her memories of Islam, of her understanding of the existence of it. She remembered an evening at her school when she was a child, maybe eight, a showing by the students of *Macbeth* in musical form, to which all the parents of the students of the school had been invited. Asha had looked resplendent, her long and already greying hair held up with small nectar-scented white flowers. She wore a sari of Benaras silk into which was woven a stampede of animals. Elephants leading the way, parrots in flight and peacocks on foot, poor souls, small butterflies in gold. The history teacher passing by had turned to her and said with genuine warmth, 'Your sari's so lovely!'

Touched, Asha had replied, 'Thank you, it's from Varanasi. I actually bought it there a few years ago.'

'Ah, one can tell! It's gorgeous … those Muslims really know their craft!'

And she had flurried on. Asha could not believe what she

had called 'the utter condescension of the woman' when they were in the car on the way back home. 'The small-mindedness of it! The worst part is in her righteous entitlement, she thought she was being generous! That she wasn't *at all* biased. *Those. Those* Muslims.'

Back home stretched out on the bright coral sofa Asha sipped a glass of wine and waved the other hand around emphatically. 'I can't believe they allow her to teach history.' Gyan finally in an attempt to calm her said, 'Oh my love, I'm sure she isn't all bad. It's just how so many are raised in this country ... to think of Muslims as ... the other. I'm sure it doesn't mean her history-teaching skills are ... lacking? I mean ...I don't see what was so terrible about it. She's just like everyone else.'

'You think so?' she asked.

'Well I think she's better than someone professing outright hate. In a dim-witted way, she was just trying to express appreciation.'

Asha looked at him for a long time, a half smile at her mouth. 'Let me explain to you about her ignorance, or as you called it, her dim-wittedness.' She paused dramatically and stood up. 'This sari,' she said, beginning to pull it off her body in slow folds so as not to damage it, 'was not woven by a Muslim. You want to know why?' She didn't wait for his reply, didn't even glance at him, engrossed in her precise movements. 'It is covered, as you can clearly see, in animals. No Muslim weaver will weave any of Allah's living beings into their craft. Replicating Allah's divine artistic hand is a sin – yes?' He nodded, waiting to hear what his wife was building up to. 'So this was made most likely by a Hindu weaver. *Historically*,' she stressed upon the word with contempt,

'Muslim weavers have refused to weave these saris. Flowers, domes, latticework, leaves – all fine. Animals – no.'

'Asha, baby, so she didn't know – what's your point?' he interrupted her gently.

'This. If you do not know enough about the other to correctly commend them, you most certainly do not know enough to correctly condemn them.'

He could have married her all over again. Daya, still in her make-up and costume from the play, watched from an armchair, forgotten, wide-eyed, confused as Asha flopped back down onto the sofa and waggling her finger, said, 'It's these false sympathizers we really have to watch out for, jaan – they're the really dangerous ones,' while Gyan laughed and laughed.

It wasn't the only time Daya had seen her mother erupt that way. Incidents that earlier held no importance for her, Daya now unearthed from her memory, to examine and understand. She recalled now how ardent her mother had been about this one thing, time and time again. She began to discover a pattern, like a child tracing a river with their finger in an atlas, following a journey, understanding why grass grew where it did, and rocks break open where they do. She was mapping the geography of her life, and which areas Asha had made fertile and planted with ideas. The areas that were now flowering with thought. She recalled a small dinner party her parents had had just before she'd left for university. It was timed by chance, not for her, and yet her parents' friends had initially treated the evening as a congratulatory one, telling stories, much to her embarrassment, about Daya's grace even as a child.

At the end of the night she sat alone, changing CDs on

a music system, a small glass of white wine on the floor, watching her parents illuminated by candlelight, in animated discussion with the friends still there. They prided themselves on the close circle of friends they had collected and cultivated over the years. Intellectuals – writers, poets, chefs and political journalists. A gay couple who made dresses women coveted. A woman who made pottery glazed in indigo, a man who had painted his wife in the nude over a period of thirty years – they were interesting, intimidating even, but Daya had watched these people as she had grown up and now thought of them as comical, as self-indulgent. They traded exotic travel stories and jokes with sexual undertones. They seemed unaware of their privilege, and Daya knew somewhere the satisfaction they took from a friendship with her parents – actual do-gooders who had devoted their lives to helping people, and had somehow managed to earn a living while doing so. She understood what they took from the relationship with the couple, the self-congratulatory air they left these dinners with, but she could not that evening fathom what her parents took from them.

Almost as if in line with her thoughts, Daya had suddenly heard her mother's always even voice rise. 'What? You cannot be serious!' she was saying. Daya glanced at her father, who was watching his wife with alarm, so rare was it for him to see her lose composure. She was staring down one half of the gay couple, the heat rising in her face, very pink now against the delicate ivory of her kurta, dotted with tiny specks of silver, now aquiver on the surface of her angry body. 'We are racist to the Chinese, the Japanese, *anyone* with those features,' she said, wincing at her own phrasing, 'including those born right here! We are racist to white people while kissing their backsides. Don't get me started on the things we say about Africans – even Gandhi was not above that!' she said, rolling her eyes. She trailed off in sorrow, shaking her head and they thought her sudden outburst was over, but she began again with renewed anger. 'Forget being racist to other people, let's simply speak about how we have treated each other.' She began spitting out words, a song of insults, '*Kaala, kaali, chinky, chamaar. Sardar ji ke baara baj gaye?*' Each word a self-inflicted wound. 'And what about caste?' she practically screeched. 'You think they're jokes but they're not. Not when even you speak about Muslims this way. Not when Christians cannot pray in peace … church windows being smashed regularly, their priests set on fire and you tell me it's a joke? Really? Think of two little boys burning to death in a station wagon, being held there by grown men with axes, and tell me you believe what you just said.' Looking her friend in the eye, her lip curling cruelly, she said, 'And let me tell you, in a world led by the strong … nigger, or slut, or even as you said, what was it? *Katua*? Is not so different …' she paused, 'from a fucking fag.' Daya watched the complexity on her father's face, his horror mixing with pride. Her mother brought a cigarette to her mouth, lit it and said, in pain, 'We live in a world where real words, words like "feminist" and "Paki" have been turned into insults, and insults like those you speak so easily, have been turned into real, acceptable words.' Then raising her glass to the Faiz poem on the wall, she said in deeply sarcastic mimicry of her husband's hopeful refrain over the years, 'But our souls must be Sufi,' before rising and striding out of the large central room, which felt now like a flower that had just lost its stamen.

She hadn't come back out and the guests had finished their

drinks and left, Gyan politely attempting to make amends. In the weeks to come people would talk of course, the couple she had insulted refusing to come over ever again. People would call her names behind her back, at other, less elegant parties. Names like holier-than-thou, Miss Goody Two Shoes, and it struck Daya now, her mother had even listed 'Paki-lover' as one of the insults she'd heard was being thrown about, when she'd called once to ask Daya if she was settled in her new home in Cardiff. *Paki-lover*. A choice insult.

When the guests had left, Gyan had sat down on their big couch upholstered ten years later in cerrulean and rubbed his tired eyes. Daya who had been carrying glasses to the kitchen came and sat down next to him. 'So what happened?' she'd asked.

'You didn't hear?'

'No, I mean, what set her off?'

He lit a cigarette and reached for the newspaper at the edge of the table. The table was a marvel, a huge single piece of wood, an entire fallen tree trunk smoothed down on one side to create a surface now ringed with many years of frosty kisses from glasses resting on it. He unfolded the paper with spread arms, the cigarette dangling from his mouth. 'Here,' he handed it over and tapped on an article. 'India voted the most racist country in the world.' Their designer friend had disagreed of course. And had ended with a slur aimed at the Muslims. 'What did he say exactly?' Daya asked. Gyan paused before answering, pained to have to repeat it to his teenage daughter. He cleared his throat, then attempted mimicry. 'Oh please! Who compiled this? Must be the katuas, always whining.' He took a long drag and reached out to tap the article again, 'He thought it was funny. Your mother did not.

He proved the article right of course.' Daya looked down at her lap and saw a fire spreading, the article aflame. She leapt up and her father too as the fire's sizzle chewed down the paper with its red-hot teeth, its orange tongue in tow, licking. She threw it onto the floor and they watched as the point Gyan had absentmindedly touched with his cigarette disappeared. The point the article had been trying to make, gone as well, the charred remains of the dirty truth floating up towards them.

Two incidents, almost a decade apart. Her mother was nothing if not consistent in her passions.

~

That night Asha had been inconsolable. When Gyan had made it to their room after clearing the ashes and sending Daya to bed he had found her red-faced and with sadness on her shoulders, from where she had thrown off her cloak of anger. 'What a horrible world we live in,' she kept saying. 'If *our friends* think this way then what hope is there?' And he didn't have the answers so he held her. Eventually, as always when either of them was in that state, they retreated to Vaikuntha below, where he made her a cup of tea. She sipped it and said suddenly, thoughtfully, 'Do you remember 1992?' He had his arms crossed over his chest and yawned a reply, but she wasn't waiting for him to respond now, she was talking, energized by the tea. 'I always thought it would never happen again, but there are days, when,' she paused, testing the words in her head before they escaped her mouth, 'I understand why it might.' He looked startled. 'I'm sorry but I do. Because I could kill a few people for their beliefs … and does that make me better? And if I with all my … my possibly false ideas of fairness can *want to* … then who's to say whose beliefs are more righteous to kill for? I don't believe I could take another Ayodhya in our lifetime.'

'We've seen worse. We've seen '84.'

'Remember how the day she died we kept switching on the radio and they just kept playing sitar music. It was maddening.'

'I can imagine it happening again though,' Gyan said grimly. 'When have Hindus in India ever apologized or repented? We really believe it is "our land".'

'Are you trying to make me feel better or worse?'

'Sorry.' Silence. He was lying flat, craving sleep and she was sitting up, still sipping tea. He circled her waist with his arms, resting his head against her hip. 'It's just the way of the world right now, jaan,' he said softly to her thigh but internally Gyan was dismayed by her unlearning innocence. Her hope that kept her going and somehow kept destroying her further. Like his mother in the last days of her life, crumbled by Alzheimer's, asking every few days where her own parents were and being reminded gently that they were gone. Every few days feeling that pain anew. Gyan always believed it was nothing but the sorrow of losing them so many times over that finally killed her. And now he saw that same shock in Asha. Need he remind her again that the world was a bad place?

They had fallen asleep there on the mattress that could fit an army and woken to Sunday morning. Daya had walked in, Barfi in tow, and the three of them had lain around, drinking fresh tea and reading fresh papers, passing pages to one another, Daya finally rejecting the news for a Gerald Durrel memoir, giggling out loud from time to time, all of them listening to the birds. They were aware that morning that with Daya leaving so soon, these were the last few days in which they would share this buoyant ritual of togetherness for some time. But they were unaware then that it would perhaps be the very last time.

At some point Daya asked if she could go up and put the television on and they lumbered up the stairs and set out bowls of fresh fruit, and buttered toast. Kamla took Sundays to herself and the house felt half full without her. They put on the TV and Daya settled in on the floor cushions to watch reruns of *Mahabharata*, part engrossed part amused by the histrionics, theatrics and make-up. The cardamom in their tea scented up the sunlit room. Asha sat leaning against Gyan, still requiring the comfort of his being, so noble and upright in a world she saw as slanted. As she watched the show with Daya, she wondered if Muslim families across the country were watching it now too. If Muslim children had watched this or that dreadful *Ramayana* with the sparkling arrows, at the same time Daya had, as a little girl of eight or nine, every Sunday morning when anyone walking the streets of India might have been forgiven for thinking the country had been emptied overnight of all humans.

Did Muslims participate in the merry mythology of the country's Sundays? (A different religion's different Lord's day actually, come to think of it.)

Mythology. Just a myth then.

But.

Had a mosque been brought to the ground because of a myth?

And what had been there before a temple?

And what before that?

Blood had bathed the country and it had brought horror for some time of course.

But then, it seemed to Asha, they had all simply learnt to wade through it.

The soles of their feet all red, each one of them a temple dancer.

~

No, Daya could not recall more than a handful of incidents when the differences between humans – religious differences in particular – had come up except to shame those who saw these variances a tad too clearly. And so she was left to learn of those differences herself.

It was raining the day Wasim and she first spoke about it. She was sitting by her window watching the sky drape the glass in a delta of skinny rivulets, a perpetual monsoon with no preceding heat to relieve one from. She was thinking of how Milni and she would dance in the rain as children. When she was younger the inaugural day of the monsoon was always marked by Milni coming over and shouting up from the gate, 'Ey Daya, come down!' She would run through the garden in her shorts, barefoot, and they'd let the water out of the letter box. They'd lie down, the grass hot against their backs, the rain cold against their faces. They'd speed their cycles through the puddles. Eventually they would dance, practising their latest routine in the rain. Knees flecked with mud, feet sinking, snails for audience, thunder applauding.

You could *feel* it, Daya thought now, watching the miserable pitter patter outside. The Indian rain was blessed, allowing the parched throat of the country to bet on life again. Before it arrived, everyone held their breath for days, moving like octopuses through the sticky heat. The smell of rotting garbage everywhere. Bathing was of no use – one broke sweat through the soap. The fans worked in vain – they barely sliced through the treacle humidity. Airconditioners were to little avail – they made the heat all the hotter later. Coolers did their job badly, sprinkling the heat upon one, like sugar water. The evening disappointed as well, promising to bring coolness at sundown but failing embarrassingly. And the nights, they failed too as you lay counting sheep and stars and minutes that felt like hours. Then in a torrent of generosity the rain would rumble in, child of clouds, dripping pure relief on a nation of grumps. The water like manna turned the streets berserk with release. The monsoon's blue Bacchanalia, and they were all – not just Daya and Milni – a little higher, a little freer, wilder, less servile, less responsible. It was, until it turned into floods that killed farmers, a symbol of national happiness. But this … she reached out to touch the glass before her and sighed. There was a reason why they said it was 'pissing down' again.

'Daya!' she heard her name being called and for a moment believed it might be Milni, calling her down to dance. But it was Wasim at the fire escape, wet and knocking. She let him in and made him a cup of Kettley.

It wasn't that it hadn't come up before. Islam was always around, but it was in the small things. In the muttered 'Bismillah' before they ate together, even if it was just burgers. It was in the facts of Friday – 'It's Friday so we'll be at the mosque, right?' Right. It was in the way Daya had begun buying only halal meat, in case they dropped by. Though Aaftab the Adulterer had decided he could not speak to her about Islam, because well, Aaftab was not speaking to himself about it, Wasim could, and that day Wasim finally did.

'Tell me something,' he began, staring alongside her out the window, tea cup warming hands, steam warming nose, his socks drying on the radiator. 'I've been wanting to know this genuinely – why do you have so many gods?' Daya thought about it and finally said, 'Well, we're a lot of people … so, I guess we needed more? So that no one ever needed to stand in line.'

'Very funny. Do you know what the group word is?'

'No, but I'm pretty certain you're going to tell me. Also it's "collective noun".'

He ignored her correction.

'A rabble of gods.'

And like this the ice broke. That which they had been avoiding, much like Daya's well-intentioned parents, was broached. Daya opened the door to Wasim's endless anthropological mind, his well of wisdom that needed constant replenishing. As fair barter, she also opened the windows to a world he had never had access to before, apart from in books that were often too complicated for him to fully understand. 'You're my first Hindu friend,' he said simply. And Daya had to admit, despite never being able to see the difference, despite being raised to *not know* the difference, they were her first recognizably Muslim ones. If she paid attention to names now, she could count on her fingers how many of her friends in Lalabad had been Muslim. And then she had to ask: how many of them had worked to *not be seen* as different? She wondered this as with each passing day she understood the many differences.

Every question Wasim presented her with, made her see more clearly the distance between Aaftab and herself. And made her love him more, for the sheer length of the bridges he had crossed to end up in her bed.

One day, Daya, exhausted by Wasim's unstoppable questions after a long day of dancing, said, 'For all you know, Wasim, God is a woman.' Part of her wanted for him to be offended, shocked too. She had just started another round, she thought, waiting with amusement to hear what he would say. But he surprised her when instead of touching his ears and saying 'Tauba, tauba,' as he usually did when he heard something 'devilish', he said amicably, 'You're right, for all I know God *is* a woman.' And Daya, now more knowledgeable, said, 'But would that not go against the word of the Prophet?' He paused and she knew he was mumbling inside his own head the words 'peace be upon him' because she had asked when they spoke of religion if it was alright to just think it rather than say it out loud as it was just faster than him constantly interrupting with *sallallahu alayhi wasallam*. 'It would, I guess, you're right, it would. But if I raise the question, and I still come back faithful, am I not twice as devout?'

She couldn't tell when he was serious and when he spoke in jest. She asked why they didn't drink and he replied, inexplicably for someone who had never had one, 'Because of the hangover.' She could not tell if Wasim's questions were at some level him seeking assurance by trying to assess whether all of Hinduism's differences were somehow flawed, for if it were a perfect religion, it would have matched his own faith's take on all matters.

She bought a Quran. Then she bought another one. 'They say different things,' she told Aaftab, and he laughed as he told her, 'Welcome to my world,' but she couldn't quite grasp what their world was made of, and why the walls guarding it went up so high, or the foundation stones so deep.

'Let me try and explain,'Aaftab said when they were alone, finally breaking his silence on Wasim and her constant exchange of theological information.

'What is your identity?' he asked.

'I don't understand.'

'What would you describe yourself as, in terms of your identity. You identify as ...?'

'A dancer?'

'Great. And?'

'A student. A daughter. Foodie, listener of rock music, reader of books, tomboy, early riser, dog lover.'

He smiled.

'Well, this is mine, and not because I feel this way, but because I have no choice but to feel this way.'

'Go on.'

'I am a Muslim first, above all things. Then I am Pakistani. Then I am my father's son. My mother's son, my siblings' brother and someday, inshallah, I will be a good husband.'

She looked saddened. 'But none of it is about you.'

'You see Daya – your identity is defined by who you have been allowed to be, mine, by who I have not.'

'That's your self-pity again.'

'Not true. Your life is a project in self-discovery. Mine is one in responsibilities owed to others.'

'And yet, it's not what you actually think about yourself. You know that isn't who you are.'

'Maybe it's who I ought to be.'

'Then you have no business being here.'

'I am trying to change it but it's exhausting. It means going against everything I have been raised to think about myself. I manage, still. I fight still. But Wasim and so many others will perhaps never be able to cross over. What's worse is most don't want to. They don't want to challenge it and be different, and they don't want to know anyone who is. And it isn't even about Islam really, at the heart of it. It's just … mindset. You'll find folks like that in all religions, in all countries,' he said at the end, defensive.

'I guess so. It's just that I believe we should choose our likes and dislikes, friendships and associations based on those core beliefs. Who and what we choose to identify as. Not who and what we cannot change.'

'Daya, in a war if you had to pick a side whose would you pick? The side that liked dogs more? That read more books?'

'Why not?'

'Because even Hitler liked dogs.'

'Well, I would rather be friends with someone because they read a lot than friends with someone because they're Indian or Hindu.'

'And that's why you're you, Daya,' he broke, kissing her neck. 'That's why you're beautiful …' He kissed her left breast. 'That's why you chose me …' And he dissolved.

~

Wasim called the next day.

'Daya! Who is Kalima and why did you not tell me about her?' Daya began giggling. 'It's not kalima! She's Kaali Maa,' she stretched the words out. 'Whatever, I'm coming over please make tea.'

Wasim could not comprehend goddesses. It was all too Greek for him. Too much fantasy, too little piety. And it was Kali who truly caught him off guard. The curves and sweet music of Saraswati he could understand but this woman with her tongue out, seemingly mid-dance step, one man wrapped in snakes beneath her foot, another's head in hand, skulls around neck, demonic, took his breath away in a way he wasn't sure was admiration. He dropped by soon after he called. 'Look at her!' he exclaimed, gesticulating unevenly at the computer screen in front of them. It was a particularly horrific image of Kali, Daya had to admit, if only to herself. 'What's wrong with it?' she said feigning innocence. He shook his head.

'This doesn't set a bad impression for good Hindu girls?'

'Better than good Muslim men only being good for the promise of virgins,' she replied.

He continued shaking his head, 'Scary, Daya, she's scary. And I'm so sick of that virgin talk.'

'She's meant to be! And what do good Muslim women get?' she continued.

'Well, if you *were* a good Muslim woman, you would get to be one of those lucky virgins.'

'Really? Share my man with seventy-one women?'

'Okay you would get to be with your husband even in the afterlife.'

'But won't he be busy with the virgins?'

'No. That's the thing, that despite them, he will love you most of all. But since you're a naughty Hindu girl corrupting my eyes with Kali, you only get to be burned alive on your husband's pyre when he dies.'

She shoved him and he laughed, thrilled he had got the better of her, she who claimed not to care about religion.

'If you find a husband, which is of course unlikely.'

Crossing her arms she scolded him roundly, 'Now you're just being rude, so let me tell you you're dangerously close to depleting your virgin supply to zero.'

'I see. Who the hell wants virgins anyway?'

They collapsed into laughter Daya shaking her head, 'So I get the man of my dreams, he promises me he loves me most then goes and sleeps with seventy women … but comes back and tells me he still loves me and we're cool. I can't tell if your heaven is really, really archaic, or exactly like modern free love.'

'In the interest of Islam, I'm going to say it's highly modern.'

'Highly.'

'Just like your rabble of gods.'

And she cackled once more.

A list (not comprehensive) of questions Wasim asked Daya in those days:

Why are they blue?

Why do you worship animals?

Why does she have so many arms?

Did the elephant guy actually balance on a mouse?

Was any of this real?

So you don't have prophets?

Who is the most powerful?

Why do the gods have six packs?

Who wrote your holy book?

How come you people find cows dirty?

Okay, if you don't find them dirty, why won't you eat them? I'd eat a pig if I thought it was clean.

Right. But have you ever eaten beef?

And she:

Why can't you eat meat that isn't halal-killed?

But don't you agree pigs are really cute?

What is Shia and Sunni?

Why do women have to wear hijab?

Why can't you drink?

Does everyone go for Hajj?

She rarely had answers for him, but he always had reasons for her.

And all his reasons told her one thing over and over.

Aaftab had come from even further away than she knew.

10

Farida, smiling, had crossed the lawn patterned in a grid of white linen-covered tables with pink carnations in vases all set up for graduation lunch. She had taken a deep breath, then dipped her head and said, 'Assalamaleikum,' to Aaftab's father who had arrived the night before from Islamabad to watch his eldest son become a lawyer. She had hesitated then as his father had looked away, embarrassed at being directly addressed by this beautiful young Muslim woman in a rose-coloured hijab. Signalling to Aaftab, he had turned wordlessly on his heel and walked away.

There on the lawn, Farida, mouth open, trembling.

And right beside her, Aaftab would never forget her wizened, kindly old father whom he had assured, his own father was just dying to meet, hand now outstretched in shaky, ungraced handshake.

She had given him a look both withered and withering – for what is love but the ability of humans to both mirror and reflect back? – he had felt it before he had had the indecency to look her in the eye. And then she had picked her dignity off the grass and led the old man away. He had looked shrunken, like a man within a man.

Aaftab, alone on that vast lawn that was preparing for celebration, felt the familiar burn of shame in his throat and then his cheeks. He balled up his fists and attempted to steady his breath then found himself gasping for it because on the back of his head he felt the sting of something that he had forgotten. Something he was even more acquainted with than shame. All those years in Britain away from the hand that fed him just to strike him, had given him grace and confidence and had healed the scars walls had once dealt his knuckles and belts had imprinted on his calves. But in taking his dark memories to a place far away, his happiness had also taken with it his fear. Now it returned to his bones, and scarlet to his eyes. His father was five inches shorter than Aaftab, and an old man, to anyone watching, but he had struck him so hard across the back of his head he had knocked the wind out of his lungs. And he had done it because he possessed a certainty that a Pakistani boy would not hit his father back. Would not dare. And it was then that Aaftab understood. He saw in front of him a weak man, who had been made weaker still by a beautiful woman before him. He saw it was his father's internal acknowledgement of her beauty that had first made him feel shame, then embarrassment, and then swiftly brought on the thick sense of disgust and inexplicable anger towards her he had put on display. And knowing all this, Aaftab wanted to laugh. He unclenched his fists but it would only be much later that he would find the tiny red crescents on his palms from where his nails had dug into his skin in anguish.

'If you wanted to fuck a whore you should have asked,' his father began in Urdu, his tone so camaraderial it chilled Aaftab's hot blood. 'I've been a young boy too, you know.

Just because I wanted to get into some girl's chaddis, I didn't promise to marry her and start making decisions my mother was meant to. If you want to fuck a whore,' he pulled from his pocket a slim brown leather wallet, 'then here. But don't you ever bring up *marrying* some British-born slut to me, ever again.' He held out four fifty-pound notes.

'She's not a whore,' Aaftab said quietly, using the formal word for prostitute rather than the slur, like his father.

'What did you say?'

'I said,' he was louder now, emboldened, 'she's not a whore.'

The reaction was instantaneous. In a single stride his father had moved towards him and gripped his collar roughly, jerking Aaftab closer.

'Watch yourself, son,' he said. 'I will take everything away from you. You hear me? Everything.'

He was raising his voice, red in the face. People were watching. Aaftab looked him in the eye, then placed his hands on his father's wrists where they sat, taut at his collarbones, and squeezed. He felt them loosen their grip and when his father stepped back, Aaftab shrugged his shoulders into place, picked the mortarboard off the ground, nodded and said calmly, 'You have already taken from me the only thing I wanted.' Then for the first time in his life, he turned his back on the man who had never failed to remind him he held the scales of Aaftab's life in his hands.

And so, the day Aaftab was to graduate from university, he was made instead to graduate from innocence. As he walked across the lawn towards absolutely nothing, Aaftab remembered suddenly his first memory of his father. He was almost two and still learning how to walk. He must have been a cautious starter, slower than others, because he understood now the adult name for what he had sensed in his father even then. It was exasperation. In the memory, he had fallen and was lying face down in his own tears, struggling to rise again from the gravelled driveway when he heard his father's voice say sharply to his mother, 'Leave him – how else will he learn to be a man?' Now it echoed:

Leave him – how else will you learn to be a man?

Farida did not take his calls. His father had not even waited long enough to hear about the job he had been promised at a city firm. It would be months before his mother and certain events managed to get them to speak to each other again. Aaftab did not attend his own graduation ceremony that afternoon and, a week later pawned the thread-of-gold and speck-of-diamond ring he had bought, for something he had once tried while in high school in Pakistan. It had calmed him one night when he had left home to drive around Islamabad, enraged as usual. A friend he'd met had taken out a sticky black ball and rolled him a joint, slender and dangerous as a stiletto. He had never smoked it again; he said it took away the anger and he wanted to feel the anger. So he would roll them for his friends, his quick fingers enjoying the crackle of the imported paper as it curved beneath his thumbs. Licking them shut he handed them over unlit. Rockets, waiting to be fired up, to take boys to the stars. And each time the joint was passed, as they drove around under cool Islamabad skies, Ali Azmat's voice floating out from the car windows, Aaftab would shake his head, rejecting the drug. Like this he held on to his anger. Held it firm and thumping against his chest. Held it tight as it wriggled there. Held it close and felt it. Until love came. And he could not argue with love. For love he allowed it to melt away. Farida had diffused the ticking bomb that was his heart and placed there a lotus instead. And now that she was gone, he no longer knew how to deal with this anger that had arrived like a shock. How to process the pain. So armed with a bottle of whisky, a stick of hash and a sheaf of rolling papers, Aaftab withdrew to face the coming army of emotions, with bow and arrow, sword and shield.

One night many weeks into his dark revelry he had stumbled into the apartment and into Wasim's room where he found him reading books on sushi – they were piled high on his bedside. 'What's up?' Wasim asked in Punjabi, trying to ignore the smell on Aaftab's clothes and skin and breath. Aaftab greeted him with glazed silence. 'Bhai?' he tried again.

'I was in the park.'

'This late?'

'I was thinking.'

'In the park so late at night? Careful out there – you know there are djinns in the trees past dark ...'

Aaftab smiled at this superstition, for a moment painfully transported to a more innocent time.

'What's going on with you?' Wasim asked, gentler now, closing the book he was reading.

Aaftab knew the boys were all asking questions amongst themselves, and he considered for one moment telling Wasim about Farida. Then he thought of all the *izzat* he had already taken from her and knowing he could take no more, not even if it eased his aching heart, said instead: 'With me? Nothing. I've decided what I want to do with my life.'

'What's that?'

'I'm going to buy a plot of land on the moon,' Aaftab's gaze was beyond Wasim, outside the window. 'Then, bhai, I'm going to take one rocket,' he pulled a joint out of his breast pocket and waved it in front of Wasim's face, 'and fly there and build a house so that no one can find me. And you know what I'm going to do next? In the land remaining around the house,' he used the joint to trace a circle in the air, 'I'm going to have a lunar garden where I will grow a special kind of weed. And I'm going to call it *chaand ka charas*. And you,' he poked him in the chest, 'will sell it here on earth for me. And we will be millionaires.'

With that he had finally fallen backwards on the bed, exhausted, and had stared at the ceiling for a moment before drifting off, the unlit joint crooked between his fingers. The next morning he had agreed to stop the drinking. 'And you will smoke in moderation,' Wasim said. 'And I will smoke in moderation,' Aaftab repeated, embarrassed.

'You have less than six weeks before your job starts, yaara; this has been going on for months. What about your finances? I saw your last bank statement, you have no more savings.' Wasim looked agitated and Aaftab nodded again, shamefaced. His father had cut his allowance off. He calculated. Graduation had been so long ago. It had been cold still … Farida had worn a brand new pale pink lamb's wool coat to match her hijab, both bought just for the day. The day she had thought she would be asked to give her hand in marriage. The firm had offered him a position starting six months from graduation and now it was six weeks away. Where had the months gone? The magic trick of liquor. To take hours and hours and hundreds of pounds, and to put them in a bottle and say abracadabra! And when you turn the bottle, nothing comes out. Gone! The rabbit has disappeared, the hat remains. Empty.

'And Aaftab,' Wasim hesitated now.

'*Ji?*'

'I know about the fights.'

'What fights?'

'The ones you've been having in bars. With strangers.'

The first time he'd hit someone Aaftab had felt his knuckles go white against the skin of his hands as if his bones might tear through it, and the world had gone red as if blood was running down his face, the way tears might have if he accepted his anger was sadness. He was fourteen years old and the other boy was sixteen, with a lip sliced open like a fish. Miraculously, Aaftab had never once come away injured and he felt dangerously close to the angels who protected him. He treated the act of raising his fists and hitting what was nearest to him – a wall, a door, a face, a jaw – as habit, until he met Farida.

Aaftab hung his head in shame to hear Wasim speak of his regression to a version of a man he thought he had discarded when he had unlocked the secrets of love.

'*Maaf karde, bhai*, but I had to say it,' Wasim said, embarrassed to have to bring it up. 'You know, I think of you as an elder brother but … people are talking.'

Still, Aaftab was quiet.

'You see,' Wasim clapped his shoulder in a brotherly fashion now, 'you're also a very big guy. So, have mercy.'

They smiled two soft, awkward apologies.

Aaftab brought himself back to the world in under six weeks by doing things like ironing his shirts for hours and walking in the park at dawn when all the happy dogs were brought out, and wondering the whole while if his father would call. He visited the mosque and later cooked elaborate meals, he read till his eyes closed and still his father did not call. He asked his mother if he should call instead, but she cautioned against it. 'He will telephone you when he is ready. You know that.' He read about perfumery late into the night on weekends, watched movies about Mandela and researched a variety of interests at the library ranging from Musharraf to the rules of darts. He spent hours there, reading quietly at a desk in a corner, too scared to face his house alone when Wasim was working late. He was ashamed at how small he had made himself before Wasim who hadn't lived with him long enough to be given Aaftab's misery. He was shrunken by shame. So now he expanded rather than contracted. He had a suit made. He went running and listened to music, and forgot slowly, like a snake shedding its skin, who he had been. He forgot the anger, he forgot the melting love that came after, he forgot the pain that followed and he forgot the blur of the days he had spent drowning. And from that raw, empty place he grew a new shell. And this one was made of steel and laced with stone.

But Daya. Daya was water and Daya was air. Daya slipped in through the breadth of a hair.

Because the other thing Aaftab did on afternoons when he could not escape his heart, was read in the park, on benches where the sun caught his eye, where girls in men's cardigans sometimes walked by. With this Daya-shaped cut in the surface of his iron skin, this rupture he was ignoring in the invincibility of his heart, he had begun his new job.

~

Aaftab's father did call. He called many months later, the day after the entire world was shaken, when it became clear who was going to be blamed for the collapse of western civilization. They did not reference the past. They spoke instead of the future.

'Maybe you should come home?'

'To Islamabad?' he asked incredulously, since his entire life had been maimed by his father's desire for him to leave Pakistan.

'Where else?'

'Let's wait and see. I mean, I just started the job in the summer.'

Silence. And finally …

'Son, you may be many things I am not aware or proud of, and even more things I'm not interested to know of … but you are still Muslim. So, think about it.'

Aaftab remembered the story of Manto leaving his beloved Bombay for Lahore after Partition. 'But you're barely Muslim,' his friends said, alluding to his alcoholism. 'Muslim enough that I may be killed for it,' he had replied.

'I will,' Aaftab said.

He did, and he couldn't stomach the thought of living in that house again, its marble floors upon which so much of his blood had been spilt. He realized this too – to leave so soon after the tragedy would ensure he could never come back again, perhaps. He didn't know then of course that fate comes to play eventually. That you cannot dodge a bullet twice.

Where were you when the towers fell?

They were not together when it happened. Aaftab was at work when someone came running in from the reception area shouting. 'Actually shouting,' he would tell Daya later. And then they were all running to the reception, the only place with a television. He was sick with dread. There was something unearthly about the repeated image. Again the plane went through the building. Boom. Again, in slow motion, like an egg slicer chopping the head off a boiled egg. And again. Like a samurai slicing a body in half. And again. Sirens and dust – so much dust it was as if they had carried it with them in their pockets from the desert – and a woman's shrill voice trying to stay calm and failing, 'Can you tell us what's happening on the ground, Seamus?' Cut to a tower crumbling. Jenga in slow motion. And again. 'Seamus?' Silence.

Wasim was at university. He was in a class he didn't understand and wouldn't pass, many extremely fit young men – and one woman he found terrifying – surrounding him. Someone walked in and had a word with the teacher whose lips Wasim remembered had turned white. He was Californian. He informed them in a choked voice. He dismissed the class. He did not come back the next day or the next or ever again. And Wasim drifted with the group towards the common room where people were crying shocked, unbridled tears. Where messages of hate were already flying. Where some could not speak and others were talking too much. And Wasim stood aside, heartbroken, failed by humanity, yet again.

~

Osama bin Laden was at dinner with his friends and comrades, preparing to eat early as usual because of his unending stomach problems. While the others laid out meat, waiting for him to speak, he looked upon a plate of warm bread in honeyed yoghurt, a few dates as soft as liquid. And there, as they waited to dine, the news came. His boys had razed a building. He raised a toast. They began to eat but not before Osama said, 'Bismillah!'– that precious word that heralds all acts including meals in Islam. *In the name of Allah*, and this is how the seated there knew when the towers fell that it was not a task completed that they were celebrating, no, it was the beginning of something new.

When his name was revealed to the world, Aaftab thought the towers and what not were all too Hollywood-esque for a man who worked in the shadows. It didn't make sense. Then he heard that step, half and full included, Osama had fifty-three siblings. The problem child always got more attention. More eyes upon him, more love. Seven years after the bin Ladens officially disowned him, the prodigal son had struck back with the colossal attention-seeking act of a man who wasn't hugged enough as a boy, and was made to share his toys with fifty-three brothers and sisters. Whose father divorced his mother before Osama's first birthday. Whose mother then married his father's business associate. At eighteen the wayward son married his cousin, and four more marriages and a couple of divorces later, decided to attack. Aaftab was not confused about why Osama had done what he had. What he could not understand was why the West, Americans in particular, did not identify with him more. It all sounded like an episode of *The Jerry Springer Show* to him. When people asked why Osama was so angry, the answer should have been easy.

Osama had not just been abandoned by kith and kin, but by country too. Saudi Arabia had taken away his citizenship.

But what led to the problem child losing his seven-million-dollars-a-year stipend, his family, rights to his home and land of birth, and access to Mecca, gateway to heaven and land of his beloved Black Stone?

Before he became the most famous man in the world, young Osama, in the late eighties, was not listening to Michael Jackson. He was using American dollars, gifted to him as if they were dates in a wicker basket on Eid, to create the destructive forces that would drive the Soviet Union out of Afghanistan. Yes, like so many arch-enemies, Osama and America started out as business associates. But what Osama did not know then was Afghanistan would not belong to the Afghans. He was nothing more than a sweeper for the Americans. 'Don't forget to clean that corner too – we want all the Soviet trash out.' And he did it, believing in his heart that they wanted to help. They too wanted Afghanistan for the Afghans. In 1989 when they succeeded and the Soviet soldiers went home with blood on their feet and more on their hands, Osama thought his work was done, so he calmly went back to his construction business, leaving Afghanistan presumably to the Afghans. He lived in Sudan where he made roads. He turned freedom fighters into well-fed labourers. And then he heard that American troops would prepare for something called Operation Desert Storm on Saudi soil. If anyone knew how to throw a tantrum and create a ruckus, it was Osama. And he did, thanks to which he found himself back in Afghanistan, this time without his seven-million-dollars-a-year stipend, his family, rights to his home with no access to Mecca, gateway to heaven and land of his beloved Black Stone.

All gone. Straight from cruisin' Arabia, to the cold Afghan caves. Governments, Osama learnt, were nothing more than bad parents who played favourites and beat their kid with one hand while demanding respect with the other. And now under his guidance, his honest labourers were transformed into terrorists.

His entire life, like anyone else's, was simply a search for balance, or a toss-up between

construction
destruction
construction
destruction.

And let's for a moment talk about his lost homeland.

Who buys more guns and tanks and bombs and blades from the United States of America than anyone else? Who gave the great USA the right and room to train their military on their lands, far from home, in exchange for these arms? Who fought side by side with the USA in Afghanistan, against the Soviets? Which country's founder, one Mr Ibn Saud was given 5,000 pounds a month from the British Government while in exile from the aforementioned land? And by 1922, 100,000 pounds a year handed over by Winston Churchill himself? Which country, once simply known as Arabia, was renamed, prefixed by Mr Ibn Saud's family name, and 'launched' in 1932 by the British government in return for strategic positioning in the Middle East? And who allowed their Ikhwani warriors, Bedouin mujahideen, army of Allah fans, to preach freely the language of modern jihad, so long as prayer and politics remained separate in the state?

Yes.

Saudi Arabia.

One must also ask –

Who said when the towers fell and fifteen of the nineteen pilots were theirs:

'It's not us. Osama is as big a threat to us as he is to you, brother!'

And who was reassured by the great USA saying:

'Don't worry. Between us – nothing will change, bro. As far as we're concerned, Osama is Afghani.'

And who replied: 'As far as we're concerned too.'

By then, he was.

Saudi Arabia. Mecca. Medina. His birthland. His beloved. Goodbye to all that. First they kicked him out, then they let the infidel in. From their point of view it simply wouldn't do, to have a madman like him on the loose, claiming to be one of theirs, while speaking out against the secret, Freedom Fry-eating lover they held so close. Was it part of his vengeance then, to send fifteen Saudi pilots into the sky? Was he hoping that the country so slick with oil would finally have to answer to their friend and secret lover the US of A? Maybe he hoped somewhere to cause a rift.

Maybe he simply did not realize that everything slides off oil? Blood easiest of all.

You know why he chose the World Trade Center, right?

At the King Abdulaziz University, as a young man, Osama bin Laden studied economics and business administration. He knew what he was doing. He hit where he knew it would hurt.

And you know why he chose to bring it down the way he did, right?

In 1967, Mohammed bin Laden, father of Osama, was being flown in a plane by an American pilot when the plane mysteriously crashed.

Then on 31 July 1988, in what they call an accident, Salem

bin Laden, the replacement head of the bin Laden family, died in a plane crash in San Antonio, Texas.

On 31 July 2001, thirteen years later (and we all know what that number means) as Osama remembered Salem he counted out what would have been the prescribed forty days of mourning. And on the forty-first day, he said, we will embark for vengeance. And on the forty-second, we shall have it. He circled a date. September 11.

You brought down my twin towers. Now watch me bring down yours.
You hit me where it hurt. Now watch me hurt you.

~

The day the towers fell Daya was in Roath Park. She had fallen asleep there, a book on her chest. When she had woken the entire park had cleared and September's cool evening air was nibbling into the earlier warmth of the afternoon. She rested her head a moment on her backpack, watched two birds bicker and then looked around puzzled. It really was awfully quiet. She reached for her phone which she had only just begun to get used to and to check with some urgency thanks to Aaftab. She blinked. She had – she blinked again – forty-four missed calls.

In India Kamla and Gyan stood side by side at the curved kitchen counter, backs to the screen of the little television there. She was cooking dinner and Gyan had been pouring Asha a glass of scotch. He had turned around slowly; he was tired that day already. 'Asha?' he called out. She was reading the papers – a habit which always amused him. 'You read the papers at night? What good is that?' he had laughed when he'd first found out. Now nothing seemed funny.

'Hmm?'

'Come here, jaan.'

A request? An order? Later she would tell him how it had sounded so much like a cry for help she had risen immediately. Then they were standing all three of them hip to hip, staring at the screen. There were tears streaming down Asha's face and she calculated how many may have been at work already. 'Start calling New York,' she said. They tried but couldn't get through to any of their friends. They picked at their dinner and then Gyan excused himself. 'I think I'll go down to Vaikuntha. You rest ...' She had wanted to hold him. To be assured of his physical presence. To be humbled by their continued existence on a planet that reeked that night of death. But she knew better than to ask him to stay when he needed to go.

Once on the ground floor he poured himself a glass of wine and sat by the window looking out at the bougainvillea. He thought of the voices he had been listening to on the television upstairs and that phrase coming up again and again – Ground Zero. The last time he had heard it he had been five years old and his parents had been discussing ten years of Hiroshima. He touched his breast pocket and drew from it a piece of paper. He stared at it a long time and thought, 'I'll tell her soon. I'll tell her as soon as I'm ready.' He was lying to himself and he knew it. Out loud Gyan said, 'Bastard, you'll tell her when you can't hide it any longer.' And he sighed because he understood, it is not just bad people who have secrets.

11

Her last year at the university had been overladen. She had found herself with actual friends, people she wanted to spend time with, as opposed to run from. Between the library, falling in love, her classes and the physical toll they were taking on her, Daya's hours were packed so tight her days often felt as if they may burst. And yet she would try and squeeze a little, just a little more in. Aaftab would say he had an hour free and Wasim wasn't home and she would rush over to tumble into his arms. Wasim would call and say, 'Lunch? I have some kebabs for free,' and she would rush over to eat with him before making it back to the studio. The library would ask her to work an extra hour and she would. At the centre of it all, what was meant to be her life's spine, dance. Dance was the pillar around which the rest was made possible.

She would meet Colin at the studios each day, nod and begin. Daya would strip out of her oversized tracksuit to reveal her lithe body. Colin would stretch and pull his leg warmers up. He never told her but he loved dancing with Daya. She fell, she got up, she bruised, she began again. She never complained or skipped a day. She was there to dance, and he loved the way she lost herself in it, succumbed to her craft entirely. Sometimes when he lifted her light body to the air, he noticed her eyes were closed, only intuition guiding her. Daya had understood long ago, in the lanes of Lalabad, that your vision does not guide you. Your instinct does. Colin and Daya learnt very quickly, very perfectly the peripheries of each other's bodies. He knew the length of her arm and the width of hips, and he knew better than any lover, the circumference of her waist. He knew how many inches back her neck fell and how many feet high she could jump when happy.

Wasim had asked once in the beginning, 'Who's Colin? Is he your boyfriend?' Daya had explained. Wasim's face became very still, and finally he'd said, 'Did you know Islam forbids homosexuality?'

'So does his religion,' she said in an equally hushed tone.

'Are there gays in India?' he asked.

His eyes widened in the silence. Finally, she replied, 'No, it's illegal.'

'But there must be some in secret? There are in Pakistan,' he pressed on.

She looked into his big eyes like pools in a forest and said, not a glimmer of mirth on her face, 'Oh armies of them!' and Wasim threw a cushion at her head and chased her around the house.

Daya had been grateful to Colin for providing the blanket between the worn old mattress of work and dance, and the cold winds of her friendlessness. Until him, her circle of friends within school hours had remained empty. As dancers departed with injuries, eating disorders, mental trauma and the exhaustion Anna had once promised they would, the numbers dwindled and there were fewer and fewer people around. It had made the survivors more familiar but less close, as the ones who remained were twice as wary knowing how easily one could disappear. The job at the library fulfilled the purpose she had taken it with – to not have to speak to people. Only slightly less lonely than the day she was born, Daya had usually kept her head down as she walked through the school buildings. Now, thanks to Colin, she would raise it on hearing his faked accent with its square edges. He would call out to her, she would turn smiling magnificently and run up, leaping into his arms to hug him. After work she had Wasim and Aaftab, who would crawl through the window into her attic or call her over to their kitchen. Like this in her third and final year at college, her world expanded and to her surprise made her a better not worse dancer as she had initially feared.

The winter production was finally announced. Anna, who had recently been made Dean, called them all into the expansive central studio of the Markova School, that room that smelt mildly and somehow pleasantly of sweat, of human endeavour. They sat in clusters on the wooden floor, Colin helping Daya into a straddle split as they discussed their favourite Bond films in ascending order. Anna walked in, a sheaf of papers in her manicured hands (always perfect to make up for her feet), wearing an oversized blood-red turtleneck sweater over grey tights. Behind her entered the rest of the staff – the teachers who had pirouetted them through the three years. The room fell silent and the scent somehow intensified. Daya flared her nostrils and waited, heart tight in chest, for the announcement. Though it wasn't true, it felt like the entire time they had been at Markova had been a build-up to this moment alone. The dancers only got to perform publicly once in the entire three years of study, and this was it.

Exasperating and titillating her audience all at once, Anna now ignored the unasked questions. 'I'd like to begin by speaking about the venue.' A distinct irritation washed over the room but if Anna noticed she did not care. 'I know you had all hoped to be the first people to perform at the new Opera House but it isn't to be the case. As you may know,' she smirked here, 'the project has been shelved.' A murmur went through the room. 'You think you feel bad? Think of the poor architect. Designing and drawing for all those months and then having the Welsh Assembly tell her they don't want it. Poor dear Zaha. Anyway. The Opera House has been shelved for something they call the Millennium Centre and it won't be ready until next year at the earliest. So … it's going to be Saint David's Hall.' More murmurs, this time appreciative, relieved.

'Now. For the performance.' The teachers behind her all shifted and smiled. The room held its breath. 'It is to be held two days before Christmas on the last day of term. And,' she paused, 'it is to be *Swan Lake*!' Anna finished with a dramatic sweep of her hand and a rare smile. They clapped and hurrahed and hugged like children and Anna waited for them to settle after which she began naming the roles. She read them out from a piece of paper and as she did Daya noticed her name was not called. A fist pressed further around her heart until finally at the end Anna waited to call out the lead roles, the ones every dancer in the room wanted and Daya knew it was either that or she would be one of the group dancers in the back. She swallowed and looked at Colin who looked straight ahead, whose name had not been called either and there it was. 'Finally, Alex will play Von Rothbart,' Anna smiled at the tall blonde boy in the first row, and looked back at her papers. 'And Daya is to play Odette and Odile, accompanied by Colin as our Prince Siegfried. Practice begins tomorrow. Rest well!'

They exited the school that evening into Cardiff's brilliant, rare sunshine, triumphant, other students smiling at them, high-fiving, patting them on their backs as they walked past.

'Odette! I don't think I can believe it just yet!' Daya said once they were alone.

'It's been my dream to play Siegfried since I was twelve!'

'Really?'

'Not really, it's been my dream to rewrite *Cats* as an African political drama since I was twelve, but what the heck, Siegfried is everyone's dream. If I had my way I would play your role.'

'Shall we swap? You'd make a wonderful Odette,' Daya said, her tone consoling.

'I'm not sure about that but,' he stopped and turned to her, 'you know what I do know? That you,' he poked her chest, 'will definitely make an amazing Odette.'

'You think so?' she was quizzical and then looking away, said softly, 'Col … we both know I got the role because Samantha lost her mind and dropped out.'

'Rubbish. Just the fact that she lost her mind shows she didn't have the grit for it.' He punched the air.

Daya's mouth fell open in shock. 'That's cruel!'

'And what you said was extraordinarily boring,' he said, hands on hips, shocking her further. Without warning or waiting for her to respond he lifted her up and spun her around till she shrieked with dizzy joy.

'Come on, let us get a drink to celebrate,' Colin said bringing her down.

She hesitated, gauging how long it had been since she had done something like that. Life post classes had so quickly become about the boys and the sobriety they came with.

'Alright,' she conceded.

They walked to The Chamber, a pub near the law school that was once a barrister's study. It had been donated to the school on the condition that the books remain exactly as they were. In his will the old man had left a blueprint for the pub, a dream he hadn't been able to fulfil in his own lifetime.

'Thank God I'm playing Odette,' Daya said as she ordered a glass of white wine. 'It's weird, more than happiness I feel kind of relieved.'

'I know,' Colin scanned the menu and asked for a cocktail. 'Do you know what you'd be playing if you weren't playing Odette? Wait, let me pay.'

'A background dancer or a handmaiden?'

'Basically.' Colin nodded, a naughty grin breaking. 'Do you know how bloody pathetic that would be? The handmaidens are supposed to be Odette's tears.'

'No! They're not. You're just being a dick because we got the leads. Let's face it – I got mine because I'm your partner.'

'No, I'm not, I swear it. When Odette goes into exile? All the tears she cries turn into handmaidens. But this much is true, you would be nothing but a teardrop if it wasn't for me.'

'It is part luck though, isn't it, that we got these roles?' Daya voiced her doubts again, thoughtful now.

'Is it? I'd say it's natural brilliance.'

'So damn vain!'

'Just honest, love.' Colin ate a maraschino cherry off a paper pineapple cocktail topper.

'Do you think they were trying to fill some sort of coloured quota?' Daya asked, her voice dropping a notch, and Colin looked up from messing with his drink, genuinely aggrieved.

'Shut up, Daya. No. No, I do not think it was that. Go check the registers. We've put in more hours than anyone else this term. So you know what I think it is? I think it's our hard bloody work. *You deserve this*. I deserve this. Now shut it and drink up!' They raised glasses and after the first sip Daya looked at him for a long second. 'I'm sorry, you're right. And great speech.' Then suppressing a laugh, 'I know you really, really meant it because you forgot to use your accent.'

Colin flopped back in his chair, 'I'm devastated. This is what happens. You ask me to play a straight white man and minutes later I forget I'm African.'

On the table next to them two students carrying placards with slogans in red and peace signs painted onto their cheeks argued about the political climate, then came to some agreement and embraced in drunken passion. Soon the pub was spilling over with student protestors off duty and was full of their chants – more joyous than angry post-inebriation. Daya wondered what the barrister would have made of that. Of all these painted students drinking cider in his study.

'It's true, it's Bush, isn't it?' she said to Colin. 'The bloody Republicans and a war for oil or whatever. You know some people are saying it's them who brought the buildings down.' Colin took a long sip dodging the paper pineapple. He shrugged his shoulders. 'You know Daya,' he stirred the bits of fruit around, 'People forget but Lincoln … Abraham Lincoln was a Republican. So, how things start is not always how they end up. And where things are is not where they will always be.' He nodded sagely, 'African wisdom.' Then he laughed. 'I'm joking; I just came up with that. But I believe it, I really do. It's all circles. Good, bad, it's all relative. I mean the Taliban are evil, aren't they? Stoning their women and all that. So maybe the Afghans will be happy. Or maybe it's for the opium … maybe oil. Maybe it's both. Maybe the American president brought down his own buildings with his own aeroplane to start a war on terror. Maybe someday we'll all say bun-ay-na instead of bun-aah-na. Who knows, Daya?' She raised her glass. 'Who knows.'

'What I do know,' Colin started, the mischief back in his eye, 'is that in a school full of white kids, in a story about some white birds, a gay black boy and a weird brown girl are playing the lead bloody roles!' She laughed. 'Taught by a Russian teacher!' he added. 'What's that got to do with anything?' she asked and he looked incredulous.

'Daya! They eat gay people in Russia!'

'No, they don't!' she pushed him in mock horror.

'Alright, but only because we taste horrible.'

And a gay black boy and a weird brown girl giggled and clinked glasses and spilt drinks and for a moment, the world did not feel like it was ending.

In the next few weeks the students would grow more not less aggressive, shouting the Mahatma's old saying while picketing for peace: 'AN EYE FOR AN EYE MAKES THE WHOLE WORLD BLIND!' And those who could see everything looked at George Bush and Donald Rumsfeld and the boys from places like Kenedy, Briscoe, Logan and Dale and cried, 'The blind are leading the blind,' and Wasim sat quietly watching the world's greatest circus – harb – unfold and muttered, 'An eye for an eye makes a world where the blind are leading.'

On her way home that night, Daya stopped by the library

to pick up Suzanne Farrell's autobiography, which she re-read whenever she needed inspiration. As she exited, she took stock of that building she loved so much. The alcoves named after British monarchs lining one side of the room, the greatest empires of history lining the other. She stopped suddenly. How had she not seen it? She had always thought of the former, the alcoves named after their kings and queens, as an apology to the British students. Now she realized she had never once thought that the person naming them had maybe chosen the monarchs first, then to pacify the swathes of international students coming into the university each year, had named the opposite seven alcoves after great empires, none of them British.

She suddenly felt very small.

The reign of kings > *A drizzle of empires.*

Colin was correct. History is a river. A man called Mohammed Omar started the Taliban to stop the practice of *bachabazi* – child rape and prostitution. Yes, the Taliban began as an anti-paedophilia group. They even briefly joined hands with the United Nations to counter the booming Afghan opium trade. But what did they end up as? A pile of terrorist ash in a cave. And the Americans – whether in dollars or in being responsible for an expanding sentiment – helped create Al-Qaeda and the mujahideen, that spilled over and became the Taliban. They created this with their honest American tax payers' money and with their overconfident way of trodding all over the earth, expecting no retaliation. They fed this hungry, lonely beast and trained it at first simply to drink Soviet blood. But to the beast a whip is a whip and blood is blood. And as we know from al-Khayal, blood has no religion.

And after their beast brought down the towers, did America disappear from the Middle East as was hoped? Did she leave Afghanistan for the Afghans and Israel to its fate and Saudi Arabia's land and Mecca for the devout? Oh no. America took the towers and turned them into a ticket. On the back of this ticket was a faintly printed map that led to the stash. And this is how the Islamic fighters of Afghanistan were used by America not once, but twice for the security of stash. And they got it, the oil, but not in their wildest dreams could they have predicted that the men they paid for one job (the removal of the Soviets) would deliver two.

That they would bring down two towers with fifteen Saudi men, sure, and one Saudi at the helm, sure, but with that one, *that crucial one*, living in Afghanistan, banished. What a glorious gift. The Americans took this gift with both hands and unwrapped it swiftly and saw in the place of two holes on a horizon more beloved than any other, a ticket, a grenade, a drone, a map, a key to a country. Not in their wildest dreams could the big white men who run America have hoped the American public, so astounded by what they had seen (for who could argue with the emptiness where once two towers had been), would bay for blood so loudly they would not hear or question – but whose blood?

And Afghan blood would do,
because Afghan blood always has.
And who will tell the fanatic, blood has no religion?

They were after the oil, not a crusade.
But who can resist the icing on a cake?

How long till Afghanistan would be for the Afghans?
How long had it been since it had been?

From 1880 to 1947, under the British, India had four, maybe five, versions of a national flag. From 1947 till present date, she has had only one. From 1880 till today, Afghanistan has had twenty-two. That will tell you everything about how long they have yearned there in those craggy lands for a country to call their own. 'I promise you this is not about the Taliban or girls going to school,' Aaftab had said to her. 'This is about the United States' addiction. Their inability to use things like the sun for their needs. And about their deep regret that they cannot have a tiny US in the Middle East. But between Israel, Saudi Arabia, Afghanistan and perhaps, soon even Iraq … they will have their mini-land.' '*A prisonhouse of nations*,' Wasim added. Like any addict, the US was thirsting and paranoid. And like any addict the US would stop at nothing, to get her hands on a little stash.

Because you can tell an addict:

All you need is sunshine, some wind in your hair,
capture it, thrive off it …
And all they'll tell you from the depths of their despair
is 'the black stuff, I would die for it.'

These days, Aaftab told Daya, things were such that there were times, he had heard, when an American soldier could point his gun at an Afghan warrior. The warrior would point one back. They would look at each other with disdain, hatred, fear, exhaustion, loathing and nervousness. And in that moment, nobody saw, but two guns would cock their heads and look at each other with recognition.

'Old friend!'

'I thought it was you!'

'Have you been here a while? You look beat up!'

'A few years … seen some blood, done my job. And you?'

'I've been in America!'

'Ah … no wars, just school kids then?'

'Very funny!'

'It's good to see you.'

'You too, brother. When we left that factory … I didn't know if we would ever meet again.'

'Well, here we are.'

'But not for long.'

'Who knows, if one of them dies, we'll be reunited for good.'

'And if neither?'

'Then I'll see you along the way …'

'Goodbye, old friend.'

'Goodbye!'

'Now,' Aaftab told Daya, 'we live in a time where soldiers and warriors imagine they do not speak the same language because they do not believe they come from the same place. So their guns must speak for them, because they do.'

12

The thrill that had accompanied being told they would play the leads very quickly submitted to a growing dread. Daya did not like centre stage. 'But you're made for it! I've literally never met anyone with your self-assurance,' Colin told her, amused by her apprehension. Daya had grown up comfortable in the safe shadow of her parents' large, wondrous personalities. They outperformed her and she had always felt as if she were a part of the audience – a role she had carried without question into life – always the observer, the solitary watchman. The day after the roles had been announced Anna had asked Daya to her office.

'Tell me, who was the first person to play Odette?' she began lightly, her legs crossed at the ankle on a corner of her desk upon which sat nothing except a glass bowl full of golf balls which Anna used regularly to ease her metatarsals, often rolling a ball over a foot while lecturing.

'Polina Karpakova,' Daya answered dutifully.

'Yes, very good. But do you know who was actually meant to play the role?'

Daya was stumped.

'Anna Sobeshchanskaya.'

Daya tried to repeat the name but Anna waved her long elegant fingers before her as if to brush the attempt aside.

'She didn't because believe it or not, she had apparently accepted jewellery from some government big shot but refused to marry him. So he got upset and they uncast her. Imagine,' she snapped a finger, 'you can lose a role over a necklace. How much do you want to bet that Sobeshchanskaya was better for the part?'

Daya laughed nervously, trying to fathom the symbolism of the story and drawing a blank. As if she could read her, Anna said, 'No matter, let's talk about the present.'

Daya relaxed her shoulders a little as Anna swung her long legs off the desk and rolling her chair up, placed her elbows on it.

'You know, nowadays, people prefer to have two separate dancers play Odette and Odile. But I'm not for that. Sure, Odile is this dark creature and the nemesis of course, but it's important that a dancer access that side of herself too.' Daya was uncomfortably aware of Anna prodding her. 'I want you to access that part of yourself, Daya. There is darkness in each one of us. It is different in each person. For me, it is my ego.' Anna made a fist with her hand and shook it to explain. 'For you though,' and now she looked deep into Daya's eyes in a way both disconcerting and so arresting Daya could not look away, 'I think it is sadness.'

~

They had finished dinner and were sitting in the living room decorated with threadbare onion-pink velvet couches and wall tapestries printed with sayings from the Quran when they heard raised voices outside. Both of them looked up because the shouting was in Punjabi, a man clearly saying, 'Catch the son of a bitch!' And then, hysterically, a sound more animal whine or whelp or yowl than human, and finally, 'Run, bastard!' Aaftab began to walk swiftly towards the front door when a sound froze him along the trajectory. A gunshot. It pierced the evening and he realized he had never heard that sound outside of a film before. Metal din. He stood still, his heart a gong inside his chest. Wasim raced past him, but as Aaftab managed to unglue his limbs and began to run in the same direction as Wasim, they heard a second shot and the two boys collided at the door, Wasim reaching before Aaftab and trying to lock it, Aaftab a step behind, trying to open it.

'What are you doing?' Aaftab asked in horror. 'Let's go, Was!'

'No!'

'We need to see!'

'See what?' Wasim shouted.

'What's happening!' Aaftab raised his voice as well.

'No, we don't.' Firm now, Wasim barricaded the door. He wasn't as tall as Aaftab but he was thick and strong and stood steadily against it. 'Aaftab! People run *from* a gunshot – why are you running towards it?' Breathlessly Aaftab put his ear to the door but could hear nothing but the agitated beating of his own heart.

They waited in silence but nothing followed. 'Can we go now?' Wasim, exhausted from preventing Aaftab's exit for what had been minutes but felt like hours, stepped aside. Outside, the streets were cold and quiet. Sunday night was settling in and there was less activity than usual. They walked towards the end of the street in the direction from which the noises had come, their shoes feeling more like lead with every step. Aaftab realized that much as he had wanted to rush out, he now had no desire to go towards the trouble. Above them, unnoticed, a star winked then fell. Fifty metres from the house they found what they weren't sure they'd been looking for. The truth is there is no way to find a stray, unless it finds lodging first. This same rule applies for deserters, dacoits, dogs and bullets. And there, like an unseasonable puddle to anyone who wasn't looking carefully, was proof of lodging. A dark pool on the pavement. A splatter. A spill. An oil stain, to anyone uninterested in the dark.

There were no police around, and no one who might have been a part of what was in sight. If it weren't for the blood on the street, the memory of the gunshot may have felt more like a shared nightmare. Aaftab's heart was still running rapidly in his chest. Wasim could feel his palms break sweat. 'We should go …' he whispered.

'I'm a lawyer,' Aaftab found himself whispering back. 'What happened here? I could do something about it. I *should* do something about it.'

'This looks like it's probably beyond the law.'

'That was a Pakistani boy for sure. You could tell from the Punjabi,' Aaftab argued. 'He was calling out to someone else …'

'… and maybe the person he called out to caught the … the one who fired the shot,' Wasim broke in.

'Caught the "son of a bitch", you mean. And if they didn't? Then there's a killer on the loose.'

'Nobody died here, even you can see that,' Wasim was eager to end the matter.

'You don't know that. Something happened here tonight

and we can't have been the only ones to hear the sounds. Why are you being so dismissive?'

'I'm not! It just might be best if we stayed out of it. This isn't about someone knicking gummy bears.'

'Oh because *that's* something to report?' Aaftab cut through Wasim's argument with sarcasm and they both retreated into silence. They walked around the blood a few times. 'Let's go, bhai,' Wasim said, gentler this time. They walked. Wasim did not mention it to Aaftab but viewed from south to north the splatter was almost the shape of England. Bloodied and turned on its head.

As they settled back into the soft safety of their living room with cups of tea, Wasim calmed Aaftab by saying he would ask at the mosque. 'They know what's going on with most of the boys around here, and any violence against one of our own … they'll have an idea. I'll ask around.'

'You think the shooter was white?'

Wasim stared at Aaftab for a moment. Where was his friend, the guide? The big brother who had taken his arm in one hand and drawn a map to the world with the other. Aaftab stared back at Wasim and he too knew in that moment that he had been distracted, had slipped away. 'You've been working a lot so maybe you don't know what's been up,' Wasim began cautiously, and Aaftab thought of Daya. Daya practising for *Swan Lake* in the nude in the blue evening light of his room. Daya pouring tea, precisely, Daya snapping gum, Daya reading in a chair, Daya swinging a cricket bat, Daya laughing like the world had ended and she had survived. He felt shaky. 'Tell me.'

'The Cleanse Britain boys have been at it.'

'I hadn't heard.'

'There's nothing to hear yet – just rumours. But there's talk that since September 11 they've decided to go hard.'

'I see,' Aaftab paused. 'How hard?'

'We don't know but that's not the main problem.' Wasim looked down at his lap. 'The main thing is, the mosque has decided to go against them.'

'That's good though, isn't it? They're racist pigs, Was.'

'No. You won't like this. The mosque …' he paused, unable to work out how to frame the next sentence. '… the imam actually, the new one, I've heard, just heard, nothing else. I've heard he's creating a gang.'

'What do you mean?'

'Like a violent gang. To combat them. And last week one of the boys from that group punched an old man who told him he couldn't park his car where he had. Gora, obviously.'

'Who was it?'

'Shehriyar. New kid, you don't know him.'

'I do. He has the mole. The Cindy Crawford kind?'

'Yeah. Lot less sexy on him. Okay, well, I heard Shehriyar punched the old white man in his face, because his son supports Cleanse Britain. The other guys said the man wasn't being racist, just told Shehriyar it wasn't legal to park there. Was being helpful it seems. But his son …'

'I see. And you think?'

'I don't know … but it's likely it was them.'

'Them who?'

'The imam's boys.'

Aaftab said nothing for a very long time, then asked:

'Do you mean doing the shooting or being shot at?'

'Honestly? I don't know.'

Aaftab looked his way in disbelief then dread, as comprehension dawned on his face.

'That's why the street was empty. They knew. They knew at the mosque. That's why you didn't want me to leave the house.'

'It's not like that.'

'But it is.'

'I've just been going to the mosque so I know.'

'So now you judge me for that too?'

'Bhai,' Wasim's eyes were very large.

Aaftab looked away then walked with purpose to his room and closed the door.

Later that night Wasim knocked on it, then without waiting, opened it. Aaftab was sitting in the dark, smoking. Wasim sat next to him. 'Bhai, I don't judge you. I just wanted to protect you. I hope you know.'

'I know,' Aaftab said. 'I'm sorry. It's just … these days it feels like the entire world is on fire, or on its head,' he finished softly. And Wasim was reminded, of who it was who had mapped Britain for him in the first place.

As Wasim rose to leave, Aaftab called out, 'Was?'

'*Ji, bhai?*' Wasim answered respectfully, wanting more than anything else to prove his love.

'Don't tell Daya about tonight.'

'*Ji, bhai.*'

'And I'll see you at the mosque for prayers tomorrow.'

~

When the towers had fallen, the religion that was everybody's backstreet war appeared on the lips of everyone. People who had not known how to pronounce it anymore than say Wiccan or Santeria, sampled the word for taste in their mouths – *Islam* – and their kafir tongues came away bitter.

When the towers had fallen, all the places from the back pages of the papers and the innards of the CIA, places like Algeria and Chechnya, Srebrenica and Ramallah, Kashmir and Mostar had risen to the front pages, to the attention of everyone, and Islam to the top of the already terror-laden hearts of the world. So terror had a new face. Terror no longer had an Irish accent. It no longer waved a Swastika flag. It did not wear red and wield a sickle. Or a machete in black hand. It was not embodied by beautiful slanted eyes above a rice-eating mouth. It did not speak Spanish or peddle drugs, or speak Italian and wear sharp suits.

Terror now had a new face and it belonged to a forty-four-year-old Saudi Arabian man dressed in white, smiling serenely and just as likely to be selling you a carpet at the Grand Bazaar in Istanbul. But as any child can tell you, those carpets can fly.

Usama bin Mohammed bin Awad bin Ladin.

Oh-sama.

Eye-rack.

Eye-ran.

Muzz-lim.

'I learnt their language, but they never bothered learning mine,' Wasim said wistfully. 'Doesn't peace have to be an exchange? What happens if it isn't?'

'Then it's called surrender,' Aaftab replied. He took a long, slow last drag of his joint and put it out. Daya was quiet. Earlier that day, student activists had gathered along the high street. At some point in anger, they had marched onto the highway that led into Cardiff and sat down at the exact point where the road joined the city. They had refused to move. People were coming home from work, were driving out of the city, living their lives. As Daya had walked by, unsure whether to join in or not, she had watched the drivers in their cars. They looked exhausted and bored by the teenagers lying down on the streets, some of whom were in skimpy clothes despite the cold, with blue hair, and expensive boots. So these then were the Defenders of the East. Of Islamic nations. Of self-rule in the Middle East. She wondered what ordinary Afghans would have thought of them. Whether they would find that blue hair and blue burqa side by side, oddly, had more in common than not. Your enemy's enemy is your friend, after all. The students looked angry and determined while chanting and then burst into fits of laughter in between, thrilled at what they were doing. Every single person in the cars looked like all they wanted to do was get home. 'Hey ho!' someone would call out, and hundreds would reply, 'The war for oil has got to go!'

RACIST WAR! The chant was being spray-painted onto the road in bright red. A scuffle had broken out between the students and the police. A few were arrested.

'I don't see what Afghanistan has to do with anything,' Wasim said.

'No one does,' Daya responded.

'Don't be daft,' Aaftab said angrily. 'Everyone can see the connection. The first-year students marching can see it. It's clear as day. Terrorism my ass! And the saddest thing is in the long run there will be a common enemy for the world and watch, it won't be America and it won't be terrorism. It'll be Muslims.'

'Maybe they'll find Osama?' Wasim continued innocently.

'What do you mean "find"?' Aaftab looked at him in disbelief. 'They're not going to find a man randomly in a cave. You really think he's in a cave?'

'Well, that's what they're saying,' Wasim looked down at his lap.

'Of course. A rich guy like him. Please, man! He's probably in a five-star hotel in Islamabad, beard shaved, pinstriped suit on and a few ladies by his side. Come on, Was!'

Wasim giggled at the imagery and said, 'You're smoking too much again,' but was mostly silent after that.

He wasn't stupid, he understood the dark threads in the fabric of his religion, but he was so engaged with the peaceful side of it that it often took him by surprise to know that was not what the world thought of it. Wasim did not drink, he did not smoke the slender joint Aaftab made each evening after work, he did nothing to harm the perfect creation of God that his living, breathing being was. He did not read the newspapers that provided images of naked girls on the cover, nor did he watch porn or eat pork or anything that was not halal. He dressed modestly. By policy he did not hurt any living thing, only mosquitoes and he was working on that too. He went to the mosque as often as he could. Many weeks this meant only going on Fridays, but he went.

That season he had gone more often, because the mosque was especially beautiful. The committee had grown flowers all along its edges and Wasim had helped plant the bulbs that had come up in a palette of colours. The mosque was made entirely of white, save the dome, which was pale green and caught the eye of anyone passing by. On a still day the flowers surrounding it looked like they had been painted onto a canvas. There had been an abundance of poppies and it made Wasim think about the story he'd heard about World War I. The one about the summer the year after the war had ended, when the barren battlefields where hundreds and thousands of men had died came up in shocking red trenches full of poppies. People were baffled until someone made the connection. The flowers had been fertilized by blood.

A century later the theory was dispelled as romanticism, but the poppy retained for remembrance. Wasim though believed with all his heart that the red flowers had drunk the iron of fallen men and risen in reminder. *A bouquet of elegies*. How else, he wondered, could one explain Afghanistan?

If religion was the opiate of the masses, he thought, the real stuff is given to us by angels who know better.

The mosque was only ten years old and when the land had been allotted for it, a man from a local white power group had threatened to bury a pig on the plot. They had nonetheless gone ahead with the construction under the helpful eye of the Welsh Police. On the day of the inauguration, members from the Christian community surrounded the mosque, making a ring around it by holding hands, their faces solemn. As Muslims stood by the mosque, waiting to enter it for the first time, they grew afraid, fearing violence. Then they saw each person in the circle surrounding them wore a small sticker over their heart that said 'Love Respect Protect diversity in Britain'. At the end the imam had invited them all in to see the new building. Of the almost one hundred non-Muslims who visited that day, only one had ever been inside a mosque before. The building felt like a small victory and each time Wasim entered it he recalled this story, told now as local folklore, and he felt thankful. Daya and Wasim had once discussed how the same would never have happened for a church in their own countries. Now Wasim wondered whether, if this mosque were to be built today, people would still protect it.

Recently a new imam had been brought in. From the start Wasim hadn't liked him and after the towers fell and the aftermath began, Wasim had dreaded what he would say. He had addressed them with a sermon given in a supercilious tone. He had said, amongst other things, 'In these hard times I praise our brave brothers who ask for Buckingham Palace to be turned into a mosque. Let your ambitions for Islam never fall short.' Aaftab who had gone with Wasim that day asked the imam restlessly, 'We have come to this land, and the people of this land have given us education, homes, jobs, respect and even kindness. Isn't talk of a "takeover" wrong or could it not breed violence in these confusing times?' The imam had smiled and stroked his beard before replying, fixing Aaftab with a glittering stare. 'You see, that is your problem. You think of Islam as confined to the places you come from. And in doing this, don't forget, you conveniently also think of Islam as something that must be practised only in those places. That you are exempt from Allah's eyes out here. But *a true Muslim*,' he emphasized the words, 'thinks of this world as borderless. A true Muslim thinks of Islam as borderless. Let me repeat for anyone with any doubts: Islam is a borderless religion.'

Aaftab's face had coloured as the entire room had turned to look at him. He couldn't for some reason distract himself from a man to his left with a flaming orange beard and ridiculously started a dialogue in his own head as to when the practice of dyeing beards with henna had begun and why today men with more natural-looking colour options did not take them. He was sweating as the imam kept looking his way, the thought of Daya's hair in her eyes repeatedly coming to him. All Wasim thought of were the towers falling again and again. And how in their place, so much had already grown.

The imam's movement was called A Borderless World, and with that name he fell beneath the crescent of the radar of anyone tracking extremism on earth.

13

'The students are at it again,' Aaftab said as he walked into the restaurant where they had agreed to meet, drizzle spotting his jacket shoulders..

'Why do you sound angry about it?'

'Do I?'

She had never seen him like this. He had an edge about him she wasn't sure she wanted to tread.

He took a deep breath, ordered a fish and chips and turned to her. 'What did you want to talk about?'

'Where's Wasim?' she stalled.

'At the shop.'

'Kebab or Albany Road?'

'Kebab. He's trying to get promoted to head chef.'

'At a kebab shop?'

'Well, it's a start, isn't it?'

'I suppose. Anyway, listen …'

'Listening,' he interjected. They smiled and Aaftab's shoulders finally relaxed.

She drew a deep breath and turned it into words. Real ones, spoken in the steadfastness of daylight, of a public setting. In the dangerous realm of reality, bereft of blankets and skin. She told him again that she wanted a lifetime but would settle for a season. 'Just until *Swan Lake*,' she said. 'You're not going to let this go, are you?' he asked, but there was softness in his defeat. Joy even. She had been asking off-handedly for weeks. With broken hands in tattered sleeves he offered her the golden opportunity of an entire weekend. Left to choose between nothing and next to nothing, Daya chose to be next to.

When Aaftab told Wasim later that evening that he had to visit relatives near London, Wasim secretly thought it a blessing. Since the night of the bloodstain Aaftab had been walking around with his face a perpetual dark moon.

Over the next few days Aaftab and Daya spun into new thickness their web of intimate lies and wrapped themselves up in it, tighter than ever. Despite the deception, Aaftab knew she had done for him what love is meant to do. No matter what they presented to the world, in private she had stripped his life of performance. Before her he was bare, all pretence discarded, every mask set aside. It was terrifying. With her he was honest. Not the sort of slim honesty that comes from staying silent but the kind of thick, heavy, vast, lasting honesty that comes from uttering truths. From spilling the beans. From saying everything.

Were they losing sight – they both privately questioned. *A trance of lovers*. Wasim was the only witness to their madness and deep down they both privately felt that if they could fool him, they had fooled the entire world. They were sitting at Daya's house playing Scrabble when she just happened to mention, 'I have a dance workshop the weekend of the next bank holiday, in Oxford.'

And Aaftab replied, 'No way. I'm going to London that weekend – I was just telling Wasim!'

'Shall we go together?'

'Sure, I'm taking the train till London anyway.'

Did it sound false? Practised?

Because privately they had said, 'We'll go to the beach. To the water.'

'Is this the weather for it?'

'I don't want to sunbathe. I don't even want to get out of bed.'

'You're sure about this?'

'Don't ask.'

~

Gyan had wanted to go abroad for their honeymoon. 'Ole Blighty, come on, you've never been!' In true Asha style she looked out the window of the restaurant they were in, hands braiding her thick hair in a gesture that could have been either absentminded or deliberate or both. 'Did you know, that phrase, Ole Blighty – it came from Hindi.' She gave him a smug look. 'Vil-aa-ya-tee,' she said the word again, faster, 'vilayti … blighty. See!' When she finally got out of him the reason he was so adamant they go to London she laughed and laughed and laughed. 'You don't really think you're going to get to meet The Who?' she said, dripping scorn. But he did and he had. And she would never let him forget it. And Gyan was often heard years later defending himself at dinner parties saying, 'I just wanted to buy the record …'

But they went to the mountains instead.

They travelled up on a bus, their hands entwined, her head on his shoulder. His parents had reserved a room for them at a quaint colonial hotel with sloping roofs and tea in cloth sachets. They had stayed there a night after which they decided the sheets were much too white and so they packed their bags and bidding the luxurious lawns, tourist-littered little apple orchard and library of forgotten books goodbye, began to travel upwards. They stayed instead with villagers, in tiny guest houses with chalky walls and creaking windows that opened up to colossal views of shard-like peaks. An entire honeymoon made of lit fires and flowing rivers. And then before they knew how, they were in Kashmir.

They were married in 1975 on the Vernal Equinox.

A month before that on the 24th of February of that year Indira Gandhi signed the controversial Indira-Sheikh Accord bringing Kashmir back to her slowly ageing bosom and reinstalling Sheikh Abdullah as the Chief Minister of the state.

On the same day in England, the rock-and-roll band Led Zeppelin released their record *Physical Graffiti* on which the number one song was a complicated track called 'Kashmir'. One of Gyan's 'richie-rich friends', as Asha called them, had brought them a copy from Birmingham as a wedding gift. They had carried it up to the mountains with them and wherever they found a record player they would take it out and play the song over and over.

'And we will have children.'

'Really? You want them?'

'Hundreds.'

'Let's begin with one?' she grinned, chin dimpling.

Asha was lying in the ribcage of a wooden shikara on Dal Lake, her head resting in Gyan's lap where she had spread a deep auburn shawl. Her hair billowed around her, and looking at her like this, upside down, he realized the extraordinary symmetry of her face. The man rowing the shikara with one of Srinagar's famed heart-shaped oars was ignoring them as deftly as he was maneuvering the lilies and the reeds. They had asked to go 'nowhere' and of course nowhere was a place he understood as only a Kashmiri could. Gyan watched him for a moment, reciting in his head.

The French wear their hearts upon their sleeve,
and Indians keep theirs in a land of dreams;
But where lies the heart of the common Kashmiri?
On the end of his oar,
beneath the Dal's weeds.

'We can begin with one, why not?' he replied finally.

'Good. We can start work on that this afternoon.'

Contrary to all expectations in those days of sexual freedom, Asha had stayed staunchly a virgin until their wedding night. When he had asked her why, she had said, 'Since it's going to be you anyway, I have no hurry.' Like this she had informed him of – casually promised him – forever. So he had waited four years. And when he had kissed every last patch of her skin, her body had finally invited him in.

~

They went, Daya and Aaftab, to the seaside. They took a weekend and drew a lifetime from it. And when they came back, neither knew how to return. As the taxi pulled up outside Daya's house she reached into her backpack. 'I have your keys,' she said quietly. 'Oh Daya,' he replied, voice cracking. 'You have my heart.' She shut the taxi door and placed her fingers gently on the window. He placed his on the other side and understood. They could feel whatever it was they were each feeling, but they could not feel it together. They could reach out, they could desire, but they could not, would not have.

~

No one knew this but there was a single point in their relationship when it seemed for one terrible moment that Gyan and Asha would not actually end up spending their lives together. It was the summer he introduced her to his parents. Asha who didn't believe in touching people's feet. Asha who when it came to jewellery preferred old silver to new gold. Who wore her long hair open down her back rather than oiled and braided neatly. Who had not in those days learnt the sweetness of compromise.

They had been together three years. Three years that had flown by in an afternoon and Gyan finally, finally asked if she would please come meet his parents for dinner. His parents who had presumed they would choose his girl-for-life. But she was his girl-for-life and he'd be damned if her handstitched bellbottoms weren't welcome.

She came wearing a sari. It was white and gold, simple, elegant. It was *Asha*. A silver bangle on each wrist. Small silver jhumkas like the tops of the minarets of mosques dangled from her ears. He couldn't find a flaw in her performance that day. But his parents had. They asked what she was like beneath it all.

'Oh you know, she's a top bird!' was his response.

'Does she always dress so simply?' his mother asked, bewildered by his answer.

'Does she smile much?' his father asked, later adding, 'She has a real taste for scotch, huh?'

He was angry with them. He fought for her. He brought her over again, and slowly again. She continued to be graceful in his eyes, and yet over the next few months he began to see what they did. Asha was inherently rebellious. And she took pleasure in it too. It was small things. She would question his father's political rhetoric. She would tell his mother repeatedly that she thought diamonds looked cheap. She pushed buttons, she asked questions that almost always began with 'But why ...', and worst of all, if she disagreed with the answers, she said so. She said 'no'. From mild awkwardness, a simple irritation, over weeks it escalated to outright war. Gyan against his parents, his parents against Asha. Asha feigning innocence: 'I don't know what could possibly have upset them so much.'And finally Gyan had taken Asha on a cold coffee drive and they'd smoked a cigarette in his car and he had turned to her and said, 'Asha, baby, don't you see, if you're nice to them, I can stand up and say, 'No, you're wrong, she's right. Good cop,' he pointed at her, 'bad cop,' he pointed at himself. 'But if you dive in each time with all your ideas and beliefs and fights, I have no choice but to side with them. You understand?'

She was silent and the glass bottle with milky-sugary coffee suddenly felt very cold balanced between her thighs as she exhaled smoke. She thought of how the condensation would leave a weird stain. Did she understand, he had asked. Oh she understood. No one knew, how Asha understood and then wrapped up her ego and took on his world by wearing the promise of his love like a cape. How she learnt the sweet side of compromise. How she tried out that role, of being agreeable, of being exactly the same as him and his family – in order to win. And her prize she thought would be Gyan forever. She'd never counted on having the love of his family. Their kindness, their joy at her gentleness, at her genuine laughter. Their delight at her way of making Gyan better, even if they didn't understand how she did it. No one knew. They just loved her for it. Asha who was used to being adored, used to men stopping in their tracks and women asking where she got her jeans ('I *made* them'), finally understood what it was like to be *loved*. And to love, beyond yourself. She would never be understood, she knew that. Not by anyone but Gyan. But maybe to be loved was enough.

She never told anyone how for a single moment in a car outside a cold coffee stall in Lalabad, she had felt horror in her heart, thinking Gyan may not be hers after all. No one knew how in that moment nothing mattered. Not her ego, not her beliefs, not her ever-ready sarcasm. She told no one of that moment of doubt Gyan had had, keeping it safe in a place where only she could reach it. Even now all these years later it gave her pause, and whenever one of their friends commented on how Gyan 'couldn't live without' her, she went back to it. To how narrowly she had escaped not having Gyan at all. It was the tiny scar upon her ego, a scratch really, but it reminded her that she was human after all, and not a goddess as people liked to presume. Like all vain things with scars, she hid it. And then she had Daya, and when her daughter was old enough to know love and all that it came with, she told her, because Daya was a piece of herself.

Daya thought of it now. As she pined, and ached and wondered. As she sifted through, then locked away the memories of the last few days, their weekend alone by the water. She asked herself: Should she have done more to bridge the gap? Was it her own fault for not seeing how hard it had been for him? For not seeing the lengths of ocean he had swum to be a part of her world. Had she done enough? Had she *been* enough?

In the days while Daya was asking these questions, post their time by the sea, as they each tried to reclaim their lives and bodies for themselves, and their hearts from the cavities of the other's chest, something took place that Daya had not accounted for.

She was walking with Wasim down City Road at noon in the customary Welsh drizzle. They were trying to pick a place to eat lunch before the sky turned the spray into a shower. A lazy morning made urgent by the weather. Just as they decided on a cafe and turned towards it, they walked, with very little warning to her or themselves, straight into Farida.

Wasim's mouth fell open in surprise and then his face broke into his warmest smile. She was in white. So much white one might have thought she was on her way to a funeral, but from the richness of the fabric, finely embroidered with pomegranates, Daya understood she was not visiting the dead, she was a different kind of angel. 'Wasim bhai!' she breathed more than spoke the words. Under her dark umbrella, her eyes were heavy with kohl and effortlessly she wore a dupatta draped around her face like a cloud.

'*Ki haal eh?*' they said almost at the same time.

They laughed. He did not introduce Daya and she felt herself step backwards just an inch, and look down to shield her face from rain with the hood of her sweatshirt. They spoke in rapid Punjabi before Farida lifted her wrist and glanced at a delicate watch. The last thing she said before leaving, almost as an afterthought, was, '*Te Aaftab?*'

'He's alright,' Wasim replied and they smiled once more, in the way people who share secrets do.

'Who was that?' she asked Wasim, though she knew. Of course she knew. If he didn't mention the Aaftab connection, she quickly thought, she would be able to simply tease him about talking to a pretty girl. A small part of her hoped he wouldn't.

'This girl from Aaftab's college.'

She wasn't prepared for honesty so she stayed quiet but she knew Wasim would say more. The novelty of the moment was too great a temptation for him to resist. She braced herself.

'She came to the house one day soon after I moved in. It was the only time I ever saw a woman there actually. How funny, I had completely forgotten about that day.' In the kind of detail only Wasim could summon, he described the peach of her shalwar kameez and how it had matched her hijab and her nails. Daya imagined her entire body, dressed and undressed, as the inside of a shell. The place the ocean whispered its secrets.

He described how they had spent all day together, the three of them, barring the hours in the middle when he had gone to work. Daya wondered what had taken place in that sliver of uncharted time. He said she had cooked them mutton just like they ate back home and they had watched episodes of a Pakistani TV series ('drama', he called it) she had carried with her, burnt onto a CD. At sunset when the crowd from the mosque had disappeared into the building to pray she had said she had to leave and Aaftab had offered to take her home in her silver Range Rover which she had driven over and parked two lanes away early that day, before prayers began.

'I've never been sure if there was something between them, because if there was I feel Aaftab would tell me … has he ever told you?' he asked but didn't wait for an answer, continuing instead. 'See, I've also never seen him give a woman respect like that or look at something that way. I mean, they would have been perfect for each other. I never heard about her afterwards, but *soch*, he's never even called another woman home.'

Never.

'Except you of course,' he laughed suddenly. '*Lekin, tu toh jigar hai.*'

Jigar. That word they used upon her like a blessing.

Urdu for liver.

Vital organ.

What followed began with all the innocence of a bad idea.

Later she would ask herself what it was that had hurt her most. Had it been the fact that Aaftab in his wisdom had never given her these stories and details himself? That their relationship, however close, had no title that gave her the right to demand access to the vault of his memories. That he may have loved Farida more? That he loved her still? That she had been a better fit? That even Wasim could see it?

Later that week Daya returned to City Road. Among the doner kebab places and car repair yards, barbers and phone cover shops, were stores advertising women's wares. She entered timidly and it was only later that she would pause to marvel at how unaware she had been about what she was determined to do.

She bought what she had come for under the disdainful eyes of two girls with henna fading on their hands. She unwrapped her purchases when she was back home in her room. The butterflies in her heart kicked, then sat still.

'Did you ever ask him about her?' Daya had said to Wasim.

'I teased him a little afterwards, but he said it wasn't like that. I called her,' he paused and laughed again, a little embarrassed now, aware he was perhaps saying too much.

'Farida begum.'

'Because of the singer?'

'Yes. And because of the begum.'

Begum.

Urdu for wife.

Highest honour, greatest title, most sought-after rank.

The joke was that their favourite Pakistani singer was Farida Khanum. And they loved her so much, they often called her Farida begum. 'Ask your begum to sing now,' Aaftab would say to Wasim, late on Saturday nights as they stayed up chatting, listening to music. 'You mean your begum, janaab!' Wasim would reply and change the CD. If Islam had allowed for its women to take more than one husband, Aaftab and Wasim would have gladly shared her love. As her songs played, they would close their eyes and travel to some distant place where hope existed always. Born in Calcutta when Pakistan was still Northern Hindustan, Farida Khanum crossed the border at partition, becoming ipso facto the favourite singer of a new nation. Recently, she had crossed the border back briefly to sing for an audience that included the Prime Minister of India. Halfway through the concert his secretary whispered in his ear that something urgent had arisen and music could not after all come in the way of running a nation. The Prime Minister sent a note up to the stage saying he regretted having to do so, but he would have to take her leave. Looking up, the note still in her hands which expressed in a way that always made them an extension of her song, Khanum Sahiba told the audience of what she had just received. And then, ever the graceful performer, she sang the greatest of her ghazals, and dedicated it that night to him.

'Aaj jaane ki zid na karo …'

Please, do not insist on departing today.
A love letter between two countries.
A request not to be abandoned,
from the smaller to the bigger,
the younger to the older.
Stay.
Please don't insist on departing today.

Farida Khanum brought the song out to the table and waved it at him. 'I've still got this, the most beautiful part.' She negotiated. He stayed.

The story was one of Gyan's favourites. 'The stuff of legends,' he had said, when he'd told Daya the story for the first time. 'She's a total rockstar! Because you see, it wasn't about a song. It was so much more.' And Daya, still young, had asked, 'What was it about?' He had laughed and ruffled her hair, 'It was about countries, about give and take, about politics, and love as well.' And then after a moment's thought … 'The song – it was between them in the way something else is between India and Pakistan. I think what she was showing us is that Kashmir is our favourite shared ghazal.'

Even if the two made peace over it, whom did the song belong to?

Can a song belong to anyone at all?

She sang, he stayed. And in that moment of peace, the song belonged to no one and the song belonged to everyone.

Wasim's mention of the singer reminded her of the conversation and something inside her felt broken. All this while, Farida Khanum had been *hers*. This tiny story gifted to her by her father, this small piece of knowledge an access point to Aaftab's world. It had given her confidence. So much so, she had once slipped a Post-It into Aaftab's pocket before he took his clothes into the bathroom to get dressed. On it had been those very words – *aaj jaane ki zid na karo* – and he had found them as he entered his shirt, and he had found it so very hard to exit her home after that. And then Wasim had casually told her that Farida, *his Farida*, Wasim had often teased him about, likening that girl in white to hers.

Later she would ask herself: And did you want to be more like his Farida? A Farida who did not have to ask anyone to stay.

~

The day she appeared before him, altered – a day she would never forget – began perfectly. Everything was as it should be. The rare Welsh sun out like an egg yolk after a night of heavy rain, a light breeze at the windows, her tea the perfect temperature. And then he messaged, asking her to dinner. Wasim was busy, it could be just them. Since their return from the seaside, scared by the things they had felt there, they had rarely been alone.

'A date?' she typed, smiling.

'A date then.'

'Roberto's, 8 p.m.?' he asked.

She considered it. The Italian restaurant was not quite how she had pictured their evening. 'Mubarak, 8:30?' she said, naming an Indian restaurant a little further away, in the Bay Area, where they wouldn't meet anyone they knew.

'Great, I'll see you there. I have a meeting that side at 7 anyway.'

Daya came home and stepped into the shower, hanging behind the bathroom door one of the few dresses she owned – a knee-length, plum shift in jersey. She slipped it on and draped a long black cardigan over it. When she looked in the mirror she was conscious of how bare and muscular her calves looked so she pulled on stockings and then her black boots. Finally she sat down with her face, forcing herself to take a long look at it. For as long as she could remember, Daya had not spent time with her face in mirrors. As someone who spent days in rooms full of them, they did not enamour her, and had been nothing more than a device to check for alignment. When she caught sight of her face there, it sometimes surprised her, then made her uncomfortable. Tonight, she forced herself to keep looking into her own eyes. What did she see? Did she know how to make magic of it? The butterflies began to kick in her belly once more. She raised her hands and got to work. A swish here, a brush there, a pat here, a twist there. She was ready. Swish, brush, pat, twist. Ready, steady, go.

She arrived at Mubarak at 8:20 p.m. She could see him seated already at a dimly lit corner table looking down at his phone. She made her way towards him, tremblingly shy now, and as she approached he looked up then looked past her. 'Aaftab,' she said as she stopped before the table and his eyes that had seen through her now looked at her, looked into her and she waited, smiling. 'It's me!' And she saw on his face complete, utter shock. She waited for it to turn to pleasure but instead she saw the simplest of things. There was no mistaking the emotion. Anger. That anger she had heard about in whispers, in memory. The anger she had never before seen. She held her breath and waited for the onslaught as she saw his face whiten, his breath quicken, his hands ball up. But he only whispered after an extraordinary silence, 'Let's go home.' And finally she was scared.

He did not speak a single word in the taxi on the way to her place.

He did not speak while she opened the door and let them in and shut the windows to her cold room and he did not say a word as she excused herself and went to the bathroom where she forced herself for a second time that night to look at her own face. There it was, askew on her head, in the bright bathroom light that revealed her clumsy attempt at tying. In dark blue and both as new and old as his anger, on her head, shrouding her hair and robbing her face of some of its light, was a terribly knotted hijab.

A story. In 1979 the brave Italian journalist Oriana Fallaci was granted an interview with the Grand Ayatollah Khomeini in Qum, Iran, where she asked him (while wearing the prerequisite covered clothing) among other uncomfortable questions, 'How do women swim in a chador?' When he grew angry, telling her it was 'none of her business' because 'our customs are none of your business. If you do not like Islamic dress, you are not obliged to wear it. Islamic dress is for good and proper young women,' Fallaci, either to provoke him or to simply feel free, replied, 'That's very kind of you, Imam. And since you said so, I'm going to take off this stupid medieval rag right now. There. Done.' And saying so, she tossed the chador off.

Now Daya undid it as quietly as she could. She wondered if he would be gone when she came out but he wasn't. He was sitting at her desk, chair turned to face the room, smoking. 'Sit,' he said, chin jutting towards the bed. She sat timidly at the edge of it, hands in her lap. He continued to smoke, ashing into an empty cigarette packet. He always smoked by the window; she had never seen him smoke inside the room this way and she watched white tendrils rise from his mouth, from the cigarette in his hand. He finished and stubbing it out, leaned back and crossed his arms over the scape of his broad chest, knees spread wide, feet planted firmly. 'So what were you thinking?'

She opened her mouth to answer and he asked again, 'No, really Daya, what were you thinking?' She closed it again.

'Were you thinking,' he leaned forward now, 'because I am a Muslim man, that this is my wet dream? That I couldn't possibly have an opinion on this that differs from the majority of my brethren? I who have had countless glasses of wine with you? The haraami who makes love to you consistently – that guy wants his woman covered, doesn't he? He doesn't just want to undress you, he wants to unveil you, ha?'

'I didn't ...'

'Or did you really belittle my religion so much, you thought this is how you could be a part of it? By wrapping some stupid cloth around your head?' He shook his head in disgust. She stared down at her hands. 'Surely you ... surely *we* are better than this, Daya?'

When he finally let her speak, hours later, she had been worn down to within an inch of her self-esteem. He had mocked her, berated her, cursed at her, and even sat in long periods of silence when she had thought he might be done.

But always he came back with renewed vigour. Finally when he'd begun raising his voice, she had said, 'Please, Aaftab, Mrs Coombes …' and he had roared back with anger, 'You should have thought of that too, when you decided to loudly fuck a Mussalmaan!' And then he punched through a framed Bob Marley print on her wall and left a crack in the glass like a starburst, and blood on his knuckles.

The shock of what he'd done, what he'd said, how he had said it, and seeing blood, restored his sanity. It deflated his anger and set it into sadness and then the tears came down his face and she asked, 'Why are you crying?' but he wouldn't look at her. And then she wept and wept, her shoulders shaking, hot tears rolling down her face, first silently and then she was bawling like a child. He rose and sitting down behind her, wrapped his arms around her, and placed his wet forehead on the curve of her neck. They sat there a very long time and then Aaftab sensed something devastating. He had taken her safe space and made it unsafe. And so he held her until her body uncurled again, like a fern from a finger she had retreated like a snail into some secret shell and it took hours of holding, of whispering into her face and hands and hair and hot tears that he was sorry, for her to emerge again. And when she did, he asked, softly this time, 'So what were you thinking?'

'I just wanted to make life easier for you,' she said.

'Why now, suddenly?'

'Since we came back from the trip …'

'I know it's been hard Daya … for me as well.'

'Exactly. And I was just trying to come up with ways to make it simpler. And …' she paused. 'And I saw Farida.'

'Saw?'

'Well met, but not really. Wasim didn't introduce us. On City Road.'

'He told me. You were there?'

'I was.'

'I'm sorry,' he said.

'Don't be. But can I ask you …' With great courage she now said, 'You never told me Farida came over after it was all finished between you two. To the house.'

He closed his eyes. They were lying on the bed now, her head on his shoulder, both exhausted from the tension and its release. He reached for her hand. 'She never came to the house before that, you know? Even though we were together when I moved in. I thought it would be a sort of love-pad for us but she said she wouldn't come, not until we were married. It's why I soon asked Was to come live with me. Before him, all the boys who'd stayed were temporary. Anyway, that day, she came to the house because I had begged her to come over just once to say goodbye. I told her she needn't see me ever again after. I had just about cleaned up and stopped drinking, and I thought I could convince her to try once more. I thought if she saw the house, saw me again she might change her mind and then we could change my father's. I just needed her to be on my side and then I felt we could do anything. So she came and spent the whole day there and in the car on the way back she finally told me she was engaged to someone else. Then she handed me a bag of things I had given her while we were together. It was cruel. She said she hadn't known how to tell me, but that day – what was I meant to do with that single day where we played house? She did it on purpose. It was so calculated in its cruelty. Till that moment I had thought she was compassionate at the very least,' he said helplessly. 'And then it was even sadder because … I no longer wanted her. And that was an emptiness I wasn't prepared for.' 'Maybe it was her revenge?' Daya asked. 'Maybe,' he responded so softly if she had been an inch further away she wouldn't have heard him. Daya held him close now and his bitterness dissipated against her chest. After some time he said thoughtfully, 'You know Farida never used to wear hijab.'

'She wasn't wearing it that day either. Just a dupatta on her head. But Wasim mentioned she used to.'

'Not at the start. She almost always wore western clothes. Really modest stuff – trousers, shirts, sweaters. Sometimes she wore shalwar kameez and then she would put the dupatta on her head. At some point during college she decided to start wearing hijab. We spoke about it a lot later when we were together. I didn't believe in it per se; the first time I had seen her in it I felt so … sad. She had beautiful black hair and to think it would always be hidden really upset me. Plus she looked uncomfortable. It also told me other things about her, things that I felt we wouldn't agree on in the long run, if this was the path she was going to take. She argued with me. At first she spoke about modesty but I told her it was nonsense because it ensured everyone would stare at her in this country rather than look away. Then she said it was a political act and I didn't agree. It was always something that came up but she just refused to take it off.'

'So what happened?'

'I don't know. When we were together I just accepted it was her choice really, but some time after we ended and after that day when she came over, I heard she had taken it off.'

'Maybe it was to show you she still loved you?'

He disentangled himself from her gently and turned to

face her, and she saw the anger had been replaced by hurt. 'I would hope any woman who loves me would know that what I want most of all is for them to be themselves above everything. Clearly,' he laughed a short, bitter laugh, 'I've been unable to convey that, but for me, that is honesty. Remember Shakespeare? "To thine own self be true." I would rather someone fight me and have their own way than change for me and compromise on their beliefs. If she believed in it, she should have worn it. That I can respect. It's her right to wear it, Daya, even if I don't agree with it. I'm not stupid. I know many women who would rather die than be unveiled and they want this and that's fine I respect the choice. But I don't think she knew her reasons for wanting to wear it. And if anything,' he looked away now, far away, over Daya's shoulder, 'she took it off when she was done with me, to hurt me, and I presume Allah is having the last laugh now because you went and put one on.' He rubbed his eyes. 'Maybe I am just a bad Muslim.' He looked away, 'That's what it came down to eventually with Farida. She called me a bad Muslim.'

'And still you wanted to marry her?'

'I loved her, even if she made me love myself less. But Allah protects. He took that away from me …' he turned to face Daya and kissed her. 'And brought me you.'

'A girl you cannot have.'

'A girl who made me love myself. Who taught me how to love. Who redefined my ideas of love.'

'And now?'

'And now I think … some distance?'

'Okay.'

'Daya,' he began hesitatingly, 'I hope you understand why I got upset. Nothing excuses my anger, I know, but I got upset because … because you are enough. I fell for a girl in sneakers. I don't want to see her in a hijab.'

'I could wear both,' she smiled.

'You know what I mean.'

'But my mother …' she began to tell him the story of the cold coffee stall.

Aaftab finally laughed. 'In a parallel universe, if we were ever to meet my parents …' he trailed off. 'But not in this lifetime. 'In this lifetime you give your hair to the wind.' She nodded. 'And Daya, from everything you've told me about her, it doesn't sound like your mother changed in front of your dad. Only in front of his parents, for him, when required.' He hugged her. 'Take some time away from me. Clear your head. I need to as well. It's all been too much … the holiday, tonight.' She nodded again, forlornly this time. 'You should know though, what I can't have notwithstanding,' and now his voice cracked, 'I love you so much.'

And then

he was gone.

~

Aaftab walked home in the dawn, hands in pockets, listening to the azan soft from the mosque's speakers at that early time of day. It was full of sadness that morning. He looked at his phone, where Wasim had messaged at some point in the night, 'Where are you?' and he replied, 'Worked late then slept there.' The ambiguity of the word 'there' eased his guilt. Less difficult to say than 'at the office'. Another lie at a time when good Muslims were all praying. He stopped and listened to the sound, let it wash over him, and decided to be honest with himself in this holy hour. When he looked within, what he found behind his anger and his sadness was his fear, lurking, smirking, waiting.

Because it hadn't upset Aaftab that Daya was enough the way she was or that she had doubted it.

Deep down, so deep he could barely feel it, he was upset because no matter what she did he feared she would not be enough.

Not for his world.

In the place she occupied now, here, in his life, she was enough.

For his heart she was *more than enough*, but nothing, not a piece of cloth for certain could make her enough to enter his world.

And was that his world's fault, he asked himself now.

Or was it his?

On that question he sat, and rested on shaking knees his whole future.

~

To complete a story. When the Italian journalist Oriana Fallaci threw off her chador and sat before the Ayatollah in all her sunny, petite, provocative beauty, Khomeini stood up lithely, and left the room enraged. She waited. She waited a day, then waited another. On the third day he allowed her back to complete the interview. Before they resumed, his son Ahmed took Fallaci aside and said, 'My father is still really angry about what you did. Maybe it's best you avoid any questions about the chador.' She nodded. They settled into their places, the Ayatollah on a chair, two translators and Ahmed sitting around them, Fallaci back in chador on the carpet before them. She switched the tape recorder on and turning to Khomeini, began by asking him a question about Muslim women wearing the chador.

Khomeini looked at her completely astonished. And then, astounding the entire room, he let a smile flutter at his lips. After a beat, he began to laugh. It seemed women removing their coverings could make bad Muslims everywhere happy.

Later his son Ahmed would tell her, 'I think maybe you are the only person in this world who ever made him laugh that way.'

14

Gyan stepped out of the bathroom and walked towards his wife. She was lying in bed wearing a faded grey nightshirt, reading a thick book in which she was underlining things from time to time. He watched her, greedy for the poetry of her face. Once upon a time he had told her, 'I've a crush on this line here,' touching the small frown line between her eyebrows that only he got to see because it only appeared when she was relaxed and concentrating at the same time. A tiny thread on her face, just one of many that tied him to her.

'Asha,' he called to her.

'Hmm …' She had been wearing reading glasses (real ones finally) for the last few years but now took them off, put the book down and looked up at him.

He adored her like this. Her most private self. Kaajal wiped out of her eyes, body soft, frown freely creasing forehead.

'I wanted to talk to you.'

She knew immediately that something in their world was askew. She put the book down and walked to him. She stood before him, eyes seeking. He did not reassure her but kissed her forehead instead.

'Let's go downstairs?' he asked.

They unlocked the ground floor and entered. He asked her to leave the lights off, so they lit candles instead. She had a weakness for vanilla-scented ones and he often brought them home to her. The scent mingled now with that of the white roses she had arranged in a large fish bowl that had been turned into a vase years ago when someone gifted them an angelfish and she had been horrified by the cruelty of keeping it swimming in a glass globe. Neither of them could recall exactly when they had begun privately calling this level of the house Vaikuntha. They just knew this – she, an old lover of Vishnu, the preserver and protector of the Universe, had chosen the name. He had argued initially that to call it 'heaven' made no sense. 'Think about it! People ascend to heaven. We *descend* to this floor.'

'No, *you* think about it,' she had replied cleverly. 'The entire world is Vishnu's dream, and he sits in Vaikuntha.'

Almost as always, she had had her way.

She went to boil water. There were peppermint leaves from their garden in a small bowl by the kettle. She placed a few in two tall glasses and poured hot water over them. She stirred in honey. When she turned from the granite curve of the little kitchenette she saw him standing across the long space, at the far end from her, looking out of the window. There was an urgency to her movements, imperceptible to everyone, including her. But he, even with his back turned, could sense it. In another sweeping alcove caused by one of the house's five curves was a swing from Gujarat, hanging from the ceiling and painted with flowers, the wooden back carved into two peacocks with chests touching, but faces coyly turned away from each other, like tango dancers. They sat on it now.

'What is it?' she began, as the swing gently moved back and forth like a pendulum.

'I'm not well.' He placed a hand on her knee.

'I know. What is it?'

'Cancer.'

'Where?'

'My lungs.'

'Okay.'

'And … it's spreading.'

'Where?'

'Everywhere.'

She went back in her mind for some reason to when they had been trying to conceive Daya. One day in frustration and anguish she had said, 'You don't understand. All I want is a baby.'

'You'll have one. We will.'

'How do you know?'

'I know,' he had said.

'Can you guarantee that?'

'I can. I promise you will have your baby.'

And now? What did he know and what could he promise her? She was scared to ask.

'Tell me a secret,' Daya had once said to Aaftab.
'You're my only secret,' he had replied.

After all this time Gyan had learnt to keep secrets from his wife. He had visited doctors, hidden bills, taken pills and spent time in the bathroom with the shower on, coughing up blood, putting off treatment and surgery. It had taken huge efforts on his part because she was exactly half of his being and to function without that half had been close to impossible. Now that he knew that working backwards wasn't possible, that the path behind him was to remain just that, that he had to face what was to come, he knew it was time to tell her. He was tired of living as half a person. He was tired of his dirty affair with death.

'How long?' She finally asked the only important question left. The swing stopped moving.

They hadn't given him time. It was all she wanted and it was the only thing he could not give her.

The guarantee of time.

The promise of it.

The unspeakable luxury.

Who comforted whom? Whose hands clawed at whose chest? Whose tears stained whose shirt? Who sobbed into whose mouth? Which one's howls emptied into which one's heart? They had been one for so long, they did not know now how to separate.

It's true. One does not descend to heaven, she thought later, as he slept on her shoulder on their vast mattress on the floor of the house in a world that had turned on its head.

In the early hours of the morning he rose to see her already awake, sitting with her back to him, dawn garlanding her bare shoulders. He sat behind her and cocooned her in his arms before whispering, 'Remember, I am yours. No earthly damage will ever undo that.'

~

Daya did not know how to become Odette or Odile. Nothing in all her years of dancing had prepared her for this dual performance and she knew she was flailing because she could see the doubt she felt on Anna's face every time Anna dropped by the rehearsal space. When Daya and her friends turned thirteen they had begun the age-old pupils' practice of putting inside the hoods of their school desks, photos and cut-outs and carvings of things they loved. Nothing gave Daya more joy and nothing embarrassed her more, because inside her desk she did not have a single pop icon or filmstar or simpering model in a gown she craved, no. She was embarrassed because she had pinned right in the centre of the inside of her desk lid, a postcard of Tchaikovsky in black and white, beard combed and head beginning to bald. She also had a picture of Barfi with eyes red in the neon glow of the camera flash, a National Geographic cover featuring Indonesian dancers and a red autumn leaf a cousin had posted her from Switzerland. But Tchaikovsky held prize position – front and centre stage – and now she felt she was disappointing him. It had been weeks and Daya felt she wasn't getting it right.

Though Anna and the faculty had been teaching them Petipa and Ivanov's original famed 1895 choreography, after the first week of rehearsals, Anna had taken Daya and Colin aside and flung another one of her surprises. She told them in her typically offhand manner, that she'd decided they should choreograph a part of the ballet themselves. Learning, Daya could do. It was one thing to learn. But to create was another. She knew that this was how Anna wanted them to pay for their roles. It wasn't enough to be the best, Anna was telling them. You had to continually strive to be better. 'Daya, I want you to create Odile's part for me, and Colin why don't you do all the corresponding parts for Siegfried? So when he dances with Odette it's one style and when he's with Odile of course it's another … maybe more sexual, because Odette is the sweet princess but Odile is our vamp. Show me something new,' she had said casually. 'Show me what you can do.'

'Her fucking obsession with newness!' Colin had rolled his eyes as they had left Anna's office that day, but Daya knew he would manage. As predicted, a week into complaining to her constantly at the library, Colin strutted up to her and said, 'I've got it.'

'Got what?'

'My choreography plan, that's what!'

Going through books on South Africa, Colin had decided to incorporate Ingoma moves into his dance.

'It's going to be amazing. I'll be like some Zulu prince.'

'Are you Zulu?' Daya asked, curious.

'Well, my mum is. I've never asked about my dad. Anyway, what are you going to do? We have to coordinate this, you know.'

~

Lying in the half-moonlight, Daya was wide awake. It didn't help that she missed Aaftab. She looked at her watch for what felt like the hundredth time and saw it was three in the morning. She was trying hard to come up with the dance parts, but every time Anna or the other professors asked, Daya would say she needed a little more time. She had said more than once to Colin that Samantha should have got the part, until he'd snapped at her: 'Well, she didn't so tough luck; get down to it, Daya.' She'd shut up, but she still believed it. The willowy redhead from Michigan who'd been the certain lead, had collapsed from a nervous breakdown days before the final cast had been announced, and deep down Daya felt like second choice.

To complement Colin's Ingoma-inspired choreography she had decided to draw inspiration from martial arts as well but now she felt the routine she had worked on was perhaps too ambitious. There was a series of 540 kicks that she simply wasn't managing to perfect. The complicated move involved starting with a pirouette then kicking up with her left leg, and before it hit the ground, kicking up even higher with her right leg and propelling herself through the air, before landing with grace. Try as she did, she wasn't finding it possible to raise her right leg in time. The move was traditionally performed by men, and Anna had looked surprised by her repeated inclusion of it, but hadn't cautioned against it. Yet.

Kicking the blanket downwards in frustration, she swung her legs off the bed and dressed, then opened the window and made her way down the fire escape behind the house. She skipped the last three steps, landed like a cat and began walking towards the park. It had been a long time since she had danced after dark. In her first year she had done it all the time, fearlessly. She hadn't told anyone, not even Aaftab. It had been something she simply did for herself, and as Wasim, Aaftab and Colin and the library, choreography, classes and work had filled her hours, she had done less and less for herself. As she entered Roath Park she was overwhelmed by the sense that she *knew* this space. She knew where the willow wept and where the road rose up. Where the conservatory doors creaked and where it was easiest to jump the fence. She knew which paths felt darkest, where there were echoes of women who had been hurt, and she knew how to avoid them and linger along the ones where you could imagine lovers kissing. She walked swiftly then broke into a light run, taking routes she loved, moving in gently tightening circles towards the lake. Just as she gained momentum and her blood began to heat Daya stopped abruptly, for there before her, crowned by moonlight and shockingly elegant, were birds upon the water.

A wedge of swans.

In the absence of Aaftab, Daya began to take her sleeplessness to the lake, where she became night after night, Odette and then more shakily, Odile. She would put on headphones, press play and as the moon conducted the music, she would dance her part. Then she would dance it again, her only audience the swans, sleepy and gathered at the edge of the water observing her sometimes, ignoring her at others. If Odette was a swan by day and a woman by a lake by night, Daya was a girl by day and winged creature by the water by moonlight. She became obsessed with the animals, collecting and carrying home feathers zipped in to the pockets of her jacket each time she returned from the lake. No one knew because no one visited Daya in these days but on the wall opposite her bed in the attic of her oak tree house she began to build a set of wings.

It started when she almost absentmindedly brought home the first feather and not wanting to lose it, pinned it delicately to the wall. The next night, with purpose, she brought another and once again not knowing what to do with it, pasted it beside the first. Then it came to her and she began to build. She built from books with paintings of birds and from watching them watch her. Slowly the wings began to extend. Outspread they began to cover an entire wall with the exact seven-foot wingspan she was trying to replicate. Of the 25,000 feathers a swan has upon its body Daya collected only a few hundred, so the art was in the arrangement. She collected smaller, fluffier feathers for the inside bits, the places where the wings connected to the body, then she sought out the longer feathers that created the magnificent serrated ivory edge that no one could mistake for belonging to any other creature.

She began to feel akin to the birds.

She knew the variety she watched were called mute swans because legend had it they spent their lives in silence, singing only once at the very end.

She knew they could fly at sixty miles an hour.

She knew that they mated for life.

In the darkness she became Buraq, night traveller, flash of lightning, legs of horse and wings of angel. She was Neith, ancient, winged creator of the universe and everything it contains within. (How and when did we begin believing this world was crafted by men?) Wild huntress and goddess of the cosmos and of weaving, like her, Daya spun into existence a world. Like her, Daya learnt she could give birth to it without a lover. Like the Peri, exquisite djinn ladies of Persia disallowed from mating with human, Muslim men, she cast her spell. Like the Kinnari of the *Lotus Sutra*, she had the feet of a swan but the heart of a woman and could dance you into bewitchment. By moonlight she was Nike, likely friend of Garuda, moving faster and faster, a winged blur, as she sped towards victory.

As night fell in the final week before she would dance at Saint David's Hall, Daya took a deep breath and began her routine by the lake. When the moment came, she felt her body lift up into the air and time stood still for her as she raised her left leg then her right, and spun simultaneously. She landed with one knee bent neatly, like she was about to ask the universe for its hand in marriage. She paused a beat then sprang up to continue. Daya had been trying so hard to kick, when all she had needed to do was fly. By dawn, she was Eos.

~

The day before the performance Anna summoned them. 'In the office,' she said, and Daya and Colin padded down dutifully like cubs in their ballet slippers. Anna was in a sleeveless red top, much too scant for how cold it was but she seemed in these days just before the final performance overheated, always on edge and burning. 'Sit,' she commanded. 'Now. I'd like the two of you to take the day off,' she began. 'Rest.' They nodded, grateful. The last few days had seen them in the studios till late into the night, surviving on coffee, eyes hollow. 'You've had your final costume fittings?' Yes, they both nodded again. 'You like your costumes? Wings not too heavy?' She directed this second question at Daya and Daya confirmed vigorously. 'And you're ready?' Yes. 'Good. Tomorrow, when you dance you know there will be people watching. Not just students from the university but important people. People from companies in London, a few Russians – one man is even flying down from New York. Annual performances are important. They are often where the future is decided.' The room acquired a serious hush. 'Tomorrow it will make no difference whether you play the principal roles or not. Mr New York may look right through you and pick a Susie or a Kim from the third row if it looks like she has more grace, more promise. Just because *I* believe you deserve centre stage, doesn't mean they will.' She looked into their grave faces, pausing for effect, her sense of the dramatic always just so. 'Now go.' A fluttering of her fingers towards the door. Rest well, eat well, and I'll see you at the auditorium.'

That night Daya walked to the lake after a light dinner, for the first time in weeks with no intention to dance. She sat down and watched. The birds had grown to know her and her presence no longer alarmed them. They would turn expectantly as she arrived, and didn't skitter if she approached them. She had begun to give them names, and could now tell them apart. The one with the strangely webbed foot she called Alexander. The one with the feather that always stuck out on his head was Gyan, after her father. The one who carried her three cygnets in her wing each evening was simply Mama Swan. The first time she had seen the babies she had squealed and stopped dancing, then realizing she had no one to share the moment with, had burst into tears. She watched them now, the moonlight turning the lake diamond-edged, each ripple on its surface clasped beneath a swan like a blanket. At some point the mother swan stepped up onto the damp bank Daya sat on. Shaking out her feathers noisily, she settled them again, cupping her body and sinking to the ground before Daya. So close. If Daya lifted a single finger, she'd be able to touch her. Breath held, expecting a sudden frenzy of crashing wings, wrist pressed to knee, Daya uncurled a hand and let it extend until it touched ivory. A muscle rippled somewhere under that monument of feather, but the bird did not move. And they sat, very still, Daya's hand on her wing, as the earth shifted and the stars realigned. Daya knew, when God was handing out qualities to all the animals, he had turned to the swans and given them the bag of grace. Daya knew she was no longer a girl playing a swan. She had become one.

15

The boys had never seen Daya dance, and just after he did, Aaftab wished for a moment that he hadn't. It made everything twice as hard. To see her in that frosty dress that looked like nothing more than pale skin on her top half, and candy floss encasing her lower half. She stood on the tips of toes that had been in his mouth. Her movements were water, her fingers feathers. Her short hair had somehow been swept up in a knot with tiny pearls sewn through it. They caught the light as she spun – dew on grass. It was one of those rare occasions she had make-up on, her lips fuller, cheekbones enhanced, dark eyes darker still. It surprised him that despite knowing Colin was gay, it hurt Aaftab to see him hold her, to see him touch her so intimately. At one point he even leaned in as if to kiss her, and Aaftab could have sworn Colin's lips brushed against Daya's. She looked at him so lovingly.

Seeing her like this, the star of the show, the heroine, the centre of her world, he wanted to announce that she was his, or as close to being anyone's a creature this free could be. He wanted to walk up at the end of the performance and take her in his arms. When she came up to curtsey, the hall exploded into applause and a little girl ran onto the stage in a baby blue tutu to hand her a bouquet of violets. Daya stood breathing heavily, sweat making her neck and collarbones slippery, making her nipples stand out against the skin-like cloth, and he stood as little more than one of the awed crowd. He tried to clap louder than anyone else but realized with heat in his cheeks how childish this was. When they got their coats and walked to the stage unaware of theatre protocol, they found a heavy velvet curtain begin to drop, and though they tried making eye contact with Daya, she seemed to look right through them. Taking Colin's outstretched hand, she walked backstage in a shower of clapping, cheering, and rose petals.

When Anna had asked who they would each invite, Colin and Daya, twin lonely souls, had both drawn blanks. 'I wish you weren't in the show – I could have invited you!' Colin told her. And eventually Daya had caved and called first Wasim and then Aaftab. They hadn't spoken much since he had left her house that terrible night. It had been easy – he had avoided calling her, plunged into work and started visiting the mosque more regularly, and she had said she was too busy dancing. Wasim had adapted, the way he always did, to their tides. Now sitting behind the stage Daya's heart pounded at the prospect of seeing him, and in front of it Aaftab felt himself break a sweat.

A bulky, suited Welshman by the stage steps asked Aaftab and Wasim where they intended to go, and when they said, 'To meet Daya,' he said with a smirk, 'Well, everyone wants to meet her, sir, so you can wait your turn.' It was only after they had wandered around, got a Coke from the cafe, looked for a backstage area and tried her phone a few times that Daya managed to get through to Aaftab, breathlessly telling him where to enter the green rooms from. The two of them squeezed in through the narrow door and found themselves in the very unglamorous bustle of the backstage. Girls and boys were running about in stages of undress, people were taking make-up off their faces, and champagne was being drunk with abandon.

They found Daya sitting in a corner, high up on a pile of discarded costumes from plays long forgotten, surrounded by bouquets, her knees up against her chest with her arms around them, icepack on feet, watching the drama like a wingless angel. When she saw them her face broke into happiness. For a few painful minutes after her performance she'd thought they hadn't been able to make it. As she'd curtsied time and again, she scanned the crowd for them. The lights had been torturously bright by the end, and as she stared out with hope, she'd felt nearly blinded. But here they were, she couldn't believe it; they were in suits, even Wasim, who had worn one of Aaftab's old ones. 'You came!' she exclaimed, rosy with glee, amazed she had ever even considered not inviting them. 'Of course we did!' Wasim reached out to ruffle her hair but withdrew his hand and placed it on her shoulder instead, in awe of her elaborate hairdo. 'You were phenomenal,' he said. 'Why didn't you tell us you were this good?' They laughed the easy laugh that was the thread that stitched friendships. Aaftab who had been standing aside awkwardly, his jacket on his arm, leaned down and embraced her, pulling her into his chest with his free arm. 'Congratulations,' he said softly.

In their hearts they heard the crashing sound of a dam breaking. In her baggy jeans and scruffy sweatshirts, her unlaced sneakers and men's cardigans he could separate her from the slender girl in his arms at his weakest. He could not place the girl with shorn hair and biker boots in his reality. It felt too far away and in that distance there was frustration but also there had been safety. But this … this beacon of grace. She sat there, knees drawn up to chest in a way he had seen her sit so many times in the blue light as he dressed to leave, or smoked a cigarette. But always a secret, always in private, her very nakedness placing her permanently in the realm of fantasy. But this Daya, so self-assured, ruling her turf, not rising when they walked towards her, not rising when he embraced her, waving softly across the room to countless admirers but somehow continuing the conversation with Wasim. Bestowing smiles. Radiant, capable, elegant, strong. So different from the Daya he had last seen – broken, tear-stained and underconfident. In that moment he wanted her, more than ever, in his reality. And not for the first time, he doubted how deserving he was of her at all.

Just then a bouquet of white peonies came sailing across the room and landed by her. 'From the Welsh Assembly this time, Miss Odette!' Aaftab looked up and saw a tall, lanky boy striding across the room, smile whiter than white, a crown at a jaunty angle on his head. He stopped short when he saw them. 'Hello, hello, who have we here?' Colin said, the sheen of perspiration making him look more striking than ever, the joy of success making his face more innocent unlike the way it made some men look less so. He was still in his costume, an outfit everyone agreed was a feat of the designer, constructed of fabric so fine it appeared to be skin. Wasim didn't know where to look so he waved politely and took a step back from all the lean, rippling, sweat-soaked muscle before him. Aaftab held out his hand and both he and Colin opened their mouths at the same time.

'Aaftab.'

Daya blushed and tried to stand up in as leisurely a fashion as possible, given the transparent tension of the moment. 'Dinner, boys?' She looked at Wasim, avoiding Aaftab's face quickly so as not to read it at all. They nodded. 'Great, you both make the plan. I …' she leaned over to pick up the peonies, '… am changing.'

In the dressing room she stripped slowly, one of the younger girls helping her. She wiped all the make-up off her face, amassing a small pile of mascara-stained cotton wool. She washed her hands and face twice and settled into jeans, sneakers, and a cuddly navy university sweatshirt. Her entire being heaved a sigh of relief. It was over. She had worked so hard for this. Her body began to ache, the adrenaline wearing off, her muscles responding now to the promise of rest, after months of being stretched and trained, torn and rebuilt, again and again. She caught sight of her reflection. Without her make-up and costume, she had expected to feel once again vulnerable, the way she'd felt these last few weeks, but she didn't. She considered removing the tiny pearls from her hair and brushing it out, but it seemed like a lot of work so she left the immaculate styling intact. Outside, the boys hugged her, now with familiarity, took her bags and walked her to the car Aaftab had borrowed for the night from Enayat taaya.

'Colin's meeting us by the exit,' Aaftab said smoothly as they put her bags in, and Wasim stopped.

'What? It's Christmas!' Aaftab spluttered, daring him to say something.

'Nothing.'

When they pulled up outside the Greek restaurant on Woodville Road, Daya texted Colin while sitting right next to him in the back of the car to say, 'Please avoid the pork?'

and braced herself for a dinner where that would be just one of the many potholes she'd have to avoid. She wanted to tell Colin to drink water with his right hand not left. And to tell Wasim it was okay if what was in Colin's glass wasn't water. In the days they hadn't spoken, something else had taken place. Something beyond them, that had reminded Daya that her troubles with Aaftab went so much deeper. The Indian parliament had been attacked and the government had swiftly claimed it was terrorist groups with bases in Pakistan. Now between alternately thanking her friends and asking them to 'Stop it!' because all the praise was making her blush terrifically, Daya wondered if the news would come up in their conversation. And so, she prepared herself on her special night for disaster.

Her anxiety at her worlds mixing was unfounded. Daya had forgotten how sociable Aaftab was. How Wasim's English was so much better than he let on. How much they knew about the world. How much Colin knew about Islam. How much he wanted to know. How Colin and Wasim both loved to cook. She had forgotten that at her core, Daya knew who she was and what she liked. She liked strong, intelligent, concerned human beings. Warm, soft, caring people who could laugh at almost anything. And who knew when not to talk politics. Thus the two halves of her world came together around her, like two halves of an apricot un-cutting, closing cosily around its seed. And she felt cocooned, loved, whole.

They began the meal with succulent Kalamata olives, anchovy salad and gloriously creamy feta on the side, zucchini soup and roast beets. Moaning over how delicious everything was, Wasim ordered more. Grilled fish in lemon dressing with the subtlest of herbs, and rosemary potatoes mixed with black-eyed beans. Shrimp, bathed in tomatoes and soaked in olive oil, a dish perfect in its balance of sweet and sour. He wanted to order the calamari as well, but Aaftab stopped him. 'But why?' he asked petulantly. 'Oh alright, order what you like,'Aaftab gave in. 'Yes, please let's order everything!' Daya who had been watching her weight anxiously so as not to upset some delicate balance before the performance, exclaimed in the affirmative. Colin nodded enthusiastically, 'I couldn't agree more.' Wasim ordered the mussels as well, and they were all grateful for it. Finally, when their plates had been cleared and their bellies were full, he called for baklava and risogalo. The sweet rice pudding arrived in blue baked pottery cups that were emptied in minutes.

At the end of the long, sumptuous Greek meal Colin asked if he could order a drink for himself. 'I know you won't partake,' he said to the boys, 'but I only know one way to celebrate this and that's with a toast.' Charm oozing, his smile bright. Sensing tension from Wasim he said, 'I'll pay for it myself.'

'Of course, go right ahead,'Aaftab said graciously before anyone else could reply, and that seemed to settle that.

Colin summoned a waiter and said, 'One ouzo please,' and then Aaftab added, 'Make that two.' Wasim looked up confused. 'What?' Aaftab said defiantly. Wasim slipped into Urdu, chin jutting, 'It's up to you if you want to act like the *habshi*.' And Daya, Daya who did not raise her voice at Wasim, no, never, had never shouted at Colin, had not broken this pact with peace even in her angriest moments with Aaftab, now turned to Wasim, her face aflame and said in Hindi, loudly, throwing the fork she was playing with onto the table, 'You will NOT call my friend that.' In that moment she was nothing if not her mother's daughter. Wasim looked down, ashamed and Daya still angry pushed her chair back, alarming Colin further. It was Aaftab though, seated next to her, who placed one hand firmly on her wrist and raised the other to call back the waiter who had discreetly retreated. 'Three please.' Wasim dragged his eyes up from his empty placemat, and avoiding his friends' faces, said to the waiter, 'Four.'

Nobody said anything in the thick, tense silence that followed. Four ouzos arrived in delicate, coloured crystal glasses. Aaftab remembered that ouzo glasses were traditionally called kanonakia – 'little canons', as if waiting to be fired. Colin picked his up and holding it to his nose inhaled deeply. He held the glass out to Wasim and said, 'Smell. Tell me what you smell.' They had done this through the meal, a friendship mounting over taste until it had plummeted over a difference in one. Now, recognizing Wasim's truce flag, Colin attempted to rebuild something on neutral ground. Unenthusiastically Wasim took the tiny glass and sniffed. Aaftab and Daya watched as one would two animals or children being introduced for the first time.

'*Saunf!*' Wasim cried.

'Anise?' Colin asked.

'Yes!'

'Yes, that's it. It's made of anise. You got it!'

Wasim inhaled deeply, excited. 'In Pakistan, when we have a bad stomach my mother makes us drink water boiled with it.'

'And here after a rich meal, you take a sip of this.'

'Prevention is better than the cure to everything?' Wasim was smiling again, and opposite him Aaftab smiled in reflection.

'Or so the Greeks will have us believe.' Colin raised his hand and faced Daya.

'To Daya, my eternal Odette!'

She started laughing, the tension gushing from her in giggles, the giddiness of the night's success rushing back, the sumptuous meal swelling in her.

'No, wait,' she said, raising her own glass. 'Here's to you, dear Siegfried.'

'To *Swan Lake*,' they both said in unison.

'To you,'Aaftab held his own glass up and looked into her eyes.

'Yes, to Daya the dancer!' Wasim lifted his glass. 'To Daya, my sister, and to her friend, Colin.'

A pan of food critics.
A float of dancers.
A clutch of families.

They all held high their little glasses above their heads, the candles flickering off the crystal and their smiling faces.

To love. All kinds of it.

They swallowed, heads tilted back, the liquid hitting their throats then their chests and finally making its way down to warm their stomachs. They split the bill, and though Colin insisted the drinks were all on him, Wasim said they would share that portion of the bill too. He joked, saying that if he'd known Colin was truly paying for them he would have ordered more, but Aaftab knew this was apology. To pay for haraam against his will but willingly. The greatest apology he could summon for Daya. To put her comfort that night above his relationship with Allah. To sin against himself, so that she may smile. And he saw beneath Wasim's graciousness the confusion and fear too of his enjoyment. Sensed already the need for penance that would come soon.

They parted ways outside the little restaurant, many embraces exchanged. Colin said he would walk home and Daya and the boys settled into the car. They dropped a groaning Wasim at the twenty-four-hour store, where he was lifting boxes later that night. It was still not quite dark, a shade of deep mauve spreading across the canvas of the sky. They switched the carols on the radio off and sat in the car outside her house absorbing the light.

'So how have you been?' he asked.

'Alright. I've been dancing and not much else actually. You?'

'I'm okay … been working and mosquing and that's it.'

'Mosquing,' she repeated and laughed.

'They don't like me much there I think, but I've been trying to be more regular.'

'Excellent,' she said.

'Speaking of excellent,' he paused, 'you were one hundred kinds of it tonight.'

'Thank you,' she was instantly shy again.

'No, really, you were so good. I didn't know anyone could dance like that.'

She didn't know how to respond. 'Well, now you do,' she laughed. Then stepping right into the puddle they were both avoiding, she said, 'Come in?'

Aaftab paused. He stood at the axis of the see-saw of his wildly beating heart. It had been some time since he had last seen her. Some time since he had last been in the ease of her company. In the heat of her body. He wanted nothing more than to walk up the steps behind her, to tumble into her. To come apart and together in her hands. But perhaps because he had never loved her more than that night, and finally felt in the brilliance of her entirety that he had so very little to offer in return, that he put his hand on her cheek and brought his face right up to hers. He kissed her, gently, wetly, on her mouth. He reached up to smooth her hair and came away with a dot-like pearl from between the glossy strands. He held her hand, kissed her again, and finally cleared his throat to answer her question. 'I think … tonight, Daya, I won't.' But there was no harshness in his tone. No strictness as there had been at times in the recent past. If she had asked again he would have rolled up the windows and followed her up the stairs. But they both understood. For once, Daya knew that his absence meant more than his acceptance. So for once, Daya did not ask him to stay.

Longing.
Is there a fuller word in all the world?
Tell me, is there an emptier one?

16

Daya woke at noon on Christmas Eve. It had been months since she had slept in like this. Her phone was angry with beeps, her alarm clock silent after weeks of groggy early morning wake-up calls following nights in the park. A beam of weak, milky sunlight streamed in through the window at an angle she wasn't used to as she was usually out by this time. She stretched with all the languor in the world and rose to make herself tea, turning the heating up. In her underwear and sweatshirt she pottered around the kitchenette brewing a Darjeeling. She smiled inwardly, thinking of how much she had learnt about tea from Wasim and Aaftab. As the leaves grew tentacles she walked to the bathroom and filled with hot water a shallow bucket, one she used to collect laundry. Placing it by her bed she settled back in with her cup in hand and her feet soaking in hot water seasoned with salt. She sighed with pleasure and reached for her phone to go through the long list of congratulatory messages, starting with one from Colin that said, 'Thanks for last night. PS: Always knew you like this Aaftab fellow … look so dreamy when you mention him and now I know he's a DISH! Merry Christmas

Eve, sleep with him and then give me details, yeah?' She laughed and opened the next message.

~

It was evening, the sky again the colour of bruises, Daya thought, looking out from where she had lain on her bed all day. She heard her name being called and rose to look down. It was Aaftab, shivering beneath her house, at the foot of the fire escape, before the wall of ivy. She waved him up and pulled on a pair of sweatpants. He entered through the window, always so agile despite his long limbs. She noticed frost on his shoes – when had it snowed?

'What's that?' he pointed to the wall with the swan wings she had constructed.

'A way to leave?' she smiled half-heartedly. Then more seriously, 'What happened, how come you're here?'

He had come to her holding *a clutch of second thoughts* to say she was a magnet before his iron will.

When their clothes dangled from their limbs like heavy foliage at the ends of skinny branches, he whispered into her hair, 'I'm so sorry,' again and again, into her collarbones, her neck, the narrow valley between her breasts. Her vision blurred and broke, whether from immense ecstasy or immeasurable sadness she did not know, and the poetry of his apology was lost to her ears but written upon her body in an impossibly indulgent font. Her physical, tangible being revolting so carelessly against her heart – one's pleasure mocking the other's grief.

They made love, she with the desperation of the thirsty, he with the comfort of coming home. Infused with longing, he once more let go of all he had been taught he should want instead of this.

It is infinitely beautiful how two bodies fit. How one spreads, and the other probes. How one part is the exact invert of another. How two sets of skin melt. How mouths placed against each other are so perfect. How hands lock. How the curve of a head fits within the groove of a shoulder. Or between two breasts. How a nipple is at such ease between the pursed tips of two lips. How the back of the throat is just far enough, nose against neck. Two fingers around a wrist. Sole against sole. Tongue in spaces made only too happy to accommodate this fleshiness. Stomach curving into back, navel in line with spine, breast within palm. Back to front. Upside down. Face to face. Mouth to toe, to knee, to thigh. The way teeth grasp a lower lip, nip beneath curves, against sinew of neck … it is infinitely beautiful how two bodies fit.

'I missed you,' she said breathlessly, softly into the night. He stood by the window smoking the cigarette he always smoked after. There was an ease in his limbs she had not seen before, separate from his inherent confidence. She watched him for a few minutes and then it struck her. He had been with other women. She knew before she asked, but she asked nonetheless. He came towards her and sat upon the bed before he answered. Nothing had ever hurt more. The entire world inside that little attic room exposed for the constructed, empty thing it was. Through her sobs he understood finally, shame. He had taken from the bodies of women he did not love. He had given his body to women whom he did not love. Worse still, who did not love him.

But not my heart. Never my heart.

When he had first come to college he hadn't understood. 'I fucked her.' The boys would say carelessly. At first it was his religion that disapproved, but later it was simply his heart. It told him that physical love on its own was hollow. As the shell is to the sea creature, the body is to the soul, no matter how beautiful when empty. But with the heart in love, he understood that two bodies joining was the ocean of heaven surfacing upon the sands of skin. The understanding that we are souls foremost. He had allowed himself for a while to function without his soul. The worst of all sins.

She lay with her back to him in silent protest and could feel him tracing lines on it with his fingers.

'Do you know what I'm drawing?' he asked her.

'The letter H for haraam?'

'I am mapping the places there will be scars, if you sever your wings and choose a life with me.'

She turned to face him, pushing him gently so he had no choice but to turn as well. His back was now to her, in an exact mirror image of how they had been lying just moments before. She placed two palms at the centre on either side of his spine.

'And this, is where I would stitch those severed wings if I did. And I would … if only you had the courage to carry me out of here on them.'

He did not. Not because he wasn't convinced of his love for her, but because he could not be certain he was offering her a better life with him. He would love her of course, fiercely. But 'Is love ever enough?' he asked, turning back to face her. 'How does one measure love? Or sadness for that matter?' she replied, her voice brittle as an autumn leaf. 'Do you want to count the thimbles of tears?' Lying so close to her, he couldn't look away, so he had no choice but to face his cowardice, the result of it, there in the glisten in her eyes. She blinked and tears rolled down her face sideways towards the pillow. She sat up and gazed out of the window and his eyes felt some relief after looking too long into hers where all the pain of the world was amassing. 'Perhaps somewhere there exists a weighing scale for the heart, to determine how much heavier it is from one day to the next.'

'Daya, please …' he reached out to pull her close, needing her warmth, desperate in his desire to press her close and erase the cold space between them. To pretend, for as long as they could.

Safe against his chest she finally said what she had been waiting to say. 'Aaftab, there's something else I need to tell you.'

~

'You have to tell her.'

Gyan looked up at his wife in her unseasonal yellow kurta from the city of Lucknow, embroidered in spirals of white flowers. As a young man he'd wondered if Lucknow was a city filled with spiders and if they were the ones responsible for the magnificent Lucknowi embroidery one saw on North Indian women the day summer arrived. He had always wanted to visit this city whose name was made up of 'luck' and 'knowledge' both, two things he was desperate to have more of suddenly. A city he would now never see.

You have to tell her.

He was trying to gauge whether Asha had stressed on 'you' or 'have to tell' or 'her'. The 'her' in question was Daya, so taking a chance and assuming she had stressed on *have to*, he said, 'Will you do it today?' But she responded, 'You don't want to do it yourself?' She held in her hands a waste-paper basket woven from different coloured strands of straw – a gift from one of the girls who worked with them. She was collecting from around the room all the pieces of tissue covered in flecks of blood he had coughed up. They looked like a bouquet of dahlias, he thought. The treatments Asha had insisted they try had quickly proved useless, and finally he had begged they stop. Asha had argued. But this one time, he won.

You don't want to do it yourself?

No, he did not. Gyan did not want to have to hear his daughter's voice when he told her he was leaving her. When she found out in a few months at most, she would be fatherless. Half orphan. Asha glanced at the clock as she pulled on a cardigan. 'It's noon there. She'll be up by now for certain,' she said, quickly calculating the time difference. 'She must be tired after the performance,' Gyan stalled. She held his gaze till he broke away again, coughing. They had agreed to tell her the morning after the dance. 'Let's give it half an hour,' she allowed.

They didn't have to call her. She called them, in response to a message from Asha congratulating her on the show finally being over. A message Asha had sent late the night before, as she had sat up watching Gyan's broken breathing, trying to conjure a performance out of the description Daya had given her of her costume.

Daya called directly, not using a calling card, splurging after her success, and the line echoed with crystal-clear sound. *Daya, there's something we have to tell you.* Asha had experienced moments of extreme frustration in the last few years when she had missed her daughter's joyous laughter, observations and cheeky comments, but now she understood the pain of missing her when she was sad, and they were taught by distance the cruelty of tears you cannot touch. Of saltwater you cannot swim in.

They ended the call quickly, Daya insisting on returning immediately. In Lalabad Gyan said to Asha through sobs, 'Who will give her away at her wedding?'

Kissing his hands Asha said, 'You always said I would. That it was an "archaic, misogynistic, patriarchal" custom.'

'But now I want to.'

'Oh my sweet misogynist.'

And Daya had placed the perfect cup of tea on her bedside where it had gone cold, and retrieved her feet from the water which did the same. Then she had curled into bed and stayed there, until she'd heard Aaftab's voice through the snow outside her window. Now, lying in his arms she said the words she had not had the courage to even think yet. The words she suspected she had been half trying to drown out by diving into his presence. 'Aaftab. My father is dying.'

~

'So, since I'll be gone indefinitely, I was thinking now might be the best time … for us to … you know …' She didn't have to say more. 'How rarely do you want to talk?' he asked, half hoping she was joking, so making a statement bolder than he believed his heart to be. She replied with shattering conviction. 'Never. I think never is best. Unless it's absolutely necessary of course.' Almost apologetically as an afterthought she added, 'It's pointless to, isn't it?'

They were speaking in the formal language of strangers. She was saying 'aap', not out of respect, but distance. There was a chasm of unsaid words opening up between them. They were on opposite sides of a valley, each one composing themselves, and that composure serving as a dagger to the other, who in turn gathered themselves further. Like this, in an awful chain reaction they each took a step back then one more and another until the distance was too wide to cross. But this is also grace. To break without breaking. To turn your wounds invisible. To give flight to the other. To let go of that which is giving you life. To say goodbye.

Aaftab dressed like the unwanted and left swiftly. He wondered if she would have allowed him to comfort her, had he not been with the others. Had he not admitted it. But the thought made him too sad, and like so much else he boxed it away. He walked home through Roath Park and halfway across it he saw a swarm of what looked like falling stars. They were fireflies, summoned by some force like soldiers of light, like confetti in a dust storm. He wanted to call to tell her that if she ran down now she could see them. But he couldn't. And Aaftab realized he was completely alone and everything beautiful was worthless, because he could not share this with her.

~

'Library?' Daya asked Colin over the phone.

'Happy New Year, milady! 4:30?'

But she decided she didn't want to see it one last time. When she had handed in her employee access card on the 2nd of January when the building had reopened sleepily, the Head Librarian, a formidable woman Daya had grown over the years to love, said, 'Chin up. This building survived two wars, Daya, and it will survive without you.' Then she handed her a book of Yeats' poems signed by the entire staff. Daya had gifted her a Hariprasad Chaurasia CD, hoping future students may find themselves wondering where the music was coming from.

'Sam's Café instead?' she texted Colin.

'Okay. 4:40 then.'

They met at the small cafe forgotten by everyone except archaeology students who frequented it religiously, perhaps in awe of just how long it had stood in that very same spot. The joke amongst the other students was that the food was so stale they had mistaken the cafe for an ancient excavation site and the coffee and cake for artefacts. But they played wonderful jazz. Colin walked in looking snug and neat in his turtleneck jumper, Daya dishevelled, scarf trailing.

'You're the only person I know who leaves home without a shower, you know,' he started, lowering his sunglasses.

'You're the only person I know who irons their jeans.'

'Touché, bebe,' he signalled to a waitress and when she ignored him, got up and went to the back to order for them, returning chatty. 'How was New Year's Eve? I met the most amazing boy, his name's Benjamin and …'

'Colin, please hear me out,' Daya cut him off.

She told him.

He nodded. He put his sunglasses back on. They sat together holding hands. The waitress finally emerged and brought them two Americanos. Colin asked, 'Is it … definite?'

'It is. I mean I think so. I guess it is.'

'I'm sorry.'

'It's not your fault.'

Neither of them laughed.

They drank their coffee in silence. 'You look like an idiot. It's almost dark, take the sunglasses off,' she said. And he did, but his eyes were red beneath.

'I'll leave tomorrow.'

Colin looked up shocked. 'Tomorrow?'

'Yes.'

'But you can't. You'll miss the last exams. Also the oral.'

'You don't think they'll let me defer to next year or something?' she asked. She hadn't thought that far.

'Markova doesn't do that. I thought you knew this.' Colin was agitated now. 'Daya, go in a few weeks once you're officially done. You will not graduate otherwise.'

'Colin,' she looked him calmly in the eye, 'I will not see my father again, if I stay.'

'And the money?'

'What about it?' she said defiantly.

'I know your parents aren't badly off, but would your dad really want you to throw away three years of international student fees?'

'I paid for my own ticket.'

'With what?'

'My library income.'

Colin who had grown up with so little, who was constantly living on less so he could pay off his student loans, who had worked hours and hours after school as a teenager to supplement those loans, could not believe how swiftly Daya had been able to make the decision.

'Still,' he said, clenching his jaw.

'Colin. Listen to me. My story is not your story. I may never actually be a dancer.'

'Well, not if you give it up, no.'

'I'm not giving up. I'm choosing. I'm choosing my father, and I'm sorry you can't, but your advantage is that you can choose dance.'

'Don't you talk to me about privilege.'

'Colin!' she raised her voice.

When he looked at her, she asked, 'What would your father want you to do if he met you today?'

Colin pressed his lips together and blinked back tears. 'He would want me to dance.'

'And mine wants me to go back. I know. I can feel it.'

'I'm sorry.'

He took her hand back in his and repeated, 'I really am sorry.'

They left, and walked through the park together listening to birds bringing dusk in their beaks. Colin placed a hand on her arm suddenly, stopping her. 'Look.' Up ahead a patch of grass appeared to glow. They moved towards it, Daya frowning, Colin looking scared. On the park floor, as if massacred by blades of grass, was a small swarm of fireflies. Colin bent to touch one.

'But they're ...'

'Dead.' Daya completed his sentence. 'They do that sometimes. Keep shining after they're actually gone. Like stars.'

A conflagration of fireflies.

The pair stood there, understanding for just a second how the entire universe works.

When they got to her front door he said, 'I'm sorry I can't say more. It's just that now I am remembering my father.'

'I know.'

'Go fast.'

'I'm going. Colin … will you tell Miss Anna? I just couldn't.'

He nodded and she exhaled with relief. 'I'll see you …?' She didn't know how to finish this question.

'Whenever we can. Sometime.'

'Sometime. Somewhere.'

She was turning, about to ascend the fire escape, when he said, 'Daya?'

She stopped.

'Wandile Mthembu.'

She looked at him blankly.

'My name. I never say it, because my father gave it to me. But now, you can know.'

One precious thing taken, one precious thing kept.

One precious thing gone, one precious thing left.

Like this, he gave her a long-forgotten prayer.

They embraced, wet cheeks and palms pressed against each other's backs.

Goodbye now, Wandile.

And Colin Orwell went home and took from between the pages of letters his mother used to send him before she found out he liked boys, a single picture of a big man holding a small boy on his lap, both of them grinning at the camera, the four edges of the photo rounded, the colours seeping lavender, but happiness abundant. He looked at little Wandile Mthembu and cried till sleep came to hold him.

~

On being asked to come along, Aaftab had told Wasim he was working late, so, on the floor of her attic room the two of them spread her coverless duvet and clinked cups of tea like cherubs picnicking on a cloud. Then they discussed all those things they secretly feared they would never have time to later. For what is later, but the future? And what is the future but uncertain? Wasim's mother, Daya's father, the history of Lalabad, the first time he knew he wanted to cook. They began to recall stories, the memories producing tender warmth. They grew merry and then they grew sad. Together they wove through episode upon episode, creating into the starless night a tapestry of the time gone by. A blanket they must finish by dawn, in order to take shelter under it.

How quickly they had learnt the details of each other. That Aaftab hated tomatoes, and Wasim always bought the shrimp salad baguette. She only ate plain, salted crisps. Silly, insignificant things. In the future they would forget important isolated incidents, forgoing them for the details of the intimate. It is the trick of Time, to keep certain incidents for herself, and leave us in the deal, the regular intimacy of familiarity. Daya would never for example truly remember the single night Wasim had dressed his best for her dance performance. The cool grey stripe in the borrowed charcoal suit, the sky-coloured tie, she could not bring to mind. But the memory of his favourite red sweater, the one he'd worn every single day for two years until Aaftab had taken the kitchen scissors and cut it off him while he was asleep, filled her already with a pang of melancholy. She thought it would be made mundane by the fact that he wore it always. That the details of it would be lost and yet, it was the image of him in that red blur that would for years make her want to reach out into her thoughts and hug him. The man so perfectly dressed in a pinstriped suit, in the single photograph of him she would later find on the university website documenting the crowd the night of the dance, was a stranger.

There were many moments that she now grabbed at with a hand certain it needed the memory, as the reality would soon cease to exist. She put down in her mental notebook that Wasim liked the colour black, even though she had explained how black wasn't really a colour. How he played cricket with his right hand but wrote with his left. Aaftab she had learnt double time, overtime. The patterns of his moles. The tiny cluster of freckles under the fine hair on his left arm – a galaxy of stars across the sky of his skin. The ordinary in their lives became of utmost importance for her to store away. The way Wasim chopped vegetables without looking at them. The way he cut garlic cloves into transparent bean-shaped slivers. The way Aaftab smoked while walking in the winter, not using his hands, his cigarette dangling from his mouth so he could keep his fingers warm in his pockets. His irreplaceable scent.

She remembered how as Aaftab had dressed that last day she had thought to herself, 'Remember this moment always.' Just like that, the wintry scent of the bedroom mixing with that of his hair and her perfume; suddenly she had found the smoke and ash wanted their space in her nostrils, and had added themselves to the mix. Now she understood that in all those moments when she had believed in love wholeheartedly, she had been betraying her own heart by asking it to forever recall the moment. It was after all betrayal. For who need recall the smell of their lover's hair mixed with smoke, unless of course they were certain of being parted? Unless of course they knew they may never replicate that moment, that they didn't actually have a lifetime to spend together. Though she had fought with herself to live within the moment, she had already been planning wisely for the very downfall she told herself may not occur. To forget is to have faith in the future of love. The unlost moment is love's greatest betrayal.

Now she did the same with Wasim. Like a film, from start to finish they replayed their time together. She hadn't left yet, and already they could both feel the tug of nostalgia surrounding them. Every story began with a 'Remember when?'

Tujhe yaad hai jab?

A flight of yesterdays.

Kya din they …

At 5:30 in the morning, Wasim rose to go.

'I wanted to give you something,' Daya said shyly as he shrugged on his jacket.

She pulled from her pocket two pieces of string.

In 1905 when the State of Bengal was broken into two, divided along a line by a British man who cleverly coloured one half Muslim and the other half Hindu like a sign of what would come four decades later (yes, a little batting practice for

Partition), the poet Rabindranath Tagore took to the streets in protest with nothing but a bunch of strings. And then he did a curious thing. Around the wrist of anyone he encountered, he tied that string. Where the British were wrapping a noose around the neck of a state, Tagore was handing out rakhis instead. For the first time in the long history of the festival of Raksha Bandhan, people celebrated not on the last day of Shraavan when sky and land had finally melted into one, but on the first day of a separation. And following Tagore, Hindus tied strings on the wrists of Muslims as a promise of safety, and Muslims tied strings on the wrists of Hindus in solidarity. And this is how they pulled together what an empire wanted to rip apart.

She tied one on him. He tied one on her.

'I always wanted a little brother.'

'There's no word for two rakhis?' he asked.

'How could there be – all the words are in their language.'

'But not all the ideas.'

'Choose one then?' she said.

'A *khaandan*,' he smiled after a moment. '*A khaandan of rakhis*.'

'Be safe,' Daya said. 'I will. *Aur sun*,' he said almost as an afterthought. '*Allah jo karega behtar karega*.' She made herself a feeble bed and lay in it alone. She had packed light, even though her heart forewarned her that she may not be coming back. It was alright, she thought. Wasim could ship her things if need be. She took nothing that reminded her of Aaftab. Not his T-shirts that she had stolen at some point to sleep in, soft and worn and impossible to look at without imagining him inside them, and then outside of them. Not the presents – the silver sting ray pendant, an illustrated book of Shakespeare's sonnets, and so much else. She even left behind the few photographs she had of him.

She had once read a beautiful book about the objects people carried across the border with them when they crossed over at the time of Partition. Everyone going one way was a newborn Pakistani, regardless of their age. And everyone going both ways was homeless, landless and with history lost. What did people take with them? Cooking utensils. A string of pearls. A dupatta. A photograph. Often nothing but their shredded dignity. What did Daya take from this home, this land, this life she wasn't sure she would return to.

Nothing.

Why was nothing so heavy? And she remembered Aaftab quoting al-Khayal to her once. 'You know what my good friend Khayal says?'

'Tell me.'

'He says: "An empty heart … is not less heavy."'

At the very last moment while trying to choose a book for the long plane journey, she saw his copy of *Anna Karenina*, nestled between texts on her shelf, and she picked it up and packed it into her bag. It was unnecessary. She slept the entire flight home.

She had left by the front door for once, hugging her sweet landlady Mrs Coombes goodbye while promising to post her peacock feathers, forgetting the hundreds of swan plumes the old woman would find in the attic the next day. She didn't see that along the wall, behind the fire escape, the wisteria came into brilliant unseasonal bloom for twenty-four hours as she flew her way across a world. As the plane had risen she had looked down on that little island and a single word had come to mind. Blighty. *Vilayati*. Foreign. And then she fell into dream-racked sleep.

She rose hours later when the sky was bleeding sunset and had just begun to close for the night. In the cocoon of her seat, staring out to heaven, she wept over what was to come.

Interlude

The heart asks pleasure first
And then, excuse from pain –
And then, those little anodynes
That deaden suffering;

And then, to go to sleep;
And then, if it should be
The will of its Inquisitor,
The liberty to die.

– EMILY DICKINSON

ACT TWO

17

Aaftab missed the old imam. A soft-spoken man from Pakistan, he had gained great respect when his son was murdered in a brawl near Lahore with some Christian boys. The imam had taken a stand and announced that if his community retaliated in any way, he would leave his homeland forever. Revenge be damned. And when they had retaliated regardless, tying a group of young Christian boys – perhaps innocent, perhaps not, does it matter? – to train tracks, true to his word, he had left too.

Where do honest imams go?

Any way the wind blows.

And the wind blew him to Wales. He had won Aaftab over right at the start by quoting Daagh and then other poets, always interpreting the verses after, as sermons. 'What does it mean?' he would say for the benefit of his mixed-race audience in his pleasantly accented English that reminded Aaftab of the best parts of home – physics teachers, theatre and friends with guitars, his father's intelligent colleagues debating each evening over tea. 'It means we believe in a single God. There is no need for rituals … all the divisions and systems – you know like what *kind* of

Muslim is he – they disappear or rather are erased, in the face of true faith. You see? It's easy. People find faith so difficult because they concentrate on the rules. But faith is freedom too.'

He would say things like, 'Being secular no longer means simply accepting that all religions exist. It means fighting back with love, *for* all religions. It means standing up. That is a true Muslim – he who holds Allah higher than any ritual or division, and higher than human hate.' This Aaftab could understand.

'Yes, it's true that there is no God but one God but might we accept people who call this God by any other name are simply speaking a different language than yours, my brothers who are all gathered in this room who all speak different languages, my sisters listening in, did Allah not create within us the space for that higher understanding? For empathy towards those who have not yet chosen to call God by the name Allah?' This Wasim could accept.

This, all this 'Utter bloody rubbish,' as they called it eventually, the Committee could neither comprehend nor condone. The elders who had so carefully selected the fellow, now frowned in first mild and then severe disapproval. 'Twenty years he studied … for this?' they muttered to each other over cigarettes at the end of prayer time. 'Next he'll be marrying our sons off to white girls,' the congregation whispered. 'We need to get rid of him,' was the whisper back.

On his last day he had stood before them, his eyes to the floor, until finally he spoke. The gathering was small as many, aware of his coming departure and the shame of his dismissal, had chosen not to attend. He gave a brief lecture on 'being good', and what it comprised. He ended with tears in his eyes and quoted, to Aaftab's disbelief, al-Khayal. 'Today you see me cry, but remember, crying is a good way to remind ourselves that we all came from the ocean. We all must someday return to the sea.' Then he wiped a tear and folded into himself.

Those who had asked he be sent away said, 'It wasn't even a poem. That's communist propaganda he's been quoting. Also, it's Hindus who fling ashes upon water.' They shook their heads, this *hellfire of fundamentalists* and Aaftab who overheard them wondered if there was really any sin in being inspired by beauty, if it brought one closer to God. Wondered how they rejected so much that was exquisite because as they insisted, it would distract him from God. And yet, it was in that beauty that he found Him.

Afterwards the imam stood outside the mosque with his fragile group of followers. 'Twenty years I studied to do this,' he said quietly, sadly. His kurta like his heart, was crumpled, his brown cardigan unbuttoned, hung like the jowls of an old dog around his hips, his right hand clutching his worn Holy Book. '*Bees saal.* Ask me anything from the Quran with the Quran in your hand to check,' he extended the book towards them. 'Any page. I no longer know where they are getting their information, but our Prophet did not utter those words. It's all in this book. Forgive me, but hadith is hearsay. Sixth-century gossip. That's all. Eventually the world will leave the gossipmongers behind.' Wasim swallowed a gasp.

That belief so simple, shared by all the good people of the world. That the rest of the world wanted to be good too. That the world journeyed using the same moral compass as theirs. That fate was fair. How foolish, Imam sahib. Time and again, this foolishness. He handed Aaftab the Quran and said, 'Wait, I will show you something.'

Soon after he had come to that cold country, he told his wife he would apply for work as an imam again. They had no more sons to lose and his wife asked, 'What will they take from me next for your radical views? Be careful they don't take you.' She wasn't happy and made it clear, but he said, 'If I don't fight, who will?' Placing his hand on hers he had said, 'You should hear what they say sometimes. There's a storm brewing … no, a hurricane coming. I need to do my part to keep the House of God standing.'

'Al-Qaeda?' she asked.

Al-Qaeda. He nodded. 'And the Taliban.'

'Have you heard anything concrete from Pakistan?'

He shook his head, 'Just rumours from Quetta,' and squeezed her hand.

'Do you know,' he asked her after a moment's hesitation, 'how they got that name?'

She shook her head.

'You know the word "qaida"?'

'You mean rules?'

'Regulation.'

'But that's Urdu,' she frowned.

'In Arabic it means something similar. Foundations. Or more simply, "the base".'

'So Al-Qaeda is the base of … this Usama's Islam?'

'No, it's even simpler actually. Al-Qaeda is just the base where they meet. It's not so much an organization as it is a symbolic Afghan coffeeshop. It's from before Usama's time. And I've heard Usama finds this most amusing that the Americans think it's some networked organization when it just began as a phrase – as in let's meet at the base, bhaijaan, see you there.'

'But isn't it?'

'Amusing?'

'No. A network.'

'Yes, but …'

She cut him off with some force, 'And who have you heard all this from? What Usama thinks is so funny? The trouble with listening to rumours is we begin to speak them. Don't tell me about this bin Hadi.'

'His name is bin Laden.'

'I don't care, and neither should you.'

He fell silent, and moved his hand away from hers, back to his own lap.

She rose to walk out of the room, but stopped in the doorway, looking particularly arresting with the cold British light touching the warm colours of her clothes from home. 'Don't forget in all this Al-Qaeda business, what it means, to be a *qaidi*.' He smiled at her wit but when she turned her back he looked at his hands in shame because she thought him a prisoner.

She had come to him the next day and handed him a single folded piece of paper.

'What's this?'

'Khol.'

He did as she asked and unfolded it. It was a photocopy of a magazine page of classifieds, with one ad circled in red ink. He recognized the masthead – a local Muslim youth magazine. The circled text, formed to look like any other advertisement on the page said, 'Vacancy For An Imam'. Under which, the following:

1. Do you have difficulty in speaking English?
2. Did you enter Britain with a false passport?

> 3. Are you living in fear of being deported?
> 4. Are you a firm advocate of corporal punishment?
>
> This is the job for you!
>
> Salary: Remuneration in the form of good quality Moroccan dates (who said we pay peanuts?)
>
> Apply to your local mosque committee.
>
> (Please note that the mosque committee is definitely NOT an equal opportunities employer and reserves the right to fire you at five minutes' notice.)

He had wanted to laugh but it came out as a choking sound.

'Where did you get this?' he asked her.

'I found it in a magazine.'

Now he took it from his wallet, unfolded it again down worn edges and handed it to Aaftab. 'I carry this as a reminder.'

'Is it meant to be funny?' Aaftab asked after a minute.

'Isn't it?'

'No.'

'Because it's reality. Except the passport … my passport is real.' He smiled.

'And corporal punishment?'

'It would do some of them good.' He turned to the tight circle of men around him.

'Goodbye, my friends …'

Where do honest imams go?

Any way the wind blows.

And then the new imam arrived and the towers fell pell-mell and there were some who whispered that perhaps the old imam should have stayed. But mostly there were those who said out loud how thankful they were in these stressful times with folks like the Cleanse Britain gang and their violence on the rise, that he'd been sent away and replaced by someone less 'wishy-washy'. Then there were also those who claimed both imams had known what would take place in September, and one agreed and one didn't, so one was kept and the other was swept. And the new imam lit the tail of hate that people had so far kept neatly behind them, and it rose up like a torch, and set fire to the sky.

Now, especially now, with Daya gone and Wasim wandering so close to the mosque, so far from the woods, with the towers gone and a lamp gone out in the world, he missed the old imam and his beautiful voice that sang smoothly the azan over the din of the town. Wasim had said to Aaftab one day – 'the azan is like a city's anchor'. In Pakistan it was where the world paused, rested briefly and then moved on. In Wales Aaftab knew it was a sound that kept Wasim steady. The familiar clock of his life. To Aaftab it rang different on different days.

Mournful after a tragedy.

Hopeful on the days leading up to the prophet's birthday.

Joyful on the first day of the year.

Tired at election time.

These days it was melancholy.

Behind that sound Aaftab heard an immense loneliness and he thought of how after the towers had fallen the mosque had started to become a chamber of echoes, allowing room for only those who wanted their own voices and thoughts reflected back at them, the imam's voice and its echo, loudest of all. For some weeks now, Aaftab knew he had been nothing but a blip in the sound. All the other blips had faded away, overpowered over time by the echoes. They had either become part of the echo or disappeared altogether. But Aaftab had continued to interrupt the reverberation like a scratch on a record. Beside him like a twin scratch there had always been Wasim, but now Aaftab had to admit even he, his good friend, had gone silent.

18

The first person Daya met on returning was Milni. They greeted each other like puppies, collapsing onto Milni's bed in embrace. 'I missed you so much,' Milni said over tea brought in on silver trays with plates of biscuits and porcelain cups. *I miss you so much*, Daya thought. The Milni she had once known was gone. All that remained of her were the long legs, now longer still. She told Daya how she was a model, a fact Daya knew but could see Milni felt more beautiful after repeating, so she let her.

They flopped down on her bed and bits of their hair entwined as they both stared at the still ceiling fan and their voices remembered each other in the raw. Milni's laughter sounded different on the phone, Daya thought. And she cursed more than came across over a phone call. Her language was littered with fucks. It was rough and her legs and face were smooth, impeccably groomed. Daya felt both older and younger than her friend in ways that made her uncomfortable, and yet there was the old connection. Milni was wet-eyed with the news of Gyan's illness and held fiercely and silently onto Daya's hand as she spoke of the effects of the chemotherapy which they had chosen to stop,

Asha accepting it would only make him go faster. She was warm about the dancing. 'You always were the best, of course you'd be Odette,' she said without any malice. But there were small things, like the brusque way in which Milni asked her maid Pushpa to complete tasks she seemed perfectly capable of doing. The girls had grown up with Pushpa who was only a few years older than them. Somewhere something had changed and now Daya apologetically insisting on doing things like carrying her own plate to the kitchen after lunch or refilling her own glass of water made Milni uncomfortable. 'It's fine, she'll do it,' Milni said repeatedly, with an expansive generosity that embarrassed Daya.

They were sitting in Milni's parents' sprawling lounge with its flat-screen television, black-out curtains and cold Cokes on ice sweating into velvet coasters before them. Even as a child Daya had found it the most glamorous thing that Milni's parents served Coke in their house. Asha and Gyan reserved it for birthdays. Lunch had been an assortment of Daya's favourite dishes and she felt spoilt. Glued to the television before them watching a cartoon race that involved a series of preposterous characters including a dog with a wheezing laugh was Milni's nephew. He was four and Daya marvelled at how the tiny child she had left behind, wrapped in blankets made of muslin was now a TV-watching, comprehending boy in a stiff blue shirt. Milni's phone rang. 'I have to take this, babe,' she said lightly and Daya winced at that word so carelessly thrown in at the end, turning her into just about anyone from Milni's world. 'Watch him, please!' she pointed at the four-year-old and rose like a large bird before exiting the room.

The race ended and the little boy grabbed the remote and began pressing buttons rapidly, as Daya who could just about turn on a television looked on with amazement. She closed her eyes and the channels flipped as tiny soundbites, a few seconds of a show before the voices and music changed. Suddenly a voice she recognized. She opened her eyes and General Musharaff's face appeared, filling the screen. Behind him, the Pakistani flag. The little boy stared at the screen then walked up to it, his small head in line with the General's moustache. He made his fingers into a mini flesh gun and pointed it higher than himself, at the General's forehead. 'Dishoom!' he said, and then turned proudly to Daya as he blew imaginary smoke off the tips of his fingers. 'Why did you do that?' she said after a moment's hesitation in which she wondered if it was really her place to ask. 'Because I hate Pakistan,' he replied confidently, expecting praise. Daya imagined if this was a quiz show on television she would hear a voice shout, 'And the answer is … CORRECT!' Except she wanted a buzzer to sound, a red light to go off and a clown to spring out and say, 'Wrong! Better luck next time!'

What did it mean to hate a country?

I hate India.

I hate Pakistan.

I hate America.

And was it the same as saying: *I hate Pakistanis*. She heard that less often. Maybe because a single country seemed like less to take on than millions of people. Whenever she'd heard British and European students say, 'I hate Americans,' she wanted to ask, 'All 300 million?'

And when this four-year-old said he hated Pakistan what did it mean?

She wanted to ask:

Do you hate the word?

Do you hate the land?

Did it mean that he hated the meadows of Neelum Valley? The river Chenab? The Badshahi Mosque and all its whispers? The Anarkali Bazaar? Leather shoes handmade for women's feet, Shan-e-Khuda mangoes, Lahore? Their General and his moustache? Aaftab?

The little flesh gun made of four-year-old fingers should have been warning enough and yet as the day drew on and Milni said, 'What about men?' Daya told her. She told her shyly but frankly, with her chin jutting out a little the way it did when she felt defensive but couldn't figure out why. 'Well done, girl! You kept it secret all this time? I mean I kept wondering because you were always with him, but still!' They were back on Milni's bed staring at the ceiling and Milni had just told Daya about an older man, a photographer she was sleeping with. 'I don't *love* love him,' she had said, 'but we're a great team … work-wise.' Now she rolled over onto her stomach so she could look Daya in the face. 'But it's good you ended it. You can't love a Pakistani.'

Daya didn't respond. Milni took her silence and turned it into a window to say more. 'You know the unspoken rules.' She said 'unspoken' with contempt, signifying she was against these rules, and yet Daya did not believe Milni was, or really thought differently from those who believed that *Daya could not love a Pakistani*. As if to confirm her fears, Milni sat up and started counting off the tips of her manicured fingers. 'No Muslims, no blacks, white guy is dateable but as long as you wrap it up before college ends, and definitely no chinkies! Maybe the ones from Singapore or Hong Kong are okay but not the ones here. Pakistanis don't even make the list!' She laughed a laugh too loud and rough and Daya's dismay began to spill from her.

It was a feeling that had sat at the edge of her heart for hours now. It had risen in her stomach when she had seen the guard outside Milni's house, a hundred years old maybe and hobbling to open the gate that weighed more than all the money he would make in one lifetime. It had leapt towards her chest when she had seen Milni's gorgeous Alsatians tied up in the driveway with flies around their bored eyes. It had crept up her windpipe when she had walked in and Milni's parents had greeted her with so much love and sympathy before implying she should now swiftly marry and should convince Milni to do the same; careers could wait but good men disappear after all. All of it came wrapped in laughter and lightness and yet by the time Milni's nephew had pointed a gun at a screen, the feeling was at the edge of her heart and now it felt like a flood.

It spilled from her skin and covered the bed and slipped off the sheets until it filled the floor of Milni's pretty pink room and rose till she felt she was drowning in it. She sat up in order to save herself, and said she had to go because it was six and her father would be awake. Then she swam out of that room that was flooded with her dismay and her own sense of failure on choosing Milni. Milni over everyone else. '*Best* friend,' she would always say. Milni who would not choose for her what she wanted most. Daya felt struck anew by loneliness.

She got into an auto rickshaw and began the long journey to the older part of the city where her parents still lived, despite everyone saying it was too far nowadays. 'Everything used to be so close by!' she had said to her mother after coming home from the airport. It was like the city had melted in the heat over the years and spread, all the houses and buildings shifting outward. 'Everything is still close by!' Asha had replied. 'The spaces in between just got filled up.' Daya had thought immediately of Aaftab. Perhaps that was it then. Nothing had changed between them; too much had simply come in the way.

The wind whipped at her hair and she felt her teeth rattle as the rickshaw went over a particularly potholed road. Daya had always quietly done exactly as she pleased. She had known what the other Indian students at the university thought of her. What they thought of her Pakistani friends, about her studying dance while they clicked in and out of the brand-new metal and glass business school. What they said. She had gone ahead and done it still. The way she still took rickshaws at night to the far side of the city. The way she wore those men's shorts people called ridiculous and sneakers to fancy places. The way she cut her hair and refused to speak until she was ready. Quietly, Daya did what she wanted. And now something about the way Milni had made that broad statement, so blank and bereft of nuance or choice, made her skin bristle.

You cannot love a Pakistani.

And her heart replying –

But I do.

What really came of so much hatred? India forgave the British 200 years of rule quicker than a crumpet brunch. Shoving past each other to enter London and coming back claiming to know every restaurant in Covent Garden, while talking like the Queen. But that little country that was so recently a part of her, India would not forgive. That little place full of ex-neighbours and relatives left behind, Grandma's favourite restaurant and Grandad's grave and some Muslims, friends with names so familiar like Mohammed and Khan and Noor and Jahan, India discarded and would not forgive.

Two nations always on the edge of war. Always with guns cocked and one eye open. Six decades spent watching a border that was more snake than cement, more river than rope. And now finally India had the world on her side. Because after the towers fell it was no longer just India versus Pakistan. It wasn't a bullying, fast-developing India versus a small insecure nation to its craggy north, like two siblings where you had to feel for the younger. No. After the towers fell, this is what it was:

The Largest Democracy in the World
(India)

Versus

The Islamic State of Pakistan
(that country bordering Afghanistan,
that country where Osama probably lives)

If you asked Aaftab about this, he would tell you about that joke he heard once as a child.

'If you have a kilo of cotton and a kilo of lead, which is heavier on a see-saw?' As a child Aaftab had answered, 'The kilo of cotton, obviously!' and his friend had run off laughing. Today Aaftab knew. India may be a kilo of cotton, but Pakistan was a kilo of lead. Pakistan with its expensive defence and blood-thirsty streets that seemed to drink from its citizens. Such a complicated mixture of love and hate for his young nation. He had been raised in the shadow of this constant idea of war and could never reconcile how a land of poetry, and mountains that looked like the lap of God, could throw up so much violence, so many sad stories and dust and blood and misplaced pride.

When you begin something new, you start with a clean slate, but Pakistan was not granted that clean slate.

Pakistan began upon the debris of disaster,
in the smoke of survival and murder,
in the unholy mess of one man's demand
and an empire's amputation.

And Daya was realizing that in India not everyone felt empathy. That the scars of partition ran deep, and that trauma was genetic. That hate could be passed on alongside eye colour, generation upon generation. That there were people who itched to say what they really felt and that no matter how many times one repeated the words secularstatesecularstate, secretly they wanted something else. And then, voila, in some magic trick of the east, one day while Vishnu, protector and preserver napped, their dirty work was done for them and the Devil granted their wish. The towers came down and the Americans burst in brandishing words like 'terror' and 'dubbelyu em dee' and a part of India smiled and muttered, 'That's what we've been saying all along, these guys are terrorists. Even the ones who stayed here and dare to pray to their god.' So they shrugged off their decency, that long uncomfortable charade, and pulled on their saffron shoes because a legitimate enemy was born. One the entire world could relate to: Pakistan, Osama's buddy. And now it was with ease that people said things like –

'You can't love a Pakistani. You know the rules – no Muslims.'

Aaftab and Daya had avoided talking about this as much as they could: the fact that it was what separated them. Two countries that people like Milni saw as parted by blood and terribly different gods, as if blood had a religion and gods were everything, but shared clothes and language and culture and history and food and family and songs and memory and love were nothing, were negligible.

Daya seated in the auto rickshaw bent over suddenly and clutched her stomach with one hand and her chest with another as if to steady her insides because everything hurt. It hurt because she feared Milni was right. That it wasn't easy. *That it couldn't work*. And she realized she had in fact been holding out hope still. In the end Milni had said, as if to reassure her, 'Daya, you've eliminated a million fights that you would have had, by choosing not to be with him.' What she had wanted to say in reply was, '*We* create the fight. *We* choose what is easy and allowed and what can work and what can't.' But she had stayed silent in dismay. Had laughed even. A false, high-pitched, awkward giggle. Now she knew with shame what she should have said. But she did not address Milni, she whispered the words into the cool night air instead and hoped the wind would carry them across the sea.

Eliminated a million fights? Whatever do you mean?
When the hardest fight, the greatest battle
Is for us to not be.

~

Twenty years since they started The Stardust Sleepers, Daya's parents employed 158 women between the ages of sixteen and seventy-three. They had two centres, one each in Uttar Pradesh and Haryana, a small store in Delhi, a thick fistful of international buyers, and a programme for literacy for the women as well as their children. It was past dusk and though she usually stopped working by this time, Asha was checking patches of embroidery that new girls who needed employment had submitted. She was placing them in three piles according to ability and talking to Barfi about it all. This season she planned to embroider the quilts with silver and gold thread, on violet blankets dyed with beets. Done with the patches she began to sort a pile of labels. The Stardust Sleepers. Over the years Asha had found the name childish, and had suggested to Gyan that they should change it. His look of complete hurt had ensured she never brought it up again.

Each blanket they made, once ready, was wrapped in fine muslin, tied up with drawstring and tagged with two brown paper labels, one that told the story and intention of The Stardust Sleepers, and another that spoke of the woman who had created the product. The women decided what they wanted the labels to say about them.

Sita is 21 and became a widow at 19. Today she lives with her mother back in Mangar Village, Haryana and has recently completed high school with the money she earns from The Stardust Sleepers.

Or:

Ramesha is 60 and became a widow at 50. She supports her five children with the money she makes as a senior designer and embroiderer at The Stardust Sleepers. Her daughter Sanya takes care of our inventory and her other daughter Reema is studying to be a psychologist.

Asha once worried that the labels came across as too simplistic, a reduction of the incredible women she worked with into two trite lines, but Gyan insisted that something was better than nothing. 'It gives a name to the maker. It rouses *some* compassion which is better than none. Ask them!' When she had questioned changing the system, their first employee Banno said, 'Nothing has made me prouder than this recognition,' and the system had stuck.

Though it would have been faster to have one woman learn a single task or step, the couple made each employee learn every part of the process and create her own pieces from start to finish. It had created a community system where each woman could help another at any point of the project. Gyan saw over the years how they took such immense pride in the end-product, running bangled hands over a piece while showing Asha, 'See my new design!' Though Gyan and Asha's main reason for insisting on everyone learning each step came from the fear that a girl might someday leave and be unemployable elsewhere due to a lack of knowledge, this was perhaps unnecessary concern on their part because in the long years that they had run the business, no one had ever left.

Now Asha sat surrounded by fabric, unable to really concentrate on the task at hand, going through the motions but not giving them their due. What would happen to all this when Gyan was gone, she thought. She gave up trying to get any work done, knowing when to succumb to her mind's madness. She fondled Barfi's ears and he saw this as an invitation and rolled onto his back for a belly rub which she gladly gave him while sinking into her thoughts of Gyan. Gyan who handled their finances. Who protected her from his family whom she had grown to love and please but whom she did not think she could bear to face without him. This man who respected her opinion on everything and therefore was the only one who could tell her when her ideas were 'utterly mad, not the good mad baby the bad kind'. She heard footsteps and Daya walked in, her hair a complete mess from the rickshaw ride. 'Tea?' she asked her daughter as Daya swung a backpack onto the dining table and kicked her sneakers off. Barfi stretched and trotted over to greet his favourite person. 'I'll make it,' Daya shouted over her shoulder on her way to the kitchen where Barfi followed her and Kamla was laying lasagna strips for a dinner that would only be nibbled at. The house as a whole had no appetite and Kamla was doing her best to tempt them to eat a little each night. They chatted about the changing weather for two minutes, Kamla making fun of the bird's nest on Daya's head. The water boiled and Daya warmed her hands over it before she brought a tea tray over to her mother.

'There's an art exhibition I thought you would like,' Asha began absentmindedly. 'It's called …' she reached for the newspaper and slipped her glasses on from where they dangled elegantly against her breastbone, '… Visions of Dissent.'

Daya dipped a biscuit in her tea. 'Sounds cheerful! When is it?'

'It's on till Sunday – we could go tomorrow?'

'Cool.'

They finished the tea in silence, Gyan's absence marking every moment sharply. When they had stopped the chemotherapy, Asha had said, 'No more,' and had shifted him without consulting anyone down to Vaikuntha. She slept there next to him and insisted it was for the better. The smells of food cooking in the kitchen made him sick, upstairs Barfi's hair was everywhere, and this way they could control who got to see him, what he heard in the house and what he didn't. This way all he heard were the birds, and all he saw were projected films, and glimpses of the garden. He watched the laburnum like grapes in a Greek painting, the clouds like cotton discarded by the wind, saying, 'The sky is the only thing in that awful colour of hospital uniforms that doesn't upset me.' After a few days of insisting it was hare-brained, Daya and Kamla agreed on the move being a good plan. He was now stationed at Vaikuntha permanently, surrounded by all the things he loved, and attached by wires to all the necessary machines. Daya could tell Asha was impatient to get back to him, and she too wanted to shower and go see her father. 'I'll be down soon?' It was only when she closed the door to her bedroom that she realized how much she had wanted to be alone, missing the irony of how it was the only way to stomach loneliness at all.

Asha remained where Daya left her, staring at the piles of cloth. She had a sudden flash of anger and remembered the white-hot rage of her youth. Something about seeing Daya and preparing to lose Gyan, something of the combination had brought on the memory of when they had first moved into this home, when she hadn't been much older than Daya was now. How angry every single thing made her. The dust collecting on shelves every few days even though she wiped and scrubbed until her shoulder blades ached. The man she loved so much turning out to be a 'total bloody imbecile'.

What do you mean you don't know how to make an egg?

Obviously I wanted the roses to keep their stems. Why on earth would I have asked for long-stemmed roses otherwise?

Do you not actually know how to fold?

Sarcasm dripped fom her voice and she would fly into fits of anger that simmered soon after but left her tired.

Gyan for his part giggled at her most of the time and snapped at her when he had had enough. They circled the house like tigers then, until they turned back into cubs.

She refused help and hated the world for it.

Then one day Kamla appeared at her door.

Kamla whose body was tight as a drum, so much so that even when she smiled her cheeks and eyes didn't crinkle like skin, but dented like leather and bounced back, shiny, dark and taut. She looked fourteen and Asha told her, 'I won't employ a child,' to which Kamla had responded by reaching confidently into her worn yellow kurta and taking out a battered ID card of some sort. It looked like something an NGO provided young girls in Kamla's position. She was twenty-two. 'Tell me your story,' Asha had said to her, handing her a bottle of water to drink.

When Gyan found them an hour later they were both sitting cross-legged on the floor of the living room sipping tea and discussing the miseries of life. Asha had cried her eyes out on hearing Kamla's story and Kamla had comforted her when Asha had complained of how hard it was being a new bride. They had swapped everything they knew about surviving mothers-in-law, though Asha with her camaraderial relationship with Gyan's mother couldn't quite identify with Kamla's story of starvation and abuse and witch doctors and whippings.

Kamla had known before they told her. She knew in her womb, in that place that was nothing but scar tissue and wound, that it was a girlchild who wouldn't call that space home. She hadn't planned on leaving, hadn't ever thought it was possible. She was kept in a room with a straw bed and a peg to which goats were once tied and fattened up and now she was kept with a rope that went from the iron ring around her leg straight to an unmoveable iron peg. She had wondered sometimes in the middle of the night how deep that peg went. She had tried to dig the dirt around it to get it out but her nails had worn down and so she had just eaten the earthworms she'd found instead. That peg went so deep into the ground she wondered if the house had been built around it the way a human is built around a spine.

The morning she left she wasn't planning to. They knew for certain by then that it was a girl because the witch doctor had come and he had touched her between her legs and said so. Her disappointed mother-in-law and her emasculated husband who was so ashamed of her body only offering him this burden had asked the doctor to cut it out and he had said, 'Why don't you try another thing …' And so, they had starved her in the hope that it would die inside her from hunger. And it did, of course it did but not before Kamla realized, quite by accident, feet lose weight too. On the morning Kamla wasn't planning to leave she stood to go relieve herself in a corner of that room made of mud and darkness and she found her feet came away free, suddenly so light, she toppled.

And then she flew. Because who knew? Feet lose weight too.

'Tell me what you want?' Asha asked.

'I want a contract,' Kamla had been taught to say.

'Sure, and what shall I put in it?'

'I want Sundays off.'

'Of course, for church,' Asha nodded and Kamla laughed.

'No, for the matinee. And put that every year for as long as I work here, you will give me two sets of clothes. One in the autumn and one in the spring and both should always be yellow.'

In the dark hours after Kamla escaped the house where she had become a goat, her husband a man who had given her less than a dozen nights of his life, and his brothers who had given her more bruises than he had given her nights, ran out into the fields and the farms to find her. When she knew she could no longer fly, she lay down exactly where she was, in a field of sunflowers. They towered above her and she asked their mighty stalks to save her, and she who had hated the colour yellow from when she was a little girl and did not believe in any god any longer made a deal with a sunflower field. 'Save me,' she said, 'and I'll forever wear your colour.'

She arrived in the city in tatters, a dead baby in her belly, a dead smile on her lips, dust in her hair and blood on her feet. Three years later, she knocked on Asha's door, NGO credentials inside her vest and sparkle in her eye.

'You see,' she said, 'flowers saved me.'

~

Asha drove them to the art exhibition the next day, after Gyan had slipped into his post waking sleep. She hadn't left the house in a long time, unless it had been to see doctors for him and now she felt both thrilled and terrified by the world, bright and loud as it was.

The exhibition was at a new gallery, slick with modernity, white walls and glass doors with tall marble vases full of blush-coloured carnations. Daya was ashamed to find herself momentarily surprised to see such a space in India. Outside, the street was filled with security guards checking bags and patting down visitors' pockets before they could enter. 'What's happening?' Daya asked. 'Our right to dissent is being protected. By private security,'Asha rolled her eyes. The problem it seemed was over a particular series of art, created by a Kashmiri student in Delhi. Tahirra Bhatt was all of twenty-three when she had won a college competition and got the chance to display her work at the gallery. No one, not the gallery owner, not the dean of the Art department of Tahirra's college, not Tahirra herself, could have predicted the uproar her pieces would cause.

The first one was visible as soon as they walked through the large sliding-glass doors. It was six feet by nine feet on the floor of the gallery and Daya would later recall thinking, 'If only she had made it a little smaller,' but she hadn't and it was unmissable. Her choice to place it on the floor – was that intentional too? Other projects that were submitted (but rejected) for the show that year included a series of lamps made from liquor bottles, a massive papier mache unicorn, and a bookshelf made from books. At the very deadliest there had been a collection of black-and-white images of two scantily clad Indian men caught in an illegal act – kissing. And then there was Tahirra.

Tahirra Bhatt had created on the floor of the gallery a map of northern India painted in the tricolor but with the tricolor turned on its head. The saffron and green had been swapped, and the student had explained how the inversion was in fact subversion. She had said that exact word – explain – like there was a way to reason this out. 'Let me explain!' loudly, confidently to the press, her sweet chin lifted. The green at the top left was in the shape of Pakistan, the saffron below became India. The conflicted land between the two had been painted not just white but to look like … snow? And bang in the middle of it was not the charkha or chakra – Daya had to look twice, but she knew what it was. It was a wheel on which viewers could play Russian roulette.

The second piece of art was at the far end of the room. In big, black, bold letters across a long wall it said:

PAKISTAN (I)

Extending from the bracketed 'I' were three arrows. One pointed to the word INDIAN and said 'Once upon a time all Pakistanis'. The second pointed to the word INDEPENDENT which had below it these words: 'The Pakistani is independent from Pakistan', and the third pointed to the word ME, below which Tahirra had written, 'Are you scared you are all the same?'

It wasn't so much the content of the show as it was the timing of it. After the towers had fallen, India had battled her own attack – the one Daya and Aaftab and Wasim never did discuss, the silence on the matter acknowledging that their friendship was greater than their countries' conflicts. That they would not be reduced to nationality. But ideas of nationality were exactly what Tahirra was questioning when she created her art so soon after the attack. Twelve days to Christmas, as New Yorkers had prepared for a sombre one, Gate 12 of the Indian Parliament was breached by a white car with five men, apparently (we never really will know) border-crossing attackers who would die that day. But there was also Constable Kamlesh Kumari. The first person that day, in the bitter, misty Lalabad cold to realize something wasn't quite right. She took eleven bullets in the gut, that place that had expanded twice for two children, that place where she knew something was amiss, that place that now expanded forever for terror.

There were five other policemen.

There were two security guards.

There was a gardener.

When you decide to be a gardener, you do not think you will die of a bullet. You think you will make roses bloom. That the only time you will see your own blood is when thorns dig in. You think you may at the very worst die of a snake bite.

Who was really the thorn in India's side?

Who was the snake from whose bite he died?

There were some who were whispering that Pakistan had ordered the attack so that their men (and the world's attentions) would be forced away from their post-September 11 posts along the Afghan border. Would be shuffled quickly to the edge of India instead and this would allow for a quick second of nuclear threat, a gap in time, a gap in that line, through which Osama could cross over, from Afghanistan to Pakistan unguarded. Because all eyes would be on I for India.

There were others whispering there was far too little evidence for the Indian government to be spending far too much in this frenzy of sending their own men to the edge of the country. Who were these dead men in the car anyway?

Daya knew the timing of Tahirra's art was no coincidence. Asha had always said to her, 'Things arrive when we need them. Stars align, everything is a sign.' She felt sweat pool in all the dips of her body. They walked into the next room which displayed Tahirra's final piece. A different wall and this one was covered in numbers. Hundreds of numbers all in red ink. There were so many crammed in that Asha and Daya had to walk up close to the wall to comprehend what the clusters of writing were. There was typically a date, beneath it an age, and beneath that, information in what looked like binary. At the top left and right corners of the wall were two jokes. The one on the left said:

What do you call a Pakistani prostitute in France?

La Whore.

The one on the right said:

How did the blind man know which girl was Indian?

It was the one who wasn't a virgin.

At the centre of this noise of numbers and riddles in red, in the middle of this wall in black ink she had written:

There are two places where Hindu and Muslim men meet.
One is on the battlefield.
The other?
Over women's bodies …
With flesh the treaty.

On a table in the room she had provided a guide to the binary. The complicated code under the dates, was a log of assaults on women (Hindu, Muslim, Christian and others) by groups of men that included both Hindu and Muslim men. 'Well, that's one way to make peace,' Asha said with a sneer on her face. 'Take the violence out together on the women. Age-old cure.' They sat in the room for some time on a red velvet sofa provided opposite the wall for viewers. A sound recording played interviews with some of the women who appeared as statistics before them. They absorbed, mother and daughter together, weeks of sadness now directed towards something new, something even bigger than what they were going through.

'Ma?' Daya said to the air before her.

'Hmm …' Asha was lost in the art.

'I have something to tell you.'

Sitting there surrounded by the fertile horror of what women are made into by religious war, Daya drew strength from numbers and became a statistic of loss. And Asha, who always had an opinion on everything, gave way to her daughter's voice that had taken so long to appear. She thought of her as a child, silent for years, and of her now, speaking in streams of words of that thing Asha knew so well – love – and she chose to let her flow and acted as nothing more than a vessel. Into her mother, that subcontinent she had once alone called home, Daya poured her sadness, her story. And Asha who knew there are no coincidences, collected them to carry as only a subcontinent can.

19

Cardiff 'Caerdydd' to Lalabad. Thirteen hours. Seven hundred and eighty minutes, every single one of which had been spent by Daya asleep and dreaming dreams of Aaftab. Aaftab with the sea behind him. Aaftab sharing with her the closest thing in her adult life she had known to a holiday. Aaftab in the few days she had known him to be entirely hers.

'Come down!' he had whispered to her on the phone at five in the morning. Wasim had finished work late and so asked if it was okay not to drop them to the station. Aaftab had said alright then, with feigned reluctance. Early the next morning he was waiting for her at the bottom of the fire escape with a large rucksack and a small brown paper bag. She wanted to throw her arms around him but had stood there staring into his face until he'd laughed into the dark and said, 'You want to make that train or what?'

On the train they sat next to each other very still for some time and as they shed the long kilometres to their destination they grew lighter and the sun appeared, flooding the sky slowly with rosiness. Daya seated by the window, fell asleep in its delicious warmth through the glass. When she woke she saw a shimmer in the distance and realized it was the sea.

He opened the brown bag and took out oranges which they shared, and then he had turned to her and finally, in that very public place, kissed her full on the mouth, citrussy and warm, dripping with abandon and untold things.

He had found the lighthouse through an advertisement in a travel magazine. He'd torn the page out and kept it in his breast pocket for days, unfolding it in private. Built in the 1700s, closed by the late 1800s, haunted, solitary, visited by birds and available to rent for short stays. They had never spoken of where they would go when they had agreed to just go. But this felt right. More than some hotel with clean corridors and room service, this felt like their love. It had secrets in its circles. *Where things came full circle.* Where they defied gravity. It is where they stopped time briefly from moving rapidly to that moment where inevitably they would have to part.

They reached the sleepy seaside town, breakfasted near the railway station, bought bread, wine, cheese and other groceries from a local seller and took a taxi to the lighthouse, the taxi driver presuming they simply wanted to see the landmark. 'It's not very remarkable at all really,' he said to them. 'I've seen much taller. But it's ours, isn't it?'

It was theirs.

For two nights it was theirs.

The village on the edge of which their piece of heaven stood was truly unremarkable, and they wouldn't have had it any other way. Its most colourful claim to any kind of fame was having been used as an airforce target training area during World War II. The training mainly entailed the royal fighter planes testing chaff – an anti-radar foil – over the village. The idea was that they would carry large bundles of aluminium foil strips, which would then be dropped within radar frequency of the German aircrafts. The foil would confound the German pilots whose radar screens would display a complete mess of targets, or a series of false echoes caused by the radar hitting metal and bouncing right off it. After the attack, the Germans – always ahead of the curve – knew exactly what the British had tried, but it had lost them Hamburg, and 40,000 civilians. Most importantly, it has never been reported whether what happened in Wales, to the unremarkable village on the edge of the sea, happened to Hamburg amidst British revelry. Whether, covered in aluminium strips of plan-foiling foil, it turned in the morning entirely and astonishingly to silver.

When they heard this fact, with the flippant air of young lovers, they called it their weekend in Tinsel Town.

A weekend in a lighthouse.

A weekend surrounded by sea on three sides.

A weekend where even the ghosts left them alone.

Where the gulls breakfasted just outside the curved glass with them and the night sky stars were neighbours and their love came into bloom and no one could look into their room and they knew they were playing the roles of those who had saved lives in the past, and this way, they tried to save their own.

They had found the key inside the old boathouse, as promised by the owner over the phone. The red metal door had swung open squeakily, the smell of two hundred years of sea embracing them. They closed the door behind them, fumbled for light switches – on the right at shoulder height, as promised. A single filament bulb came alive above them and lit up the stairwell inside which a long iron spiral of steps moved upwards towards everything. They bolted the door and joked about never leaving again, but their voices were shaky.

The tower was dim, and they made their way up cautiously. At the top the spiral staircase seemed to disappear into the ceiling, and Aaftab reached up to release the hatch. It was easy to find, as promised. He unlocked it and flipped it open, a square of light appeared and he climbed through it, lowering a hand for Daya.

Nothing prepared her for the brightness hitting her eyes after she emerged from the long stairwell. The room was so striking she cried out in exclamation, a child's sound escaping her mouth, words not enough to express the quantities of delight. Save a small bricked-off area for a bathroom, the room was one intact globular marvel. Daya lay down on the bed and sighed the sigh of a girl come home.

~

In Wales, Aaftab dialled his landline in Pakistan and imagined it ringing at his father's desk in his study in Islamabad. Imagined his father picking it up, clearing his throat the way he always did, just before answering, 'Assalamaleikum.'

'Waalekum salaam.'

'Aaftab?'

'*Ji*, Abbu.'

'*Khairiyat?*'

All okay? What he was really asking was *why are you calling me*?

'*Ji*, Abbu. I just … I just wanted to say I'm ready.'

'Ready?'

'For you and Ammi to choose my wife.'

~

Daya had been gone a week when Aaftab had found amongst the bills and bad menus that were slid under his front door each day, a crisp white envelope with a stamp that depicted a whale, apparently convalescing in bed. He didn't understand the picture, but that writing, he would have known with one eye closed, a hundred years from now. He sat down and took a deep breath. He put it away, unopened. He rolled a joint and reached for the envelope again. Lighting up, he slit it open and began.

My dearest Aaftab,

Do you know how the whale got his throat? Don't worry, I haven't lost my mind, it's a story by Kipling. It's part of his Just So Stories *written for his little girl who died. He called them that because she always wanted to hear them exactly as they were. 'Just so', so to speak. For all his daft racism, I just adore Kipling. Don't tell anyone I said so but I'll let a wee bit of racism slide for the sake of talking tigers, singing bears and Kim's adventures.*

I wasn't going to write to you. I promised myself not to and I know you prefer us speaking instead. But I asked at the airport post office if they had any special stamps and they brought out this one. So, hello.

In an hour I'll be on the aeroplane and by the time you get this, I'll be in India. I'm not sure how long I'll be gone but it may be for a very long time. Things may be very different by the time we see each other again. What I'm going to say next will strike you as really, really odd, all things considered, but I've given it a lot of thought and I'll only say this once, so take it before I change my mind. Aaftab, please for your sake (and mine), stop rejecting every girl your parents send you a photo of. You've tried to hide the fact from me, but I know they're asking. It's time. It won't be so bad, I promise. It will be better than giving yourself to girls you barely know, as I now also know you've been doing. Maybe our parents do have our best interests at heart, and who knows, with half that battle won you may even be lucky enough to find a lovely person. Not as lovely as me, and certainly not as lovely as you, but lovely enough. And isn't enough … enough?

As for us. We should have met as perfect strangers. We should have met at an airport. Should have bumped into each other in a busy street in Kathmandu or shared a table at a crowded coffeeshop in Cairo. A berth on a train in Mexico. A cathedral in some obscure European city. We should have met anywhere but here. Sometime in the future maybe we will have a day where we can talk, walk streets, hold hands, eat, laugh, maybe even kiss … and then go back peacefully to whatever it is that isn't each other.

Forgive the outpouring and me saying all these things that I couldn't in person. It's raining right now and Wasim once told me about a flower that turns transparent in the rain. Maybe it learnt from humans? Maybe we learnt from it … the Skeleton Flower. So here I am, stripped to the bone in the rain. Here's my transparency:

I no longer want to feel the guilt of holding you away from your fate, and I do not want to feel the sadness, of holding myself away from mine. Understand, it is my immense love and not a lack of it, that says the next words …

Goodbye, Aaftab.

The truth is, we are fighting what we refuse to see, that a future together is not simply unlikely. It is, as you once said, impossible.

Yours,

Daya

'But there's still so much to talk about,' he wanted to say to her, the way he would say often before he left her house. Wanted to hear the comforting way she would always say, 'Some other time?'

Some other lifetime.

He had folded the paper and brought it to his nose, searching for her scent, before putting it away. Soon after, he had taken her advice.

~

The lighthouse looked down onto a sparse coastline. They were sitting on the iron balcony that ran like a collar around the building's neck, legs dangling, nothing but an eighteen-metre drop to the sand and pebble beach below and the wind whipping around them at sunset.

'It's so stunning,' Daya said wistfully.

'It is. But I find beaches without palm trees strange. Maybe because that's how they always appear in the American movies.' He waved his arms in the air exaggeratedly and said, 'Californiaaaaa, bro!' She laughed.

'Do you actually even like palms?' she asked.

'Yes, but I like pines more. I love the way they smell. Did you know there are over a hundred varieties of pine?'

'No, I didn't, but if someone else had told me that I would say: I bet Aaftab and Wasim know all hundred and then some.'

'Very funny. Which do you like?'

'I don't know. British trees sound so proper. Like old men in parliament.' She made a mock solemn face and said in her poshest British accent, 'Hello, Mr Adler! Oh hello there, Birch. All well? I saw Oak and Willow in the conference room with Mr Maple earlier!'

Tumbling laughter. Then breathlessly Aaftab said, 'I like gulmohars.'

'Gulmohars?' she inquired, scrunching up her forehead, unable to recall.

'The orange ones!'

She nodded in recognition. 'They flower for such a short time, right? My mother once dyed a whole batch of blankets with them.'

'No you're thinking of Flame of the Forest, those are different. Meatier. In Islamabad gulmohars refuse to last. I tried growing them but the moment the temperature drops, the plants wilt. It's the only reason my Ammi agrees to visit Karachi – to see them.'

Daya smiled, moved by his sudden sharing. He spoke so rarely of his parents. 'I like neem,' she said softly. 'When I had chicken pox as a child they made a neem paste and put it on my back.'

'Well, there are no scars there,' he smiled. She blushed, thinking of how earlier they had entered the room and immediately made love, with her bent over at the window in ecstasy, the entire sea in view, waves crashing.

'I like neem too,' he said, bringing her back. 'I like how it looks. You know, when you lie under a neem tree you can see the leaves cluster and form circles.'

'My absolute favourite are banyans though,' she said and laid her head on his shoulder, viewing the horizon as a vertical line.

When he spoke he said *drakht*. When she did, she said *pedh*. Together, they said tree.

The British had left and made them each 'the other', and what had stayed was the British language, making them both the same.

'Banyan drakht,' she said softly, imitating him, tasting the Urdu.

'Palm pedh,' he repeated after her in Hindi.

Like this they tried to cross a border.

As for the one language that bound them. Unhappy at it belonging to the rest of the world as well, they simply undid it. And like this there arose a fourth language like a bridge, separate from all the languages they already spoke.

'Do you think,' Aaftab said thoughtfully, trying to light a joint in the wind which had risen as the sun set, 'that we butcher the English language?'

'Who, us?'

'No, not *us* us. Us as in desis. Indians, Pakistanis. The rest of us.'

'Does anyone own a language?' she asked.

'But we say things wrong. Take Wasim, for instance. Yesterday when he couldn't make it to the station he said to me, "Sorry but I'm spreading myself on thin ice." What does that even mean?'

'You're asking me what Wasim meant? You know Wasim speaks a language that is entirely his own. You're the one who told me to listen for the layers. In fact you're the only one who vaguely understands it!'

'And you,' he smiled. 'It's funny, isn't it?' Aaftab started again. 'No one feels touched to hear you speak English. No matter how great an effort someone's making. You feel touched to hear someone speak Swahili or Spanish or just a few words in Hindi.'

'Or Malayalam,' Daya added.

'What's Malayalam?'

'A language in India.'

'Ah. Or Burushaski.'

'Buru-what?'

'Pakistani language,' he grinned then turned serious. 'You get what I'm saying though? There's an expectation that people should just speak English.'

'But they conquered the world, Aaftab.'

'So what? There are a billion Indians in the world but we desis get excited when someone says "chai".'

'It's their entitlement, you're saying?'

'Yes. And then to expect us to speak it exactly as they do,' he shook his head, amazed once again at the realization.

Daya remembered an evening in Lalabad not long before she had left. She had been out with friends. A party at someone's house. Not so many people, good conversation, cheap wine that she was only just learning how to drink, crackers and cheese melting in the humid evening warmth. Eventually it had rained and when it stopped they'd moved to the roof of the house. Post cloudburst the sky was brazenly beautiful with glittering freckles on indigo skin. They sat around smoking, ashing into empty beer bottles, flicking bottle caps to see who could hit a mark on the wall. A boy with an eyebrow piercing began to relate a story about how he had heard just the other day someone say yachett.

'No way!' someone else chimed in.

'Yes. He said, "Can you believe he owns a yachett?"'

'So what did you say?'

'I said, "Do you mean yacht?"' What else could I have said?'

'And how did he react? Was he embarrassed?'

'No. He laughed and said, "Oh whatever, potato-potahto."'

After much giggling from the group a slender girl in a sari spoke up. 'I like that Indians speak English that way though.'

'What do you mean?' Daya asked, curious.

'You know, I like that Indians have created their own English. Our pronunciation, our phraseology ... what's wrong with it? It's fusion, that's all.'

'Confusion is what it is,' the pierced boy with the yacht story mumbled.

'But it's not,' she continued. 'It's definite. This is our version now. So we say "cut the phone" and "close the light" but that's literal translation, isn't it? And why shouldn't we make it ours?'

Why not indeed.

They left behind their language, but surely they must remember that old British proverb. The one Aaftab and his friends used for cigarettes in school desks.

What was it again?

Finders keepers, losers weepers.

If anything, the British knew this: what finders do is make something theirs.

~

Aaftab sat at his desk in his office. 'Mahogany wood,' the partner had said, knocking on it twice the day Aaftab had joined. He looked around now. It was a tastefully done space, two desks at angles, imitation antique desk lamps, a potted areca palm flourishing in the corner next to an armchair in powder blue. He was grateful for this office. This office that

Daya had never been to and now never would. He lifted from his desk the tiny globe that sat there always, a paper weight cleverly made. It was a sphere, like the earth, and flatter on two sides than a perfectly round ball would be, but one could not tell where. To the human eye it simply appeared round. And yet it sat and did not roll when placed on a desk.

He turned the globe slowly in his hands the way Allah did the earth. He traced the tiny countries there with his fingers. What was Pakistan? What was *a country*, he thought. Sixty years ago, could he have married Daya because that line had not been drawn by an Englishman across a map? Before one country became two and later three?

One day, some years after Pakistan had become an independent nation, someone in a crowd had said to a young Jamal al-Khayal who was expounding the dangers of nationalism to those who would listen: 'Forgive me, al-Khayali, but maybe it was easier to be open-minded before. At that time, this country didn't exist so we didn't have to defend it.'

'Didn't exist? According to whom?' he had asked.

'Forgive me, but God had not yet made Pakistan,' the boy said.

'My friend,' al-Khayal smiled, 'God has still not made Pakistan, and countries do not really exist. Now tell me, what do you really think needs defending?'

Aaftab located Pakistan on the globe and prepared to meet a girl he was meant to love, because she came from this country they were both so lucky to call theirs.

~

They had spent every single moment of those two days in the lighthouse touching. He slept with his arms wrapped around her, his mouth resting gently on her neck, his thigh thrown across her hips. If she tried to move, all his body parts shifted with her like they were two stars in the same constellation. A perfect brown jigsaw. He had held her hand while she brushed her teeth. Had rested his feet upon hers while eating. Encircled her waist with his hands while they cooked, amusing her with the sudden surge in his usually more reserved affections. 'You're acting like you may not say goodbye at the end of this weekend. I ask for a summer, you offer me two days, and now I feel you may give me a lifetime yet.' She had laughed while saying it and yet he had seen in her eyes that dangerous thing – hope. He had asked himself later, staring into the mirror in the bathroom, 'What are you doing?' And the reflection had replied, 'But I love her.'

~

In Lalabad with nothing but sadness filling the curves of her childhood home, like a snow globe full of tears, she found her mind filled with the memories of those days that she had tried so hard not to indulge in afterwards. She paced her room in circles as she heard Kamla chopping onions ferociously at the dining table outside.

~

Aaftab's knee kept touching Enayat taaya's uncomfortably and though he wanted to think about the task ahead of him (literally, as she was seated opposite him), he couldn't help but think of the feeling of his uncle's knee and its nervous bouncing, grinding against his as they sat side by side.

Noor looked up. She sat by her mother in a mint green shawl, a look of worry on her face. Their eyes met briefly before they both looked away. They had been allowed a dinner alone together in a restaurant with her parents at a different table. He had asked his mother to request Noor's mother to allow for this and Aaftab with his soft eyes and law degree was granted it. He had come to pick them all up with Enayat in tow, a stamp of authenticity, and the family had insisted the pair have a drink before dinner. Orange squash was passed around after which he seated her in the back of the car, holding an umbrella over her to protect her from cold late January downpour. Both families piled in, his uncle next to him in front, her parents flanking her like bodyguards at the back. So this was a date, he thought.

At the restaurant which Noor had chosen but Aaftab liked, they got a corner table – suitably candlelit and bestowed with rose stems. Noor's parents, true to their word, made themselves scarce. Seated with his uncle at a second table behind a pillar, they were out of earshot which gave Aaftab some relief as he realized they probably couldn't hear him either. He looked up and again saw her staring at him like a seal above the menu. They ordered and once through with the niceties, Aaftab turned to her more decisively.

'So tell me, how many brothers and sisters?' she asked, her voice nervous.

'Four.'

'You're the eldest?

'Yes.'

'And what does your name mean?'

'Aaftab?' he was surprised at how rapidly she was running through her list of questions, and then he winced, the memory hitting him in the stomach. Daya had asked him the same things, one evening soon after they had met, outside the library, in simpler times.

'Aaftab? The sun,' he repeated now.

'And what does yours mean?'

'Daya? Mercy.'

~

It was in the lighthouse that Daya had said, 'Every time we make love, we're straying across a border.' And he had replied, 'No, Daya. We're rejoining lands.'

On that beach where the horizon was an inky line that divided the stars from their reflections, they listened sadly to the sound of the millionth wave of the night as it crashed against the shore and tried hard to stay, but was pulled back yet again, against its wanting will.

~

Somewhere in the corner of a dimly lit restaurant with red velvet chairs and brass candlesticks, Aaftab was inching his way closer across a table. He had begun the evening slouched back in his chair, had felt himself straightening to hear her better, and was now leaning towards her, watching her mouth form words. 'Pakistan is boring,' she was saying. 'I'm so happy we moved here.'

'I find Pakistan pretty interesting, but I'm happy you moved here too,' he said, surprising himself.

She giggled and inadvertently leaned forward as well, her knee hitting his gently under the table. Though it jolted them both on the inside, she did not move it. What further caught him off guard was how she now took matters deftly into her hands.

'So … why do you want an arranged marriage?'

'I trust what my parents want for me.'

'Rubbish!' she said lightly. 'A boy living in the UK suddenly calls home eager to get married? I don't believe it. Don't tell me you haven't had girlfriends?'

'I have.'

'Then? Why didn't you marry one of them?'

'It wouldn't have worked.'

It was the truth, he told himself.

~

Daya couldn't bear it. She'd barely eaten dinner and was back to pacing her room, picking up and putting down objects and drowning beneath the memory of all the promises he had made in a building whose only reason for being was water, all the truths he had given her in a seashell spilling over with love disallowed by a line in the sand, a line between two lands. She checked the time and was surprised to find it was past 2 a.m. She calculated. He'd be home from work by now. So Daya broke her own rules. She picked up the phone, and dialled Aaftab. Lalabad to Old Blighty.

'Yes, hello?' he answered politely, expecting anybody.

'Aaftab, it's me.'

'Haan bhai, what's up? All good?'

Whenever he called her 'bhai' she knew he was with

people. It was their code – officially unestablished, intrinsically understood.

'Shall I call back later?' she asked.

He continued in his jovial public voice, 'Tell you what, let me call you.'

He put the phone down and looked up again.

'So where were we?'

'Right here,' Noor replied with a smile.

Later he watched as she played with her empty teacup, a crescent stain along its edge from her mouth making it somehow so intimate. They had stayed out well past what was agreed on, and Aaftab knew that just behind a pillar there sat an elderly couple with his uncle, yawning. He handed Noor her shawl and they stood, crossing the restaurant back towards chaperoned reality. When they were directly behind the pillar, perfectly hidden, she swiftly placed a hand on his arm, a light touch for a split second and said, so softly he would later be able to question if she had said it at all, 'Thank you, I had such a nice time.' Their eyes met and before he could respond, she was walking towards her parents, hands by her sides, dutiful smile in place. So this is what it was like with someone who understood the rules of his world.

~

Just before the darkest part of night began to give way to dawn and they lay as one body instead of two, unable to sleep out of sadness that the weekend was so close to ending, he had said, 'Tell me, all those things we never have the time to talk about.' Outside it was high tide, waves gathered around the base of the lighthouse. The only way to leave now was to sink or swim, so she dove in. She told him about her love for him and how she could no longer fight it. How she had never felt these things. How her entire life was a regret till this point because she had not known him, and a waste henceforth because she would not have him.

And in turn he told her.

'I have loved you, Daya. I have loved you so much and I have longed for you. I have wanted to reach across tables and rooms, across the world, believe me, across all its shitty rules about religion and countries and across old men's ideas of wrong and right, all the things keeping us apart and I have wanted to take you in my arms and keep you there.'

~

Aaftab parked Enayat taaya's car outside his house, said his 'Khuda hafiz, see you at the mosque' and decided to walk back home through Roath Park. It was past midnight but he needed the air. It was too late to call Daya back in India now, he thought for a moment, calculating the time difference. The grass was wet from rain and he made his way towards the benches, sitting down despite the damp at his favourite one, the one he'd been sitting on the day he'd seen Daya. He smiled now thinking of that day, then allowed himself the thought of Daya, briefly, before putting it painfully away. He smoked half a joint he'd been saving, then patting the bench softly, began walking home.

The stars were strung above his head and a new future began to emerge before his eyes. With each step he felt the wild clear away and a path however slim and wedged in by weeds opening up before him. He saw that maybe this was the easier path.

'And what about yours?'

'My name?'

'Yes.'

'Noor?'

'Yes?'

'It means "the light".'

When his father had emailed him her photo after their phone conversation, Aaftab had replied, not without some irritation at his own affected tone, 'Mashallah, she looks like she will make a wonderful wife. I am blessed.' And his father had responded, not without some sarcasm and even a dash of cruelty Aaftab was certain, 'What more could a young Muslim man ask for?'

Really, what more?

For Mercy.

20

Aaftab finished his walk at a slow pace. He turned into his lane and noticed the mosque, white as bone, so fragile in the moonlight, as if it was made of paper. He saw the grey owl, Lucida's mate, fly by with a screech and he noticed that the door to their house was open and the lights were on. Something about the bird's low-flying yowl had felt like a warning. He started to jog. 'Wasim!' he called out. 'Was? Was!' Louder now. He entered at such a pace it wasn't until he stopped that he noticed he was standing amidst the debris of his life.

Every single carpet had been slashed along its length.

The wallpaper had been sliced loose, giving it a series of gaping mouths that seemed to laugh hideously.

On the wall in the living room in red paint still wet like a wound, the words:

YOU WILL LEARN

He raced from room to room shouting Wasim's name, his voice hysterical, unrecognizable. Later he would realize how stupid this had been. How the person or people who had broken in may still have been there. In his bedroom his duvet had been slashed and feathers from it still floated around the room like ghosts. How close he had been – not minutes even, maybe mere seconds – to being in the same space as whoever had done this. He would understand this in retrospect. He called Wasim. He called the police. He began to clean.

When Wasim arrived he found Aaftab on all fours in the kitchen, feathers clinging inexplicably to the knees of his trousers. He had not taken his jacket off and there was something that repulsed Wasim about this. This man who notwithstanding Aaftab's drinking days, he had only seen upright, so dignified, so proud of the expensive clothes he had worked so hard to buy, reduced by violence to this. Wasim joined him wordlessly, taking from Aaftab's hands the bag he was holding and beginning to fill it with shards of glass he had been picking meticulously off the floor. As he stood to deposit them outside where already Aaftab had made a small pile of things that could never be used again, Wasim noticed something. The door to the small cupboard in the corner of the kitchen that troubled him so much, was open. He walked towards it and hesitatingly swung it all the way open. It was empty.

'Aaftab,' he called out and pointed.

A chill went through the room like spirits passing.

'They're gone,' Aaftab said finally.

He walked over and ran a finger through the dust that had collected in neat shapes around bottles that had stood still there a very long time. Two squares for two whiskies.

'Well, at least we know who did it,' Wasim said, voice dripping disgust, his usually graceful mouth twisted. 'Fucking yobs.' Wasim didn't ever curse and the words sounded like a different language, coming from him. 'I heard they have some of the cops tied in,' Aaftab replied. 'And that they try and operate in areas where they know the cops will cooperate.'

'I wouldn't be surprised. Their dads all probably drink together at the pub on weekends. I mean … where are the cops?' Wasim asked, more of the room than of Aaftab. As if on cue, two men in uniform walked through the front door, left open after all these years because somehow that felt safer now than being enclosed in a space thick with aggression. Aaftab and Wasim told them what they knew. Cleanse Britain. Local lads. Ethnic tension. Nothing stolen but the booze. A lot of damage to property. 'They were probably drunk when they broke in,' Wasim said.

'Can you boys stay somewhere else tonight?'

'Not really.'

'Well, can you sleep in the room with less damage?'

'Anyone who has anything against you, Mr Aaftab?'

'Not that I know of.'

'Any reason why Mr Wasim's room would have less damage?'

'It has less stuff?'

The first thing Wasim had done was check if his mother's bottle full of earth was still in its place in his cupboard. It was. In fact, the only thing that had been damaged in Wasim's room were the curtains and the book on his bedside. It looked like it had been stabbed with a knife, leaving a deep gash. Aaftab touched it that night like it was a wound and his fingers gauze. They both lay in Wasim's bed, every sound a dagger, unable to sleep. They waited for morning, not talking about the house, chatting instead about the date with Noor, Wasim overjoyed by Aaftab's report. And then, hell broke before dawn had a chance. Just before light Aaftab's phone rang and when he saw it was Pakistan calling he picked up, hoping despite the bad news of the night to give his parents the good news they had always sought from him. *Qubool hai* – I accept. He opened his mouth to speak the words and then he heard his mother scream – not just over the phone line but over the clouds and seas and deserts and mountains that separated Britain from Pakistan. She was saying just one thing, over and over again in Urdu in a screechy, broken wail.

'You son of a bitch.'

He had never heard her swear before and instead of asking what was wrong he said, 'Why are you speaking this way?'

She began to howl in response.

'What have I done now? I was just going to tell you how well the meeting went. I'm happy, I'll marry her. You should be happy too.'

'Oh my son-of-a-bitch,' she moaned. 'I did not raise you to have girlfriends. To have affairs. What good Muslim woman do you think will want you now you son-of-a-whore?'

'What are you going on about? Ammi please ... this language,' he said helplessly, embarrassed by the curses.

'You have far more to be ashamed of than my language, Aaftab. But I will tell you this. You are no longer my son and your mother must have been some devil's whore. So I will call you and her whatever I want.'

He tried asking her, reasoning, but finally put the phone down and thought of calling Noor to check how much of their conversation about their pasts she had relayed to her mother. How much had then been relayed back to Pakistan?

His life these days felt like one disaster stacked onto the last. Daya's leaving, Daya's letter, his home, now this. Frustrated, he put his familial woes into a box and decided to follow up with the police instead.

~

The officer-in-charge was an elderly Welshman who looked almost too kindly to be a figure of authority.

'It's early to say this, but it seems there are no fingerprints anywhere but yours. Well, it's either yours or Wasim's. No one else's.'

'I see.'

'Do you though? Look mate, you know fingerprinting is a real hit or miss, sort of. But when I'm *only* seeing the both of yours amongst the fresher ones ... You understand, we cannot rule out anybody.'

'We cleaned up right after it happened.'

'Well, you shouldn't have, you know better than most – it's a crime scene.'

'I was in shock, as you can presumably understand.'

'I know you're wound up, Mr Aaftab, but that tone won't get us any answers.'

The policeman asked for Wasim to visit the station and as Aaftab waited outside, asked him questions.

Why was his room intact? Where was he really that night after Aaftab left for dinner and before he showed up at the kebab shop? Did they have any differences? Why was the liquor gone?

Afterwards Aaftab talked to Wasim for a minute and going into the station, said, 'He hasn't done it. With all due respect, that's daft, it's his house too.'

'There's no jealousy? That you earn more, for example?'

'None.'

'Are you certain?'

'Let me put it this way. Even if I weren't certain, even if you found your suspicion to be a hundred per cent true. Even if you could prove it to me – I would not press charges.'

'Well, that settles it then. Any idea who it might be? We can't seem to find any leads on the boys you mention. The CB blokes. In fact, we're pretty sure it wasn't them because as you may have heard they were all in London.'

'At the protest? Those bloody louts?'

'If you can call it that. Lot of hype. Seems like only eighty people showed up.'

'It's *only* eighty to you, sir, but imagine me being in a room with those eighty bigoted people.'

The old policeman regarded him for a moment and replied, 'Just so you know, there was a counter protest on the opposite side of the street. Anti-racism, anti-Islamophobia, anti-war. There were more than 200 people in that one. You're safe, mate. Now tell me, anyone else you think it could've been?' Aaftab shook his head. 'It would just take one or two of the Cleanse Britain lads,' he said, 'and they'd have the perfect alibi too.' But he knew it was unlikely for the police to go about questioning every boy who had ever attended a meeting of this close to imaginary, unregistered organization that worked in violence from the shadows. Besides, something else wasn't adding up.

~

Obviously it hadn't been the white boys. How simple that might have been.

They hate us because we are Muslim.

So simple. Lacking all the complexity of:

They hate us because we are bad Muslims.

They had entered the house at 9 p.m. after they were certain both boys had left. They had begun to search for what they'd needed and sprinkled hate as an additional ingredient, an afterthought, right at the end, a few minutes before they left. The glasses did not require breaking. The pillows did not need to be ripped open like that. And yet there was pleasure in knowing these things would cut and choke the inhabitants later. They had exited stealthily through the open window in Wasim's room when the owl outside had suddenly screeched. 'Allah hu akbar,' the eldest had muttered, and in a series of swift swoops they were gone. They waited in the side street until they heard Aaftab begin to scream and then under the cloak of his panic they left, taking with them what they needed.

Wasim may have noticed the missing bottles in the kitchen but he could not point out what he had never seen. What he had never known to be there. He could not say, 'Aaftab, check for the yellow tin box in the last drawer on the left side of your desk. Check to see if all those letters from Daya are there. Are they missing? Check to see if you find train ticket stubs to a town with a lighthouse, one with Daya's name and one with yours. Check if your hash from Morocco, sold from one bad Muslim to another, isn't gone. If the photograph you keep of Daya is still there. The one of her in the nude by your window, from the day I had gone to the doctor.'

Aaftab didn't even like photographs. He didn't like how he looked in them but he wondered if it was simply something ingrained in him in his youth. That a photo is a replica of Allah's masterwork, and therefore haraam. Maybe hearing that so many times as a child had made him weary of them. He hated the flash on cameras and the blinded few moments after that. He disliked being told to smile. The thing that most troubled him about photographs was the feeling over the years that those were his only memories. Other days faded away and he was left always with one bright memory of a time period – the one in the photograph. 'Try to remember what we did in those days,' he would ask a friend. They would inevitably come to a day that had been photographed.

Initially he had liked that Daya and he had no photographs together. He was the one who had insisted on no evidence. No paper trail. Initially, not even his cigarette stubs were left longer in her house than he could help. But then she had begun to write letters and who can resist the romance of letters? Not Aaftab, certainly. And then, that one time, he had taken a photograph of her. Wasim had had a doctor's appointment and they had just made heartbreaking love. She had stood up to stretch and wandered over to the window. He wanted to remember, to hold on. He had taken it on his phone and was looking at it late one night at work when he felt the urge to truly possess it. He had attached his phone to a computer in the office by a cord and had transferred the image then pressed print. It was 2 a.m. and there was no one else there. In the otherwise silent printing room he listened to what ink sounded like when forming Daya's curves on paper, imagining the breaks in sound to be the parts of her the light was drawn to. When he lifted it, the page was still wet, Daya in the nude, glistening. He blew on the sheet and she shivered. He placed her by his computer and worked till 4 a.m. At dawn he had folded her up to make her pocket-sized and took her home. And now he had lost her.

His mother hadn't mentioned specifics.

The last thing she had asked before she hung up was whether he'd been sleeping with a girl.

She had said the entire sentence in Urdu, but the word 'affair' in English.

As if her world did not allow for such things.

He had denied it then put the phone down, irritated with Noor.

He had gone to meet with the police.

Wasim was interrogated and then finally, exhausted, was let go. They went home and drank tea from plastic mugs the neighbour had lent them.

And finally at sundown, Aaftab rose to roll a joint.

And that is when the drawer had come away lightly, no longer heavy with the weight of his various sins. His blood had gone so cold, he was convinced that if you could look within him in that moment and isolate the complex framework of his veins, it would present itself as one human-shaped snowflake of red crystals, webbed and icy. And the answers clicked into place.

For some reason in the hours that followed he kept opening the drawer from time to time, convinced it would be there. His precious yellow tin box with the old tobacco company's name, bought from a speck of a shop selling Indian antiques in Lahore. 'Vazir Sultan Tobacco Company, Hyderabad, Est. 1927,' it had read. The letters all raised like braille from a time before tobacco was taxed. He opened the drawer, touched the base, the wood grainy beneath his fingers. No box, no papers, no photo, no hashish, no letters. And it troubled him not just because they were gone but because he imagined those boys so bereft of soul opening up that worn paper and seeing there Daya in all her sweetness. They would not be able to see past her teardrop breasts to her massive heart. Or below the swoop of her waist the treasures beneath, or see how, in stillness when captured, the dancer became the dance. Daya of steely gaze and freckled nose and dusky shoulders and mangled feet. Daya who said things suddenly into the silence. Things that were true and hard to say. Imagine a mouth that had never told a lie. She told him once, 'If someone asks about us, I'm not sure I can deny it!' But she had learnt to. She'd learnt the wicked art of silence and how it was the perfect twilight between innocence and guilt. Between responsibility and freedom. She had learnt to avoid a question and to walk home in the dark. To make love in the afternoon silent as salamanders. To hold hands in parks and let go the moment someone came and slip notes like a spy and undress like a bullet. She learnt the world anew as full of secrets and enemies and whispers and rules and she learnt why it was called a *bodyguard of lies*. She learnt how to dance around those lies until she trusted no one, least of all herself, and he loathed now that he had done this to her. That he had not been able to keep her safe. It hurt him that he could not eventually protect her, and he was so grateful that she was not there. Not near him to smell his shame. Far from his godless, forsaken self that did not deserve her.

Despite their judgement he knew she had not broken any laws. She was safe, somewhere, even while her words were swallowed and mocked by those who would never, could never understand the poetry of a woman in love. Some part of her was safe, even if it was not the part she had given him for safekeeping.

He would never see her letters again, he thought, and that was a wound he did not know how to heal from.

~

Daya had waited by the phone until dawn but Aaftab had not called back as promised. When she realized he wasn't going to, she got up and walked downstairs to Vaikuntha where she lay down in one corner of the giant mattress, as she sometimes used to as a child. The house was keeping odd hours and no one asked why she was awake at 5 a.m. It was understood that hearts did not break or wake exactly when one expected them to. She tried to remind herself that Aaftab was doing this for both of them. That he did this as much for her, as for himself. That it was she who had broken the rule by calling. It was late the next day when Daya saw a message from Wasim.

Wasim had been grateful he'd had work all afternoon and into the night. The house with its walls gaping open like a dead fish's sad mouth was depressing, and the police were still coming and going. He had been questioned for most of the morning and had gone to the kebab shop later, tired. Before he had begun work he had suddenly, intensely, missed Daya. The whole damn thing would have been easier if she were around, he thought. On a whim he'd messaged her, trying hard to fit everything into one text, not wanting to pay for two international messages, annoyed at the abbreviated versions of words. They were so ugly, he thought, just before he pressed send. Then he'd washed his hands and prepared to worship with his knives, in a way that wasn't prayer but brought him peace nonetheless.

She read it now, imagined him trying to keep it short, to the point.

Hi Daya. House had breakin but we are ok dont worry. Can u believe cops thot I did it? Missin u a lot. Sum gud news. Aaftab met a girl thru parents. I think its a yes! Chal jigar, take care.

Jigar.

That word they used upon her like a blessing.

Urdu for liver.

Vital organ.

The only organ in the human body that when injured, cut off or scarred, knows how to regenerate.

Daya pressed delete.

~

Aaftab understood finally what had happened. Or thought he did. Finally he heard the echo of the eldest one whispering 'Allah hu akbar' bounce off the walls and tell him the truth.

It wasn't the white boys. He knew who it was. 'You will learn,' the message was clear.

It had taken weeks to turn the mosque. Weeks. Not months or years as Wasim had predicted but weeks, as Aaftab had always known. By the time the problems really began, Aaftab was saying they should be praying facing the west with their asses to the east, so pitiful was their Islam.

Within weeks of the new imam coming, there were boys standing around like vigilantes outside the mosque post prayer time, taking note of who was attending, while taking up great spaces on the street with their father's cars, some that doubled up as taxis at night. Aggression swelled their chests and they smoked around the corner from the adults, whole cigarettes roughly sucked down in minutes while talking about a better Britain. Within weeks Wasim noticed there were fewer women coming in to the back room through the side door. They simply stayed home after the new imam gave an impassioned lecture on the correct place of the Muslim woman. What's worse, he could see how it emboldened some of the men. How they looked inflated, wild-eyed after it.

What they didn't know was that the women had begun to meet in secret at a house not far from the mosque. They met to speak prayers together but one day one of them reached behind her neck to untie her headscarf and one by one they all did. A Bangladeshi girl let her hair down her back and an Egyptian woman ran her fingers across her closely cropped scalp. 'Those are beautiful!' one girl called across the room, gesturing to the aquamarines in a Pakistani girl's ears. And like this, Islam brought them together. They would meet to pray and they would stay to heal. One girl's bruises opening another girl's heart. One girl's undone braids bringing back another's childhood.

They began a post-prayer cooking club where for many weeks books were exchanged more frequently each Friday than recipes. The charity book rack outside the mosque had been emptied of free books and in their place, people now put their shoes. The day Aaftab saw that, something cracked inside him and he felt within himself a need and a responsibility to attend prayers again at the mosque more than he had even after the night of the bloodstain. It was a persistent feeling, an urgent need to be a part of the voices – or the only voice –

that prevented such things. Books disappearing alongside their women. The urgency had grown until he had asked at work if they would give him Friday afternoons off for his prayers. They had said yes without hesitation. A keenness in these dark times to prove they were not part of the dark side. That they tried to support all the ways people claimed to come closer to the light.

And he had been going. Even with all his accumulated sins he went. Now he thought that had been a mistake. He had openly challenged the imam, he questioned constantly what was going on at the mosque, he chatted with people at the end, collecting and, dare he admit it, creating opinions. It had all been stupid of him, he saw now. Someone like him, so easily labelled a bad Muslim, had no place telling the ones who believed they were truly good which version of Islam was correct. And now they knew about his sipping whisky and smoking charas. They knew about his Daya. And Allah was having the last laugh because it was no longer just the boys at the mosque who knew. His parents knew too. Half the mosque probably knew. All his father's friends. His uncle. His siblings back in Pakistan. But who didn't know what was going on? Two people.

Daya. Daya did not know, perhaps would never know. Daya who had a world that did not intersect with his apart from at one point. Wasim.

And Wasim who did not know. Whom Aaftab did not know how to tell. Because telling Wasim how he knew who was to blame meant telling Wasim everything, all the things a little yellow tin box finally could not contain.

Two people who made up his entire world. And who amongst mortals is ready to forego a world?

21

Wasim finished at the kebab shop and checked his phone. Daya hadn't replied. He took off his apron and rolling his shoulders to release the tension of a busy Saturday night, began walking home, his breath creating small puffs in the cold air. He wanted to go back to yesterday evening when he had left the house looking the way it had been. Peaceful. His phone rang and he took it out of his pocket hoping it was Daya, but it wasn't.

He always had the same conversation with his mother. Without ever sharing the details of his life, he always reassured her he was doing fine, then she asked if he liked being a doctor. He said he wasn't a doctor yet. She made a joke about him fixing her aching legs when he became one. He still hadn't found the courage to tell her that there was no degree in medicine waiting to attach itself to his name. But there was a P.E. degree. Which in Pakistan he knew meant nothing more than 'gym instructor' and that had no glamour attached to it in her mind. That's what he had thought as well, when he first started the course. Over time, he had developed a deep respect for the work. He wanted to tell his mother that had he done his P.E. course properly, he probably could have fixed her legs but he had not yet dreamt up how to explain to his parents at the end of his time here, that not only was he not going to be a doctor, he wanted to be a chef. That he was learning from TV shows and they were such good shows. From discarded DVDs purchased from discount bins. He was embarrassed to admit he did not know if he could ever afford to eat in the restaurants he wanted to cook in. That he had never tasted the food he thought he wanted to make, so when he tried making it at home, he wasn't sure what he was meant to be tasting and yet he believed he could do this.

She was droning on about his brother's wedding. 'If you were here we could have got you both married at the same time. But it's good when you come back as a doctor you can get a bigger dowry and a prettier girl also.' He thought of how in this country men paid for certain kinds of women. And in his country, women's families for certain kinds of men. He was drifting in and out of the conversation, making the appropriate sounds. 'In a few weeks we will go see the girl's family. It's all set more or less but we will pay them one visit. Your brother wishes you were here, obviously.'

'How will you all go?' he asked, knowing how scarce money still was for his family.

'Bus. We will take the bus.'

All those hours on the road after which the entire family would pile into one room in a guest house. A room with a sink and a cot. They would give the cot to their mother, his brothers would sleep on the floor. He felt a surge of guilt when he realized he felt glad to not be there. And because of that he said, 'I'll try to come.' He was almost home from work now and he told her so. 'Okay go, go … let me know about your plans to come here. Khuda hafiz.'

He entered the house which felt almost intact again. Aaftab had worked his magic. He had even pasted the wallpaper back with glue, wherever he could. He entered Aaftab's room. The feathers were all gone, the spare blanket that Daya sometimes used when they were watching movies, on his bed. Aaftab wasn't there. They usually mentioned to each other if they would be out late, so he imagined Aaftab had just popped out to buy cigarettes. Again his phone rang. It was a number he didn't recognize.

'Assalamaleikum?' Wasim answered out of habit, even though Aaftab had told him a hundred times to just say hello.

'Waalekum salaam, brother.'

'Who is this?'

'You can call me a friend.'

'Hello friend,' Wasim said jovially, playing along, wondering who it was.

The person on the other end laughed. 'Sorry about what happened in your house, brother.'

The smile on Wasim's face froze. He started to break a sweat and something in him clicked as he realized what was happening. He sat down on Aaftab's bed, his breath caught in his throat. Suddenly it made sense to him. It wasn't the white boys. Of course it hadn't been the white boys.

'Alright, friend,' he said, his voice grim with a desire for justice. 'What can I do for you?'

'You know who we are?'

'I have some idea.'

'You know it was us.'

Admission. That was easy. Wasim remained silent.

'But we did not come for you, brother. We came for your friend.'

How can you both be my 'friend', he thought now. So he said, 'You understand *he is my brother*?' through gritted teeth, heat rising.

'You call him your brother but don't know his deepest secrets. He has hidden from you his true life. You think we stole the alcohol just like that? We stole it to protect you from being near sin.'

'I can take care of myself.'

'You do not know what he's hiding. You think we only came to take things but it's not true. We came to give you something too. We came to give you the option. We aren't in a place to perform true jihad yet, but you can join us in our mission to remove the borders that seek to contain Islam. We know you understand.'

The moment they said it, he was certain. A Borderless World indeed. The imam's rhetoric. He listened as the young male voice continued. He was sure now that it was Shehriyar, using a stronger Arab accent than necessary. It sounded slightly comical and that emboldened Wasim. He knew Shehriyar. He was just a kid. He listened as the voice said, 'Your brother has turned his back on Allah – we never thought such a day would come when one of our own …' Shehriyar trailed off with a deep, disappointed sigh. 'Will you do the same too?'

In response he measured out his words, part sorrow, part rage, part disgust, part amusement. 'And I never thought I would see a day, when brother turned on brother. In my world, that doesn't happen. Not by my hand. Khuda hafiz, *friend*,' the last word swollen with contempt.

He looked up and saw Aaftab in the doorway. He didn't know how long his friend had been standing there. He realized his hands were shaking. After a long silence he said,

'Tell me then, my brother, what is it you have hidden for me?'

Daya had once asked Aaftab, 'What made you first love Wasim?' and he had answered without skipping a beat, 'I loved him because I saw very quickly that we loved the same things. I'd never met a boy who was happy watching clouds before, you know? We loved the same food and the same old songs, we were both touched by nature and loved Ghalib. And then he loved you.'

'Then how can you blame people for loving those who love the same god as they do?'

'Because the other reason I love Wasim is he is not afraid to challenge me, and teach me new things about the world.'

Wasim did not speak a word. Not a single word. Not when Aaftab told him about Daya. Not when he told him how far it had gone or for how long it had continued. Not when he revealed it had sometimes been right here in this house, on the bed where they now sat. Not when Aaftab paused and looked for Wasim's eyes but Wasim would not give them to him. Not his eyes and not his mouth. Not a word, not a look. Aaftab gave him the truth, the whole truth and nothing but the truth, so help him God.

At the end, Wasim stood without a word, nodded without looking in his direction, walked towards his room and closed the door behind him.

He lay in bed a long time surrounded by his thoughts. They circled his head like cartoon birds or stars, after a man was hit hard. He could not imagine sex, let alone it taking place between his two closest friends. He lay there weighing out what he knew about the things Allah minded, and what he knew about love. All night he asked himself to whom he wished to give his empathy, and what that would say about him. At daybreak he was no closer to his answer than he had been at nightfall and he lay in bed weary, touching the scars on the book Shehriyar and his friends had sliced open. As he ran his fingers over the pages stabbed through the middle, he decided he knew one thing for certain. He knew *this* was wrong. He knew this could not in any world be right.

As if on cue his phone began to ring sharply. It was an unknown number again, but a different one from before. He picked up and didn't say a word. He did not say hello. He did not say assalaamaleikum.

As-Salaam-Aleikum.

Peace be unto you.

They did not deserve such a greeting, he thought.

And if they responded, Waalekum salaam –

And unto you peace too –

It would have been a lie.

So to spare Allah this human hypocrisy, he kept silent.

'Brother,' the voice began.

Brother. It was funny how it was never white people who called each other brother. It was black men to black men. Arabs to Arabs. Muslims to Muslims. Brown skin to brown skin. Bhai, brother, akh, hermano. And when white men said it – 'bro' – it sounded ridiculous. For what brotherhood had they ever had to forge? Who had they ever had to fight together as a family?

'Shehriyar, I know it's you so you can stop the pretence.'

'Oh but it's not,' the voice said, and Wasim realized it wasn't a lie. The voice was different. Older, more sinister. He had heard it before but he couldn't place where now and his tired mind zipped around the faces he saw regularly huddled outside the mosque, talking big, in whispers. He felt a rising panic. Which of the older men was it? There were so many. He had been so certain of who it would be and now that it wasn't Shehriyar he lost his footing and with it his confidence.

'Brother, we had a question,' the voice said calmly. 'It's a simple one. Do you not believe in our moral jihad? And will you not join us in choosing what is right, in showing the correct way to those who stray from the path of the Prophet, peace be upon him. In punishing those justly who fail to see and spread the true glory of Islam, unfettered, in these dark and often confusing times in these lands of harb and war? We did not take your friend's items and show them to his family for fun. This is a serious thing we speak of.'

Wasim took a sharp breath inward, audible perhaps to those listening over the phone. His free hand flew to cover his mouth, his eyes widening to become two massive pools of green.

'No,' he mouthed into his hand and bit down on it hard. It was the imam. In the long silence, Wasim's mind raced and finally the answer came. It came from his bellowing heart, it came from the moral compass forged in him as a child, it came from his wonder with the world and it came from the depths of his despair at how fast that world was changing into a place where he felt less and less at ease each day. His answer came from his anger at the television and the newspapers, at people judging him for his name, a name that meant grace, and that he tried so hard to live up to. It came from a place he could not have reached on his own, a place where he chose forgiveness for his friends. It came from the calculated knowledge that until the imam did not know that Wasim knew it was him on the other end of that phone call, he could say whatever he wanted. He could say exactly what he would have said to Shehriyar because this man was no better than him. And so he did.

'I will never join you, brother.'

'Very well then, it seems you have decided you are not a true Muslim.'

'That's not true. Now you tell me something. What makes you more Muslim than me, brother? Since when did I have to earn my right to Islam? Let me tell you: your jihad is easy. Your jihad sees everything in black and white but does not see the shades in between. What a sad world you live in, brother, to not be able to see the full spectrum of Allah's beautiful world. Listen to me.' His voice cracked as rage and tears and heat rose to his eyes. 'My jihad is light.'

He was a good Muslim, he knew this in his heart, in his breast pocket where he kept Allah always. And this small bit of knowledge made him fearless.

'Go. I will never join you. And now I must go too, because though I hear no azan, I know it is time for my prayers.'

He hung up, before they could respond.

Outside he heard Aaftab rise and go towards the bathroom, despite the early hour. He heard him leave the house soon after, despite it being Sunday. Wasim laid out his mat and as he knelt there that morning he understood that prayer was fine, but it was only when you placed your heart before God that you understood what it meant to truly worship. After he was done, he slipped into the kind of deep sleep that came from one thing only – a conscience that was clear.

22

They spent all their time together, Daya, Asha, Gyan. Barfi asleep at the foot of the bed and Kamla coming in and out with things required. There were nurses – three of them in shifts to provide round-the-clock care – but they weren't generally allowed into the inner sanctum of Vaikuntha unless it was urgent, or they needed to administer something. Besides, there was little point any longer, save his comfort. When Gyan was awake, conscious, Daya would ask him questions. Twenty-one years with him seemed very, very little and she could not fathom what the future was going to look like. She asked him things to distract him from the pain. To distract herself from the sadness. To know everything she could of his thoughts and ideas in the short time left.

'What did you write when you used to try and write your novel?'

'Already talking about me in the past?'

She coloured and he laughed at her discomfort.

Then she teared up and he pulled her hand to his chest. Even that small action tired him.

'I wrote the same story every time,' he said softly as she wiped her face with her free hand.

'Every time?'

'Every time.'

'Which story is that?'

'The story of how I met the girl I love.'

'Where did you meet Ma?'

'At the Acacia Inter-College Festival.'

'You're lying!'

'No, really, ask your mother.'

'If you could cook one thing what would it be?'

'Don't be funny, you know I can't cook anything.'

'Anything?'

'Nothing. Tea. I can make tea.'

'But if you wanted to!'

'Dosa. I would learn how to make the best dosa in the world.'

And finally one special day she asked with curiosity:

'Why did you call me Daya?'

For the first time Gyan paused. She thought he had fallen asleep or into his land between worlds again but his eyes were open, looking towards Asha now.

'Because it means mercy,' he finally said.

'What's the use of that?' Daya sulking. Daya sorrowful. Daya full of self-pity.

Asha looked pained by her tone, so Gyan continued very slowly, rasping with each word.

'Daya, you see, mercy is born of two things. The first is wisdom. Awareness. Knowing that the world requires mercy, an understanding ...' he needed water and even though they'd been warned against it for fear of pneumonia in his already destroyed lungs, they obliged him. He sipped from a small bowl with a spout Daya held up. Glasses had become too much effort for his slack mouth in the last few weeks. He gestured to Asha to continue as Daya wiped his wet chin with a handkerchief embroidered with a G.

'An understanding that the world needs mercy. Needs forgiving, constantly.'

Gyan, whispering now, 'The second thing is hope. Hope that if shown mercy, the world … any situation can change.'

Asha adding, 'The hope that compassion can in turn breed compassion.'

'So knowledge and hope?' Daya repeated.

'In other words,' her mother said, holding a hand out to her husband, 'Gyan,'

he took her hand and held it tight, 'and Asha.'

'Happy twenty-first birthday, baby,' Gyan smiled.

And Daya who had always felt so adrift and rootless, so aloof and alone, felt in the scoop of her throat, the large, hot, unexpected feeling of finally belonging.

~

They were married on the Equinox, a day of perfect balance when the sun and the moon shared exactly the same amount of space in the sky. On that first night Gyan took her home and made the world turn over many times. His friends had covered their bed with rose petals. There were hundreds of them all in white, her favourite kind, and when she woke up the next day and stood to draw the curtains, they clung to her back in soft clusters, and she looked for a moment in his waking eyes like an angel resting her wings in the morning light. Four times a year since, Asha had changed the direction of the mattress they slept on. On the spring and autumn equinoxes she flipped the entire thing over. On the summer and winter solstices, she turned it back to front and then front to back again.

In her abandoning of their bedroom for Vaikuntha, this was the first year since they were married that she would not do this. On the vast alternate mattress he had once summoned for them to live a full life upon, he lay. Some days propped up by pillows, some days on his side though it made his breathing more laboured. She wiped his forehead with a damp cloth. She didn't allow anybody else to touch his body until Daya came, and even then, she watched over the process. She put cucumber cream on his feet and elbows, played sitar music softly. Underneath the medicine and the poison his body emitted, she could still smell him. Sometimes when he was sleeping she placed her nose near his scalp, letting hot tears form in her eyes and succumbing to his aura, so delicate around him now. His strong beautiful body that she had loved so long, was coming apart in her hands. She was not ready to be without him. She was not ready to be alone.

~

It was in this time that Asha received a call one day from her old friend, the half of the gay couple who had abandoned friendship over a dinner and a statistic. Asha answered the phone with a single word.

'What.'

'Don't hang up. It's Atul.'

'I know who it is.'

'I want to come see you.'

'Now isn't the time. Gyan isn't doing well, Atul.'

'I know. I want to see him too.'

'Oh, to clear your conscience and all that?'

'No. Not that. To check on you. I'm worried, Asha.'

And because it had been so long since someone had wondered whether she was okay or had offered to come and check on *her*, she broke.

'Come around eleven tomorrow. He's more energetic at that time.'

'Okay.'

And then, as she did with everyone, but felt the need to do more with someone who hadn't seen Gyan in three years, she said, 'Please prepare yourself. He's not the same.'

Not the same.

It was as though he had been scooped out of his skin.

His bones had never been nearer to the surface.

Or perhaps it's truer to say his skin had retreated to the bone, looking for the last pieces of him to hold on to.

But every time he opened his eyes, she saw in them the same boy who thought in earnest that she wore glasses. That he would get to meet The Who.

Atul arrived at five to eleven.

'You've never been on time before,' Asha said as they settled into the sofas with cups of tea. She had worn a light shawl that he had given her many years ago and he noticed her peace offering. He had brought with him a book for her, a history of Romanian textiles.

'I've never been wrong before.'

She kept her gaze steady on him, not saying a word. She wanted a complete apology. This was Asha, she wouldn't take flippant admittance of guilt as anything more than what it was. The apology was separate.

'I'm sorry.'

'How come now? Did you feel sorry for me? With Gyan about to go, etcetera?' She was being rough and she knew it. But to be the opposite was something she reserved solely for Gyan now.

'Asha, come on.'

She looked down in shame, like a petulant child.

'You know we broke up?' he said now, speaking of his partner. She nodded.

'After fifteen years. It wasn't easy. This last year, it made me think of all the other times I had been wrong. All the times I had been … righteous,' he mocked himself. 'And I kept thinking of you. And then I met someone. And what do you know – he's Muslim.' His face coloured.

'What a simpleton you are,' Asha smirked. 'Our very own Dick Cheney. Now that it's your life, it's different, huh? The personal … the political.'

'No, it's not like that. You don't know how many times I've had to hear the words "katua cock".' A sharp, hard laugh escaped his mouth. 'No one believes it could be love. The idea is that because he's Muslim, I'm in it for the fun.'

'It's odd, isn't it? I'm sure no Muslim thinks of being Muslim as particularly fun.'

'Not right now, no.'

'And yet, our interactions with Muslims in friendship and romantically are meant to be some whimsical lark or feather in our caps.' She shook her head. She knew deep down that with every word she defended Daya and the boy she had told her about too. 'How's it going though?' she asked, softening now.

'Not so good. We wanted to go to America for a convention. He didn't get the visa.' He shrugged.

'It's okay,' she patted his knee. 'Why go to that hellhole anyway.'

They laughed together after a very long time, and something released palpably, the air around them loosening.

'And you?' he finally asked.

'Me what?'

'How are you?'

How was she.

Asha was not just angry, she was not just sad.

If only grief were so simple.

No. What Asha wanted to say was this:

She wasn't able to do the math.

She thought her deeds made her a good person. She gave all her old clothes to the poor. She fed the street dogs on their lane. She sent money to organizations that promised to save tigers and she never, ever wasted water. She planted her own vegetables, she bought organic fruit in the hope of protecting farmland. She spoke to the children who came begging at traffic lights and urged them to go to school. 'It's free, and you'll get food there.' One little boy with his two front teeth missing had said to her, grinning, 'I don't need to go to school! I know what I want to be!'

'*Kya*?' she had asked, humouring him.

'*Amir!*'

Rich.

But all the money in the world could not buy what she wanted now.

Why this? Why her? Why now?

The things that make up grief, they defy math.

'God must really hate me,' she said anguish and amusement mingling.

'That's not true Asha, God loves you.'

'How can you say that? It's not fair.'

'You're thinking of the one thing you do not have. And that's not fair Asha.'

'It's the biggest thing. Without it nothing is worth anything.'

'It's only God's chosen ones who have this much to bear. These are the biggest tests. And I believe if you pass them you will be closest to God.'

'What about those people who were killed in churches in Rwanda? And all those mass graves in Kashmir? And those Dalit girls who were raped and murdered because their brothers married upper-caste women? All those people who die in car crashes. You want to tell me they're lucky?'

'The dead are always lucky. It's us who must bear pain.'

'Because God hates us.'

'No. Because God sees infinite potential in you.'

'But not in Gyan?'

'Maybe his purpose is fulfilled.'

She pondered over this, smoked what was now a rare cigarette, and finally said, 'I want to believe you … but I'm so scared that some things just are.'

'It sounds awful but being thankful is the best way in these times.'

'Gratitude?' she smirked.

'You have your health. You have your daughter. Imagine going through this without either.'

Shame crossed her face.

'Asha, you have had a happy marriage. Those things don't exist – they're like fairies.'

'I believe in fairies,' Asha said softly, and smiled at last.

She asked if he wanted to meet Gyan. He nodded and Asha said, 'Alright, but no tears. We have a no-tears policy.'

They walked down to Vaikuntha and Gyan turned towards them, a skeleton held together by tubes, his hair scant on his head. Atul struggled to keep his face together and Asha moved forward, swift and bright as light, arranging pillows and cushions, chattering away, none of the tired bitterness that had surrounded her just moments before visible. It was like all the colour in the room rushed to her. 'Atul,' Gyan croaked, and Atul, his face earnest and ashen, leaned towards his friend to hear what he wanted to say. Gyan whispered through a grin, 'You bloody ponce … it took a dying man for you to get over your big fat ego!' And then he laughed his Gyan laugh. Full of irreverence and wisdom. And Atul broke the rule and cried.

That night Daya went over this conversation again and again. Asha had relayed it to her and neither had said, 'But what if he's wrong? Where does that leave us?' Daya stared at her ceiling where she had stuck glow-in-the-dark star stickers as a child. Her father had mapped out the sky for her and she had placed the stars where sitting on his shoulders she could reach them. Now she stood up on the bed in the dark and reached for them. One by one she began to remove them. They bothered her, not because of the greenish light they emitted but because she found herself repeatedly wanting to wish on them. When she had brought down the very last one she scooped the stars up in her hands and made her way to the garden. There she dug a shallow pit with her fingers and poured them into the soil. Maybe someday a tree of stars will grow here, she thought, and children will pick them like wishes. Then she returned to bed where she fell asleep with bits of earth on her hands.

~

Not long before the end, one of the curved curtain rods in Vaikuntha dislodged itself and the curtains fell. They came down so soundlessly, one wouldn't have known at all if it weren't for the sudden sunshine that filled the room. 'The light is making so much noise!' Daya would say to them as a toddler, when they woke her up for school in the early days. Asha tried at first to fix it herself but found the brackets in which the rod rested had fallen too. Because she could not bear to call a carpenter into that space that had become more private than ever, she asked Kamla to bring her an old bedsheet, a hammer and nails. Though he was sleeping, Asha placed a pair of headphones playing The Beatles gently onto Gyan's ears, and prepared to nail the sheet to the wall quickly, so as not to disturb him.

When Kamla walked back in with the sheet, Asha began to laugh. She laughed and laughed until she had tears streaming down her face. And then she began to cry. Kamla who was no stranger to the alternating hysteria and melancholy of grief, left her alone, closing the door behind her. Asha did not hear it shut, as in Gyan's first days of illness she had padded the edges of all their doors with strips of velvet so as to let him sleep more peacefully. With tears running down her face and chin and neck Asha lifted one corner of the bedsheet up and pressing it against the wall, hammered into it a nail to secure it there. She then did the same with the other side. When she was done making this makeshift curtain she sat down next to

Gyan and lowered her head gently on the side of his chest that could still take her weight, if only for a few moments. He had not opened his eyes but he placed his hand on her head like a blessing in his sleep. She could hear his ragged breathing inside the cavity of his chest.

Cavity, meaning hollow.

Cavity, meaning decay.

She looked towards the window. The hanging sheet was covered in tiny blue flowers, so faded now that against the light they turned almost invisible. She had always insisted they were forget-me-nots and now they really were. She wouldn't remind him, *she couldn't remind him*, but it was the first bedsheet they had ever made love on, all those years ago. It was the memory of that moment that had broken her loose from the cocoon of safe grace. She closed her eyes. She was exhausted. Of course it would be that particular sheet, she thought. Ever since their life together had begun, the world had been nothing more than a series of coincidences, the sanctity of which they had never argued with.

His eyes still closed, he stroked her hair. He would not remind her, he could not remind her, but the song that had just begun on the headphones was the old song he had shyly played for her, that wondrous first morning after the night they were married.

23

Aaftab and Wasim avoided each other in the long days after the confession, and then finally they could no longer and began eating their meals together again. They stopped making excuses to not be near each other. Like a couple who have decided to give their marriage a second chance they approached each other gingerly, relearning personalities. What they had liked about each other in the first place, what had changed over the years, the things they needed to learn anew. Like this days passed and just when the dust of all that destruction began to settle, Aaftab entered his office one morning and was invited directly into the partner's room.

It was a larger version of the room where he worked. Two desks, far more imposing than the ones in his office, larger windows, larger potted plant, higher ceiling and better upholstery. 'Sit Aaftab, sit,' they began. Water was poured. Throats were cleared. Aaftab decided to take the first step. It was something he hated doing when white people were awkward about starting a conversation; it felt apologetic to him, and yet he did it so often. It was always:

'Did you want me to take the later shift?'

'Oh, should I do Saturday and you take Monday instead?'

'You want to have pizza actually?'

Always sensing what the other wanted and succumbing to that very British habit of *not saying* and saying it for them. Adjusting. It's in our blood, he'd thought exasperatedly, more than once while accommodating. And now he did it again.

'Everything alright?'

More throats cleared. The two men before him in sharply cut suits, men he respected and looked forward to seeing each day, danced around each other, eyes darting, stammering and sipping water.'

'Well.'

'Well …'

'Well, you see …'

'Well, the thing is …'

Aaftab looked from one to the other, waiting.

Finally the elder of the two took a decisive sip and began. 'You've been here a considerable amount of time now, Aaftab, to know … to know what kind of firm we are. We're … we're very …'

'Open-minded,' the second, younger one chipped in.

'But in the last week something odd has been brought to our notice. We had a complaint.'

'Maybe a tip-off?' the younger one again.

'A tip-off – call it what you want – about your activities at the firm. Now Britain is in an odd place at the moment, there's a lot of anti-immigrant sentiment flying about, a lot of hot heads and such …'

'Anti-Islamic, you mean,' Aaftab said, smiling affably, once again making it easier for the white man before him to say what he needed to. 'It's okay, you can say it.'

'Well, yes, anti-Islamic.'

'But that's not the problem,' the younger one said, suddenly sterner.

'Oh?' Aaftab was genuinely puzzled. He looked at both of them blankly. 'I'm so sorry but what are you talking about exactly?'

'Well, we don't want to believe this but in the last week we've been approached with the information that you have been using the firm and your position here to manipulate immigration documents for the kind of young man who would set fire to this country in an instant.'

Silence. They were no longer looking him in the eye.

'They say they have evidence of your activities.'

'Like what?' Aaftab said in amused disbelief.

'Like a few months ago when you asked to go for your prayers each Friday. They say it was for your meetings with the group.'

'What group? That's ridiculous. And it's hearsay. Where is the actual evidence?'

'We understand it may not be true, Aaftab, but these are delicate times. There is, like we said, so much anti-immigration sentiment …'

'Anti-Islamic,' he cut in again, this time making it harder and not easier for them.

Silence.

'I've been at the mosque every Friday until recently. You can ask anyone.'

'We did,' the elder one said softly, troubled. 'They said you're never there.'

The younger one now spoke up. 'Aaftab, we have no choice but to ask you to take some time off until further notice. Yes, there's no hard evidence but these are very special circumstances and we've never dealt with anything like it before. We haven't pulled this out of some magic hat. Your imam, who's trying to clean up society and avoid such things, he vouches for it as well.' Leaning across the table with an outstretched arm he said, 'We'll get in touch.' And Aaftab stood, his head sounding a gong, and looked straight at him. 'It's *aaf-taab* actually. Not *aff-tab*.' He shook the hand briefly and walked out.

~

The doorbell rang and Wasim answered it. Two policemen in uniform asked for Aaftab. 'He's not here. He's at work.'

'Mind if we wait?'

'He might be a while.'

'Right.'

They stepped out to discuss the matter and Wasim tried but failed repeatedly to get through to Aaftab.

~

Aaftab left work angry and confused, but mostly defeated. All he wanted to do was call Daya back. To tell her everything. Spill his shame onto her lap. Sitting with Noor at the restaurant that night, he hadn't allowed himself the joy he should have, when Daya had called. Now, he thought sadly, he wouldn't know where to start. Would she be angry? Worried? Disappointed? He put his phone away and began to walk home.

~

'Here he is,' Wasim said, surprised.

The policemen were still trying to decide what to do when Aaftab had turned the corner. Now they looked as bewildered as Wasim did, to see him saunter down the street in his suit, mid-morning.

'What can I do for you?' Aaftab asked the policemen, wearily.

'You can answer a few questions.'

'Alright.' This day couldn't possibly get any worse, he thought.

They asked him one question. Where was he the night his house was broken into.

He told them again, the same story.

And then they told him.

'The man you claim is your uncle, Mr Enayat Sheikh, this lady Miss Noor Abdullah, her parents, all said the same thing, mate. They have no idea who you are.'

So everyone knew.

'Why would I have her number? I have emails and messages to prove this stuff!'

'Look, mate,' the tone was sterner now. 'We don't know, but if we're to believe what some of the elders at your mosque here are saying, you've got a bit of a roving eye. They said they know you, but didn't want to be associated, exactly. Also you should know, there are some who don't think you were anywhere but here that night.'

'Blaming the CB boys,' the second policeman shook his head in disgust. 'We don't know what you're up to, mate, but we'll be back.'

'I'm the victim here, it was my house that got broken into!' he was raising his voice. Wasim put a gentle hand on his back and pushed him into the house. 'Please let us know if you find anything else, sir,' he said, and closed the door politely.

~

Wasim and Aaftab sat together quietly after the police left, until it was late in the evening. 'So what do we know for sure?' Wasim asked, then began to answer his own question. 'We know the imam's boys broke in here that Friday and stole the sharaab and … your other stuff. You think Noor is in on it with them? I mean, they did come when you were at dinner with her and now she's denying the whole thing.'

'Could be. I doubt it though. Does it matter?'

'It doesn't. Anyway, they mailed your parents photos of everything, yes?'

'Yes. Not just my parents. My little brothers and my sister and Enayat taaya.' Aaftab's youngest brother had finally forwarded the email to him but had also sent a message saying their father would skin him if he found out so Khuda hafiz until forever.

'And they told your firm that you're some kind of crazy fundo helping wannabe jihadis get visas into the country.'

'He nodded. 'Apparently the imam said he's trying to get rid of extremist lads like me so he wanted them to know.'

'Like you?'

'Yes. It would be funny if it weren't so sinister. I'm fucked, aren't I?'

'What did they tell the cops?'

'That I'm a womanizer and was some loudmouth at the mosque. That I used to have tons of young Muslim boys dropping in at our place before you lived here. Like I was running a cell or something. Anyway, that's enough for them to want to know more. I mean, any day now the police will land up at my workplace.' He looked up, panic slowly setting in as he connected the dots. 'What do I do, Was?' He knew this – they couldn't take him in based on any of these allegations. Not yet. Still, the allegations were building up and Aaftab knew that 'not yet' was swiftly turning into a 'now'. He knew the greatest intoxicant was another man's blood.Wasim was looking even more panicked than Aaftab now. Gravely, with ice in his throat he said, 'Aaftab,' an odder and odder expression growing on his face. 'Where's your passport?'

He knew before they checked the other drawer of his desk. It was gone.

Without his father's connections, without his firm, he did not know how to move forward. 'Should I go to the embassy?' he asked. It was too risky, they both decided. 'You're just an ordinary guy. What if it's true that governments are secret friends? If you're listed as a...'

'Don't say it,' Aaftab cut him off. 'If I report my own passport stolen, how does that put me in the wrong?' he lashed out, frustrated.

'It tells them you're looking to travel. If you're listed as some kind of threat, this adds up. No embassies.'

Aaftab wilted visibly. 'I'm going to go,' he said softly, more to himself than to Wasim. 'I'm going tonight.'

'Go? Go where?'

'There's no time anymore. I'm calling Idris. There are boys at the mosque, boys who have overstayed visas or come in to this country on lorries rammed between computers or crates of oranges, who will lie and say I got them in just because the imam asks them to. They will happily go back to Pakistan or

Tunisia or wherever the fuck they came from illegally, just to feel like they've participated in cleansing the world of a haraami like myself. I'm calling Idris.'

'Okay, but not from your phone. From mine.'

Idris was one of Aaftab's friends from college, from the era when boys would drop in by the twos and fours at all times of the day and night. Idris and Aaftab had become close almost instantly, drawn to one another because of their mutual love of poetry and their dormant stance on Islam. Idris Idris as he was named and as they called him was a member of a wealthy family from Qatar who had made their fortunes fishing. At twenty-one, when he was home for the summer, he'd been engaged to a local princess whom it was rumoured he told quite frankly at their engagement party that he preferred men. When she said she was okay with it as long as he kept her well, he had laughed and explained how he was not alright with such a life because he was who he was and that was that. He was now living out the scandal back in Wales where his family had provided him with a luxurious apartment by the Bay and an annual allowance that kept his body clad in designer clothes and his shelves full of books. He wanted very little more and had agreed not to discuss his 'kafir ways' as they called it, openly, so long as he didn't have to ever go to the mosque or suffer an engagement again. He was their man.

'Idris Idris?'

'Aaftab, man? What number is this?'

'I need to see you.'

When he wasn't reading or inviting boys from the bars at the bay up to his elegant pad and serving expensive bottles of Merlot, Idris Idris spent his days indulging his one other passion. Idris Idris loved sailing.

Before dawn the next day, at the darkest end of a night of doing a hundred thousand things, none of which he felt prepared him adequately for what was coming, Aaftab met with Idris at Cardiff Bay where he was taken into the boat parking area meant for owners only. 'You guys wait here.' Saying this, Idris walked off leaving Aaftab and Colin in the eery space full of echoes and strange mercurial smells.

After they had spoken to Idris, Aaftab had said, 'We need someone with a car, who isn't from our world at all, else we start walking at 3 a.m. or something. I'm not calling for a taxi, that's for sure.' Wasim had been the one to come up with it. 'Colin. There's no one else.' Now Wasim waited in the car so in case someone came, he could drive off, unattached to the episode. Aaftab hadn't wanted Wasim to come with him at all, but Wasim had just said, 'The early birds who flock together get the worm and the feather.'

'Does Daya know?' Colin asked Aaftab, as the two of them stood together in the dark.

'No.'

'Are you going to tell her?'

'We aren't really in touch. And I'd appreciate it if you didn't tell her. This way what she doesn't know can't hurt her.'

'I won't. You have my word.'

In the darkness Aaftab began to sob. It came upon him without any warning and echoed like a whale sound trapped between the water and the cave-like space they were in. Colin put an arm around him and sat him down on the damp ground. They leaned against the wall and looked at the boat, spotless white, bobbing in its place on the water. When he was calmer Colin asked the important question.

'What are you scared of?'

'Everything.'

Colin knew fear better than anyone. He had once said to Daya while arguing with her about what was going on in the world, 'You think I don't understand terror? I was born on a continent where men were whipped out of grass skirts and onto boats, in chains, to bring them to lands without seeds. The only seeds here were terror, and they planted these under our skin so that anyone born with this same skin would wear terror in it, for generations.' He said to Aaftab, gentle but firm. 'Nah man, I'll tell you what. I think you're basically scared you aren't going to live the life you always thought you would. But so what?'

Aaftab looked up in the dark, listening.

'I grew up thinking I would live my whole life in South Africa. I grew up with visions of a wedding with a girl in a white dress … babies. It's the life I was told to have, and so I imagined it. But I could never imagine the girl's face, so I changed the picture. It isn't the picture most people have, but it's okay. Sometimes we change the picture. Sometimes it changes before us. Life is just going to be different from how you imagined it. That's all.'

Aaftab nodded, understanding.

'And listen. Your people have been fleeing for generations. But they have also been conquerors wherever they have gone. So, go.'

Aaftab nodded. Yes, yes, yes, he would go.

Idris returned. 'Your man should be here any minute now.' It was chilly and Idris rubbed his hands together.

'How much do you pay for this parking?' Aaftab said conversationally, with a lightness he wasn't feeling.

'Too much.'

'What's the fellow's name?' He was asking things to keep his mind from thinking other things.

'I'm not going to tell you. That way in case ...'

Aaftab nodded. In case he was caught. In case, in case.

'You can call him Captain Ahab.'

They smiled wry smiles.

Something occurred to Aaftab. 'We'll be gone a long time?'

'Yes, my friend.'

'Where will you say the boat is?'

'I will say I sold it.'

Idris could see doubt through the shadowplay on Aaftab's face. 'I've arranged it already,' he relented.

'What do you mean?'

Idris looked downward as he replied, 'I've actually sold it. I've given the papers to the fellow to whom it's promised. He's an Irish lad; no one will ever think to look for him. If you ... *when* you reach,' he steadied his breath, uneasy for the first time, 'when you reach, the boat will not come home. She's going straight to Ireland. In fact, it won't even be her.' His eyes turned dark and his voice dropped. 'They'll swap her,' he whispered.

Ahab walked in.

Wasim came in behind him and began to load the boat with Aaftab's two small bags. It was a sailing boat with a single cabin below, meant for joyrides and summer afternoons fishing and drinking champagne. For a different kind of escape.

Wasim embraced him.

'Remember. *Hijrat*,' Wasim said.

Earlier that night as they'd packed his bags Wasim had told Aaftab softly, 'I know you think you're a bad Muslim, but they say if you do find yourself in a land of harb, without Islamic law, there are two ways to respond.'

'Two?'

'Yes, two.'

'I see. And what are those, *maulana saab*?'

Wasim ignored the taunt. 'The first is jihad, as you know. Our jihad, not a jihad of bombs but of love, of overcoming the ego. I know you tried that.'

'You don't say,' Aaftab's bitterness spilled from him. 'What's the second?'

'*Hijrat*.'

Migration.

'Go, Aaftab. It's time. Go where they will not misunderstand your name, your religion, your way of practising it, your language, your pain. Just go.'

'Is there such a place?' he asked.

'Well, if you find it, give me a call,' Wasim smiled.

'And when they ask you where I went?'

'I will say I don't know, and it will be the truth.'

Wasim had tried to understand based on the clothes Aaftab was packing where he would go. But he couldn't and Aaftab refused to tell him, and they both knew it was best that way.

The boat entered like a knife into the waiting water, egg-white sea foam spraying its sides. It was still more night than day and Aaftab could count stars just before each one faded away into the coming light. The stars that always reassured him because despite what it looked like, there was order to them. He could sense the sun begin to rise at his back and knew they were moving westward. Behind him his entire life, before him the Atlantic. As water opened up and the shore retreated, he wondered about where he was going. Inexplicably he remembered something from his useless list of facts. During the Second World War the *Mona Lisa* moved home six times. She travelled in ambulances, lived in a Cistercian Abbey, lived with bishops, and even stayed in the fabulously turreted fortress the Chateau De Montal before she came home to the Louvre, six long years later. Now he thought, 'The *Mona Lisa* was once a refugee too,' and it gave him some comfort to think someday perhaps he would share this thought with Wasim.

Wasim told Colin and Idris he'd walk home. At the edge of the highway, before he turned down into the stomach of the city he took from his pocket Aaftab's phone and wiped its history. He removed the sim card, swallowed it and tossed the phone onto the highway. Then he took out his own phone and stared long at the message. It was typed up and ready, and all he had to do was press send. He considered deleting it. She deserved to know. He squeezed his eyes shut and pressed the green button.

Daya. I know everything. Aaftab told me.

24

The morning he went, Asha thought of the morning he had officially proposed.

Under a full moon, in a hill town, peaks hidden behind clouds but sky alight with moondust. He had gone down on one knee, like in the movies, and he had not said, 'Will you marry me?' No. Blessed with the hope that came from knowing purest love, Gyan had said, 'Will you grow old with me?'

Soon after they were wedded, Asha had awoken one morning to Gyan sitting up, reaching under the blanket and pulling her arms out. 'What on earth are you doing?' she had asked, annoyed. He had been scared, he said, by how deeply she'd been sleeping. 'I couldn't tell if you were alive or not!' he'd said sheepishly. Then he explained how bodies in sleep were so akin to the ones God had claimed for himself, they needed an obvious sign of life upon them. This sign, he claimed (or rather, exclaimed, because everything Gyan said was in exclamation) was a human's hands. 'In sleep they curl up, and the fingertips always retreat towards the mounds of Venus,' he pointed out the palm's 'love-lump', below the thumb, as he referred to it. 'Why do you think that is?' she asked, curious but still irritated. 'Because loving is the greatest sign of life, fool!'

'Very funny,' she rolled her eyes and turned over to sleep once more.

'No, listen,' he pawed at her shoulder. 'It's true. It's the body's way of holding on to the soul in its sleep. When a person dies, their hands uncurl.'

She looked at her hands and she understood. Death showed the flower fully blossomed, the petals all open, the life lines complete. It was their joke over the years if one of them had slept too deeply – 'I had to check your palms to see if you were still holding on!' For weeks Asha had woken each day petrified she would see his fists laid flat. Then finally the day came.

The morning he went, Asha's only words were whispered to a bedroom made empty by his final absence. Lying flat on her back on her side of the mattress, she turned to the emptiness beside her and replied to his long-ago proposal.

'I will never stop wanting to grow old with you.'

And then she fell silent, for a very long time.

The same morning Kamla found Barfi in his usual spot in the sun on his navy cushion on the floor of the living room, curled up like a dumpling. 'Come, Barfu,' she called him for his walk. He did not stir. Two souls had left the building that morning, hand in hand. It must have been easier with a friend.

A host of angels.

Gyan had asked that his ashes be thrown over the Indian Ocean instead of the Ganga. 'All rivers must reach the ocean eventually; think of it as a shortcut,' he'd said, his eyes twinkling. Daya and Asha made the trip to the southernmost tip of the country together, the entire thing a blur of baggage tags, clipped instructions, and clammy held hands, but when she smelled the ocean air, Asha understood he had asked this not for him, but for her. He had never cared for rituals. He'd believed strongly in the eternity of souls, and she understood now standing by the ocean, her feet covered in foam, sand between her toes, her trousers rolled up and wet, that this was him still taking care of her. In the moment when she turned the steel box over and the wind took charge, carrying the last earthly pieces of him away, she did not feel abandoned as she had so deeply feared she would, but loved to the very core of her being. In that moment, she knew, no one could have loved her more.

Daya was the one who cried. She cried for her father and how little time she had had with him at the end. For his jokes that constantly annoyed her that she now wished she could laugh at. She cried for the hundreds of beautiful ideas he had placed inside her heart without ever telling her he was doing so, so that when she walked around its corridors she would suddenly bump into something peculiar like sympathy for the fig fruit because Jesus once cursed a fig tree for having none. 'And young JC turned to the tree and said, "May you never bear fruit again, horrible tree!" But you know, the poor thing, it was just out of season,' she could hear Gyan now in her head, telling the story comically, and she knew all these quiet things in her heart had come from him. She wept because she missed him and because she missed Aaftab and she had to learn now, like her mother, how to live without.

~

After the goodbyes, Daya thought to call Wasim but found she couldn't muster the will. She had replied to his message saying he knew 'everything' with a message of her own saying all she knew was that her father was gone, and that she would be in touch when she could. 'I'm so sorry, jigar – call only when you can,' he had said. She had sent Aaftab a message as well, saying Gyan was gone. He hadn't responded and this piled on top of the massive betrayal of his engagement, his confession to Wasim and his enforced lack of communication hurt her so much, that while she knew Wasim meant well, it was simply too painful. This is what Aaftab had left her with finally – his silence when she needed him most, and Wasim's questions, when she needed them least. In her ear she could still hear him whisper, in the lobby of a hotel, '… to the grave,' and she swallowed the words 'how dare you' over and over.

Wasim drowned slowly in the silence from both Daya and Aaftab. He wanted to tell her that Aaftab was gone but until Aaftab called, he didn't know how he would answer when she asked – where? So, with some relief that she didn't want to talk, he gave her room to mourn in peace, forty days at least, but his life felt ruptured. To avoid going absolutely mad in that time he had begun speaking to his mother every morning.

He would wake up and make himself tea, the house a space of echoes, then to avoid the largeness of Aaftab's absence, he would call his mother and listen to her plan the trip to meet his brother's bride. There was comfort in it. In the simplicity of her problems. Hotel rooms and bride's clothes. Would she be pretty enough? Was the outfit the correct shade of green? Would the bus driver let them stop enough times for them to pee?

'Assalamaleikum,' he began.

She crackled through the way she always did. He put on the table the calling card from which he had scratched a thin silver strip to reveal a cheaper dialling line to Pakistan.

Half the time the cards didn't work and he remembered how for this reason Aaftab called them lottery cards.

'Ammi.'

'Wasim!'

His brother's fiance's family had offered to have the groom's entire family stay at their house.

'Shall we?' she asked.

'What do you mean?'

'Does it look cheap that we aren't staying in a hotel? Does it look like we can't afford it?'

He wanted to say – but we can't, so what's the problem. Every time he said something like that his mother would respond, 'You have forgotten how things work here,' so now he reassured her that it didn't.

'You're sure? It's so many of us, and one more if you come.'

He had forgotten this promise to her.

After Aaftab left, Wasim was asked time and again where he had gone. He was asked by the police. He was asked by the boys at the mosque who looked shocked when he walked in for his prayers the next Friday like they had never called and threatened him. Like the imam himself had not. Wasim said his prayers and glazed over while the imam spoke. He was saying, 'One boy asked me, "I want those things alcohol gives me – magic and madness and freedom and exhilaration." Yes, he said those words. He said, "I want to fly like that." I promised him that Islam will provide him that after death.' Many in the rapt audience praised the lord softly but Wasim had zoned out and risen swiftly at the end. He nodded politely when Shehriyar sized him up, as Wasim chatted about how cold it was with an elderly man he sometimes bought meat from, and left quietly, avoiding Enayat. He had considered not going but more than bigotry, he hated cowardice, and he would not give them that. So he went and it looked to the world like he truly had nothing to hide. After a little while they stopped asking him where Aaftab was. No one had enough evidence to warrant searching for him. And no one reported him missing.

For the rest of the world, it seemed to Wasim, Aaftab was gone and they simply didn't care.

For Wasim, every minute was silence. Every moment anxious. Aaftab had left him money for a few months' rent but now the largeness of the house felt terrifying. He didn't want to be in the kitchen. He had never before realized how lonely he was. It occurred to him that without Aaftab and Daya, life in this strange town was pointless. Daya refused to call him back and Aaftab may as well have been shark food. Listening each day to his mother he thought perhaps he would after all go back. Not in time for their trip, no, but maybe in time for the wedding. He had enough money saved up, having lived so frugally while in Wales. And though the boys from the mosque and the police had all finally left him alone, he no longer felt safe anymore. Ease escaped him.

When he had first come to this house, Wasim had with his hard-earned money, little by little bought the things he would need to make it *feel* like home. He bought, without consulting Aaftab, pots and pans, woks and ladles and things to chop and grind and peel and grate. Aaftab had only known how to buy ice trays and frozen goods but Wasim had brought heat. As his first summer in Wales arrived though, something took place that Wasim hadn't prepared for. The heat he brought paired itself with incessant rain and no matter what he did he could not avoid the mould. Wales was a drizzly country, Caerdydd a wet city. Every morning when he took out his heavy chopping board to cut the onion and tomatoes for his omelette, he would find on the damp edge of the wood the beginnings of tiny flakes of white mould. He would scrub them off with some annoyance, and then begin work. The next morning it would be back. He kept thinking he would at some point purchase a plastic chopping board, but he never did, the romantic in him put off by the idea.

Of late Wasim had not had the will to cook for one person. But that morning after the call with his mother, he urged himself into the kitchen. He had cracked the eggs for an omelette and whisked them, then he had pulled his chopping board out and with a sigh taken it to the sink out of habit. It was there by the window that he noticed, in the days he hadn't cooked, in his human absence, the fungus had had a chance to thrive. Instead of the usual white specks that appeared on the edge of the board, Wasim saw the delicate curls of a plant, a pattern repeating in grey velvet, each bud matching the next, reaching for life. And with awe he realized the miracle of what the wooden board was doing.

It was remembering itself as a tree.

No amount of scrubbing and straightening could take that away from it. Wasim knew this because for years now he had felt the same way inside his jeans. Like he was always trying to both suppress and remember that he was more.

Maybe, he thought, as he later gently placed the chopping board in a patch of soil and flowers behind the house, maybe it was time to go home.

25

The house stayed quiet, covered in white sheets and scented by medicine and *mauth* for days. After Gyan left, Asha slept in Daya's room and they took to keeping Daya's lava lamp – a present for her sixteenth birthday – on each night. Sometimes Asha would stay up all night, going over years and years of love, salty memories, and time expanded like a lotus. She allowed herself an immense tenderness. Sometimes she would wake and find she had slept two days and time had caved and disappeared. Other times she would not want to wake for it meant leaving him, so she would sleep just to dream him.

Days passed like this and then she decided with some shame to fix things. For some time their home had functioned as a hospital and now Asha wanted to live in it again. She began by giving away boxes and boxes of clothing to Kamla, who for the first time accepted the offerings. For years Kamla had insisted on her two pairs of sun-coloured clothing and nothing more. Asha had asked her more than once, 'Is it really because of the sunflowers? You can leave that idea behind now. I think the flowers will understand.' Kamla always just smiled and said, 'A promise is a promise,' but the truth was that she had for years kept only the clothes on her back and one extra set because she had lived in the expectation of the requirement to run. All these years and the fear had not left her bones. The less she had, the easier it would be to leave, she told herself. But now as Asha handed her boxes full of lovely-coloured clothes Kamla took them *chup-chaap* without a word. She knew this was Asha's way of healing, so she took them to her room on the roof, wearing each day a new one for Asha until finally one night Kamla admitted to herself that maybe this was Asha's way of healing *her*. The time had come. The sunflowers would understand.

She put the last two sets of yellow clothing in a bag and taking a day off work carried them to Lalabad's once-glorious river. Standing above it on a bridge, Kamla could see light glinting upon its surface. With one strong hurl of her wiry arm she let go. Then she watched as the slow-moving water carried away a few billowing pieces of yellow cloth. She was free. There was nowhere to run and she was perfectly safe in her stillness.

Like this Asha and Kamla swapped sartorial choices. After gifting her friends and Daya and Kamla everything she could, for herself she chose seven of her softest pink tunics – first flush, the shade the sky is when the sun begins to graze it with the crown of her head – and chose to wear only those, comforted in the colour of babies and newness and birthing and buds. This was not an ending, this was a beginning. So she chose to wear the colour of falling in love.

~

Daya had avoided Milni since the day she had drowned in her dismay. It had been easy – she said she wanted to spend all her time with her father and she did. In trying to restore normalcy she called her now and they met at Milni's ('My place is still too depressing,' Daya had said) and lay on her bed chatting. With some reluctance Daya told her friend that Aaftab had disappeared. 'Just like that. He never called me back. I heard he met a girl for marriage and … that was that.' After an initial 'I'd warned you,' Milni was sympathetic and even managed for a short while to cheer her up. Before Daya left, Milni made a suggestion. 'There's this guy. He's great if you want to maybe get a drink or something?'

'Okay.'

'Okay?'

'Okay.'

'Tomorrow?'

'Okay.'

So Daya put on her best pair of jeans, a navy-blue sweater and her mother's silver earrings and made her way to a quiet bar to meet them. She got there early which gave her the chance to acquaint herself with the place. It was chic, dimly lit, playing Oasis, serving wine in stemless glasses. They walked in soon after, Milni in a short sparkly dress and boots and he, looking like he couldn't believe he was not butter. Milni introduced the strangers and they ordered drinks. More red wine for Daya, a vodka for Milni and 'A whisky for the gentleman, please!' Milni said to the bartender. Rohan had chosen a single malt Daya had once heard Aaftab say he liked, and she had to shake the sudden sadness from her shoulders. She turned to him and asked about his work. He spoke at length about his business and made her laugh and she noticed he had perfect hair, and sneakers she wished she could own. He refilled her glass without missing a beat. 'I need the ladies' room!' Milni announced, picking up her little handbag and striding off, winking at Daya from behind Rohan's back.

'So,' Rohan smiled.

'So,' Daya tried her best to make that word sound charming, or cute at the very least.

'What would you like to know about me?' He smiled a big open smile and Daya had to admit he had very good teeth.

'Okay … What does your name mean?' she asked.

'Rohan? I haven't got a fucking clue!' He laughed and downed his whisky, asking with a gesture for another.

'I have a question,' he said.

'Shoot!' Daya spread her hands, attempting to convey openness to whatever it was he wanted to ask.

'Milni says you're a dancer.'

'Well, I studied dance, yes.'

'So if you're a dancer dancer, how do you plan on making money doing that?' he said, curious.

And you? Daya who had become so accustomed to British politeness, thought, taken aback, how do you plan on making love by dealing car parts in your father's factory?

She opened her mouth to say something but saw Milni, much to her relief, returning. 'I'm suddenly so tired,' she said, putting a hand on Milni's arm and squeezing it slightly. 'You guys carry on!' They offered to drop her home but she said no, thank you, it was too far. She got into a taxi and when it reached she entered the house looking for Barfi, then remembered he was gone as well and she lay down on her bed and embraced loss and cried till sleep came.

~

She woke up late and wandered out to a house flooded with spring sunlight. She took an apple from an indigo pottery bowl on the dining table and drifted into the living room looking for the papers which she realized no one read in the morning any longer. Asha would only read them before bed tonight. She stood for a moment before the painting of Faiz's poem tossing the apple from one hand to another. The apple was from Kashmir, a favourite variety of Gyan's, who refused the American apples sold in the markets of Lalabad, over-plumped and polished with poisons. 'Carpets, kahwa, apples and saffron,' he would always say of Kashmir. 'The spoils of war.' She looked now from the apple in her hand to the long strokes of calligraphy before her and recalled Wasim telling her that Faiz was wedded in Kashmir. Had Faiz eaten these apples? Her thoughts drifted and she wished she could read the script. Those lines of language that fell like art does to a page.

In her love for Aaftab, Urdu had begun to fascinate Daya, the way it once fascinated her mother in her love for Faiz. 'To read our great loves better, we must learn all their languages,' Gyan had said back in the eighties when Asha had started learning Urdu. 'Body language?' she had replied cheekily, poking him in the ribs. Urdu and Hindi were not some distant cousins. They were siblings. One inexplicably Muslim and the other inexplicably Hindu. And yet they possessed scripts made from two drastically different fabrics. One of clouds and the other from the branches of trees. One crafted of curves, the other from lines. Could brothers separated by air and appearance still read each other? They said it wasn't true but sometimes, high up in the Himalayas, you could see a cloud caught in a tree, and that was where they still embraced. For what is the horizon but a border? And what are they both but imagined lines?

Daya was drifting, thinking thoughts her father might have thought when her breath caught in her chest. She dropped the apple and began to race towards her bedroom, her heart pounding. Kamla hearing the apple hit the ground, exited the kitchen and saw Daya run in and then out of her bedroom and out the front door, leaving it open. Ignoring the rogue apple, she followed her hurriedly, as Daya took the steps two at a time, turning on the last one and heading straight for the garden. She heard Daya shout 'MA!' and decided not to follow.

'Ma!' Daya found Asha pruning the bougainvillea bush in their front garden, behind the massive white sheets that had covered the mattress in Vaikuntha, her parents' studio. They had finally been washed and hung out to dry and Asha appeared between them, reaching out to the flowers, the dusty orange petals dancing under her hand. Flowers had always responded to her like puppies. 'Ma, what does this say?' Daya held out a book. 'I'll need my glasses – just a second.' They went inside.

After she told her, Asha closed the copy of *Anna Karenina* and handed it back to her daughter. Daya's heart felt crushed within her chest. And then, it began to bloom.

~

He hesitated, then opened the last page and handed her the book.

'So what does it say?' Daya asked the beautiful boy on the bench, in the Pathani suit and skull cap.

'What do you mean?' he blinked.

'I don't read Arabic.'

'It's not Arabic, it's Urdu,' he replied, amused.

'Well I don't read Urdu either,' she smiled.

'You're not Pakistani?' he asked.

'Nope. Indian.'

'Oh.'

'So what does it say?'

She hadn't paused. If his nationality had taken her by surprise, she hadn't shown it.

We are all the same. Bones, muscle, souls, blood, shame, hate, joy.
Love.

'It says,' he paused and she waited for him to best translate the Urdu. He cleared his throat. 'It says, "I know the end of this story, everyone does. So why do we keep reading?" Or umm … something roughly along those lines.'

'What did you mean by that?' she sat down next to him.

'I just meant,' he began, now engulfed by his lie, giving the theory some thought, 'it's *Anna Karenina*. We all know the ending, right?'

'Right, so?' Daya asked.

'So why does generation after generation read this book? I asked myself, "Why do we do that?" and in that moment, I think I understood life itself. You see, life is beautiful, *because it's lived*.

'Profound,' she replied, then began giggling. The truth was, the boy was profound and childlike and wise and wonderful and funny all at once.

Months later he told her, 'The day I met you, I was coming from the mosque, that's why I was dressed like that, obviously. And I had prayed for something that came true.'

'And what was that?'

'The thing I told you. About why we keep living, keep striving, when we know we must eventually go.'

'You had prayed for the meaning of life?'

'No, I had prayed for a reason to live.'

~

On the day he would meet his soulmate, Aaftab woke up and decided he would go to the mosque for his Friday jumma prayers. It always felt like a decision he made and he liked that. He disliked feeling like it being Friday made the decision for him. He wasn't opposed as such, he just wanted to have the choice. He had changed into the new clothes his mother had parcelled him recently from Pakistan. A reward for his piety. As he went through his prayers that day, it struck him that he always asked for the same things, none of them true.

Good health for Ammi and Abbu (despite everything).

Good grades for his siblings.

Goodwill for fellow Muslims.

We pray for the things we are taught to. Ask for what we are told we should want.

What did he really want?

The answer was so simple it shocked him.

Love.

So he asked for it.

Afterwards he had walked past Roath Park at ease. The sun glinting on the oaks had called him in and he had stopped to read the book he had taken from the charity rack outside the mosque. He had felt suddenly while sitting there another presence, something that calmed him. Almost like a scent, but scentless. Like a memory, but of something that had never taken place. He had looked up and seen her there, had stolen a glance at her, so peaceful in the gentle spring light, and had understood – this would be the girl he would fall in love with.

On a whim, into the back of the book he had quickly scribbled in Urdu.

Asha looked up and saw her daughter's waiting face and she understood in that moment, everything. 'It says,' Asha paused, smiled. 'It says, "Ya Allah, thank you. She's beautiful."'

He had sometimes asked himself later what he might have done if she had been able to read Urdu. If she had understood the writing. Would he have lied and said it was about the book? Or would he have told the truth, and said it was about her? That he had known without knowing? And sometimes wistfully he had wondered – if she had been able to read it, would she have understood his love, right at the start? Would she have understood how much of a reason she had given him, from the very first moment? No matter what the inevitable outcome? And wouldn't that outcome have been different, if she could have read it at all?

When Aaftab was thirteen and had just begun to wear longpant and comb his own hair in a neat sweep to the right of his skull, leaving an ivory parting on the left, his father lost his temper at him so terribly one day, he beat his eldest son's head against a wall till it split like a pomegranate along the seam and from there a piece of his soul escaped. On the day Aaftab met Daya, he knew only one thing with certainty. As she stood there before him, light dancing behind her as she swayed, asking question after question of him, he felt the seam once more begin to unstitch and then her laughter begin to fill that hollow space. Like this, Aaftab felt the missing piece of his soul come home. Like this, Aaftab knew.

~

Wasim put the phone down gently. That morning he had woken and called his brother to see if they had reached the bride's town safely. They had set out on the big trip the night before and he had wished more than ever that he could be there with them. The call hadn't gone through and he realized the bus must have been delayed, winding through some area between phone networks on its journey southwest of Rawalpindi, towards Quetta. He waited. When his phone had rung just now, it was the bride-to-be's brother. A man whom he had never met but had heard so much about in these last few weeks. His future brother-in-law. 'Bhaijaan,' he addressed Wasim.

'They've reached?' he asked.

All of them. One bomb. Sixteen people. And among those sixteen, all his brothers. His mother. His father who last minute had agreed to come. Gone.

Later he would ponder the word he had used to ask if they had reached.

'*Khairiyat?*'

Have they reached safe, is what he was asking, rhetorically.

But there was no word for *khairiyat* in English, or none that he had heard yet, that conveyed safety and warmth and well-being like this word did.

That the lack of this word had now taken away.

Later, when he wanted desperately to lay blame somewhere, he would ask – but does a bomb have a nationality?

And was there a name for a land lived in by the followers of Islam, ruled over by Islamic law and yet in a state of war? Wasim did not know any longer where this Land of Peace, this Dar al-Salam existed. But he did know the entire world was bent and broken not by Dar al-Harb or the Lands of War, but by *Dard* al-harb. The Pain of War.

He placed a CD in the music system. The tinny old music of undivided India began to play and he started to make himself a cup of tea. Not in the kettle but in a pan. He mixed tea leaves and water and milk and brought them to a boil. When it was done he covered it with a plate to retain the heat and capture the flavour and walked to his bedroom. He opened the doors to his cupboard and searched through it, arms extending deep into the layers of heavy winter clothing like a snake moving between sleeping tiger cubs. Just before his hand hit the back of the cupboard he felt the smooth edge of a bottle. He extracted it gently. He took the bottle to the kitchen and took out a mixing bowl. It was the sort of bottle his mother always used for storing pickles in after she had flavoured them with the heat of the sun. He knew this would hurt, but he took a deep breath, unscrewed the lid and began pouring the contents into the large blue bowl. Then as he did with flour whenever he made rotis, he began pouring water into the bowl with his left hand and mixed the content with his right. All these years in England and he still mixed with his hand, the way he was taught to as a child. He stirred until the mixture was sticky and smooth, and then he washed his hands. He poured the tea from the pan into a cup, picked up the bowl and the cup both and carried them to the open window. Outside there was a light drizzle. Inside, the song changed.

'Will you come home?' the man who would have been his

brother-in-law had asked. 'Maybe soon but not immediately,' he had said, and the man had understood, because he was the one who had informed Wasim, the house was locked and the bodies that once lived in it entirely lost. There was nothing to bury but memories.

He took a sip of tea and leaned into the bowl. He took a deep breath and smelt the smell of the wet earth of his homeland. He closed his eyes and breathed in again. When he opened them he was smiling, but two tears fell down his face into the mud in the bowl. He would never smell this smell in the place where it came from, ever again. He knew this with certainty. But for this afternoon alone, he was six years old, in a courtyard in a house in a village in Pakistan. The winter rain had come, and the earth was readying itself for spring.

~

The next morning he waited. It had been enough days. He was sure that today, today it would come. He needed it to. And it did. The call came. A random number, a country code that looked like India. Most likely a calling card. A lottery ticket. He didn't pick up. It rang twice and the person hung up. He left the house and walked to a nearby payphone as they had planned, days and days ago. He waited. It rang. He picked up and said that one word:

'*Khairiyat?*'

'I've reached.'

They exhaled together.

'Where are you?'

When Aaftab was certain Wasim hadn't been followed, he told him quickly. Right before he put the phone down he paused and calling forth courage in his mouth, said, 'Will you tell Daya?'

Wasim wanted to say he would, if Daya ever called back. If she ever again spoke to him. He wanted to tell Aaftab her father was gone and she needed him so much, but he had spent days on the water and sounded so bereft of hope, all Wasim said was, 'I will, bhai.'

'Thank you.'

'Oh yaara …'

Just before he put the phone down he said, 'Bhai?'

'*Bol*,' Aaftab had said, sounding distracted already, nervous.

'You take care. Khuda hafiz.' He ended the call, without giving him the burden of his news.

~

Daya fell awake the way most people fall asleep. Not with the gradual drift of pollen in the spring but the sudden burst of evening lightning. Her waking moments never lasted more than a second. She had slept with the book in her arms and the cover was bent out of shape, warping Tolstoy's face. She had tried calling Aaftab's number the day before but it hadn't gone through. She considered calling Wasim now. Then as if the thought conjured him, Wasim called.

'Daya …'

'Wasim?' She hadn't recognized the new number.

They felt the silence expand and not contract between them, on hearing each other's voices.

'You should have told me,' he said finally. 'One of you should have.'

'I know. I'm sorry.'

'Did you not think I would understand?'

'It wasn't that.'

She wanted to explain to him how they were ashamed of themselves, never of him, but he felt like the one without a secret. He had been made the outsider. He had been made to feel unworthy of their quiet place and combined magic. And now he asked her all the questions he had wanted to ask Aaftab but that cruel circumstance had made impossible so that he had had to hold his tongue with one hand and punch a wall with the other. How fast everything had unravelled. Now Daya answered for both Aaftab and herself, which made it better in some ways but also worse in others. They were still a unit and he was still on the outside. They argued. What finally calmed him was her saying loudly, 'I don't even know where he is!'

Wasim fell silent then.

'That's why I've called,' he said quietly.

'What's wrong, Was?' she asked, fearful now.

He told her everything starting with the night of the gunshot. And then finally –

'Safi. He's in Safi.'

'Where's that?'

'Morocco.' Just as Idris had promised. 'I know people. They will take you by road to the Pakistani embassy in Rabat. And from there you will be able to go home. It may take some weeks, months even before they come, but in Safi you'll be safe, you have my word.' And to Ahab: 'Do not dock in Rabat. I repeat, do not dock in Rabat. I know you will be tired but continue to the fishing village of Safi.' Then to Aaftab: 'Smaller town, less checking.'

'I see,' Daya didn't know what else to say, it was all too much to put together.

'Do you?'

'Thank you for telling me all this. But it's my turn to say you should have told me before. I've spent days thinking he wanted to have nothing to do with me.'

'I'm sorry.'

'It's okay. I love you, Was. *Apna khyaal rakhna.*'

'And you. And Daya … I'm really so sorry about your father.'

'Allah hafiz.'

'Allah hafiz, jigar,' Wasim said, tired. There was no anger, there was simply nothing left.

~

Wasim sat in the same spot till sundown. Neither Aaftab nor Daya had asked him how he was. Perhaps that then was love. That nothing else mattered to them anymore. He was still curled up in bed when his phone rang, late in the night. He was cautious about answering it these days, more so because almost no one had this new number, but it was Daya.

'Was?'

'Yes?'

'It's me.'

'I know – why are you awake?'

'It's five. I couldn't sleep so thought I'd call. I wanted to ask – how are you?'

He told her everything and at the end they both held their phones as they might have each other, comfort reduced to a voice, voices expanding to become comfort itself. When they said goodnight, Wasim smiled sadly and realized that his heart felt a single degree lighter. That he was no longer convinced he was on this earth alone.

Perhaps this then was love.

~

Kamla had left just that morning for the first holiday of her life. She would be back soon but Asha had urged her to go.

'You haven't been home in a long, long time.'

'But this is home,' Kamla had insisted.

'Go. Go to the seaside, go anywhere!' Asha repeated.

So she went.

'Where have you decided to go?' Asha asked.

'Back to my parents. Just to show them I'm fine. Give them some money. See if they're okay.'

'They're alive?' Asha wanted to know.

'So I've heard.'

'Good. You'll be fine?'

'I will.'

'Go. I'll be fine too.'

Kamla looked disbelieving but could no longer argue with Asha.

Asha had taken the house apart room by room. She had insisted on doing it alone and had gone through years and years of their possessions, holding on to some, discarding others, smelling some, howling over others. Now there was only one thing left. She approached the last room. The room she had not had the courage to enter. 'No, say it,' she told herself. *The courage to enter without him.* The room that took up an entire floor of the building, a huge cloud-shaped hall of a room that a reluctant property broker had once said was a funeral parlour. Though Asha would not enter it, Kamla had continued throughout the long period of mourning to take care of Vaikuntha as they did before Gyan left. She watered the plants, though sometimes with nothing but tears. She dusted the little clay animals the couple collected, fixed the curtain finally, and replaced roses in vases. For reasons unknown to her, she still filled the blue jugs with water each day, hoping perhaps that Asha would come down but Asha had stayed stoutly upstairs. One jug of water on Gyan's desk always, and one by the mattress on a low table where he'd also kept an ashtray smoothed from a single piece of rock, besides whatever he was reading at the time.

Asha stood at the door to Vaikuntha. If this truly was heaven as they had called it, perhaps she would find Gyan there. Her hand felt like lead upon the handle, then she pushed and she was inside. Everything was silent save the violent sound of her heartbeat. The sheets had been washed earlier that week and were back on the mattress. She was scared of not smelling Gyan on them for the first time in her life.

Sun streamed in from the long, curved glass windows on the left. A few were open and the curtains rose gently to let the breeze pass. The thin white drapes were sewn with tiny silver bells, and she heard them now after what felt like years and they sounded like his laughter. Like the twinkle in his eye. She moved into the space and it began to embrace her. Even the air tasted of their love. She lay down on the mattress. She wept and wept. She fell asleep. She woke and drank water. She stretched and reached for the book on the bedside table, a carpentry manual – the last thing he had read, or rather, had been reading before they had had to read to him, and then he had only, inexplicably, wanted them to read Beatles biographies out loud. 'He's going back to what he loves,' Daya had said quietly one night and it had been true.

Asha walked around the room now, realizing for the first time since they'd bought the house, how very vast it was. His parents had called it indulgent and perhaps they hadn't been wrong. But what had they been indulging but their love? And now faced with the long years she would have to live without it, Asha was glad for their youthful impulsiveness. She walked to the music system and noticed Kamla had forgotten to wipe the dust from it. This made her smile. There was an old game Gyan and Kamla used to play, where she would challenge him to find one thing out of place, or wrong, or messy or undone in the house. He never could, and she would stand there triumphantly, arms crossed, duster over sharp shoulder, eyebrows wiggling. Asha pressed play and Nina Simone's voice filled the room. She stood in the centre and swayed, singing softly, eventually sinking to the floor, crying again.

Finally she stood up. She held her own arms in her own hands, hugging herself, and then took a deep breath and walked up to that spot where Gyan had spent hours and hours, reading books, scribbling notes, typing on his computer, with his feet up, or his legs crossed, sometimes standing when he was restless. She did not know if she could face it. Even when Gyan was alive she never sat there. His desk was his space. It was beautiful, inlaid with camel bone and brought over from Rajasthan as a tenth-anniversary present from her to him. In a house where nothing belonged to only one of them, they both always called that desk his.

Now she approached it like an intruder. She had very rarely been on the opposite side of the desk, always instead sitting before him in the tall, blue velvet armchair he had placed there for her. She touched the arms of his chair, thought of his elbows resting there. She sat. His hips had made room for hers. Looking out to Vaikuntha from this end of the house she realized what a beautiful view Gyan had had all these years. The entire vast spectrum of their love on display. The desk had two old silver frames in its corner, one with a photo of Daya as a little girl, fresh from ballet class, grinning ear to ear, pigtails lopsided, an ice cream cone in her hand. The other had a black-and-white image of Asha, taken a few years ago. She hadn't liked the photo and asked him why he had replaced the old one of her considerably younger self. 'I don't want to be that man,' he had said.

'What man?'

'You know, the one that stares at his wife's younger photo, like he's preserving her in a jar. You're real and you're mine and you're so beautiful even now even though you've gone a bit blind so you can't tell. But I want to look up and see *you*, not some young hottie. I mean … been there, done that, right?'

She smiled now at the memory. Thinking these thoughts had already stopped hurting with that awful ache of the last few weeks. Now it felt dulled, and the memories had stopped being an outright dagger and had regained some sweetness. She wanted the pain to go away entirely but knew that was perhaps impossible. Instead she had begun building a box inside the right side of her chest where she planned to place that pain. A second heart, only for him, so that the first she could keep for herself. She opened the drawer to the left and found his old passport, his face smooth and full and pink with health. She couldn't look at it for long and closed it now, shakily. The desk had droplets on it and she realized these were her tears and she was crying again. She opened the right drawer as distraction and saw one of his many folders, pushed into the space that was too small for it. She pulled it out and smoothed it down. Gyan had kept meticulous track of their finances and other matters to do with the business in hundreds of folders like this one, over the years. She opened it with an anxious thought. 'I'll need to learn how to do this now …'

And then she stopped and everything stopped.

Because it said:

He bowed to her like she was God and he knelt before her like he was preparing to pray. He entered her like she was the entire world, from the east like the sun enters the day with nothing but the need to fill it with light. He desired her constantly, like a devotee, even travelling to her memory each night in an impossible pilgrimage, doomed to be with her and only her. They met when he was twenty and she became his goddess and his religion, his temple and his sin.

They shared a flowered bedspread
a single cigarette
a few cups of tea
and ten thousand dreams.

They shared rain falling on demand
and the taste of two people merging
the intimacy of rivers with the sea
and how God had intended them to be.

And they forgot how to dress
and they remembered how to speak
and they gave up the past
and they let questions be.

And now within a chest full of secrets
and a closet full of lust
lies a stained bedsheet of blue flowers
covered in memories and dust.

It echoes of bruised thighs
flushed cheeks
and a million sighs
and of lovers who just for one moment
couldn't have asked for more.

And the pages were wet with tears and they were full of words and her heart was exploding because she understood Gyan was done. Gyan had finished. She rose and walked swiftly over to the kettle and made herself some tea. Then taking a sip and a single deep breath, Asha sat down in Gyan's chair and became the first person in the world to descend to heaven, as she began to read the story of how a boy met the girl he loved.

Postlude

He is sitting on the old city walls by the water, watching wave upon wave touch the shore. It is emerald and turquoise, this water. *Firozi*, he thinks. He dangles his legs and eats warm bread from the baker and cold oranges from the fruit-seller. If he jumps he will fall ten feet and then land on the narrow beach. Behind him is a small road leading to the town. He watches birds as they swoop and dip, kiss the water and rise again. The water glints where they touch it, as though their mouths are carrying gold. In the distance he can see boats out catching sardines. *A drift of fishermen*, he thinks, and smiles for a moment. The town behind him is mostly silent. He has heard of a lighthouse nearby and plans to visit it one of these days. That thought tires him now and suddenly the sun seems very bright. He closes his eyes. The insides of his eyelids are red and warm and full of images. He opens them again and the world is blue. He turns to go but knows that he has hundreds of hours ahead of him in which he will not have anything to do. It is the long emptiness that is torture. He gathers the paper bag full of bread and oranges and turns, swinging his feet around to the short side of the wall. As he stands he takes one last look at the beach. There he sees something almost translucent, between the shimmers that dance off the water, walking towards him now in silhouette, against a horizon so long you can see the earth's curve, a boy and a girl … and now he is weeping, and he is laughing, and he is running towards them faster and faster, because he is certain he knows them both.

Acknowledgements

I began writing this book in 2007 but put it away a few years later when I realized I knew enough about neither the world nor love. Thirteen years rack up a lot of debts, and though I have tried to recall them all, forgive me if you do not find your name here but ought to. It is very much in my heart.

Tushaar Mehra. Thank you for believing in me so much, that when I showed you a few scribbles more than a decade ago, you put me immediately in touch with Shruti Debi, saying, 'This should be a book.'

Shruti. You who had the wisdom to say no to so many pieces of writing before finally saying, 'Yes, this is it.' The truth must be told: you are neither agent nor editor, but fairy godmother who played perfect midwife to my parchment baby even while bringing a real one into this world. Thank you for your tenacity; it really has seen this book through, but thank you equally for your humour; it is what saw me through. I adore you.

The extended Misras, Parikhs and Rays.

Ishaan Nair, my first and fiercest champion. Chandni Arora, my forever boo. Thank you both for believing long before I did.

Auroni Mookerjee, thank you for introducing me to

Sheema Mookerjee. Sheema, many of the things you advised then, echo even now.

Siya Bhalla, for that conversation all those years ago and for giving me Aaftab's 'flooded river of traditions' and the poem in chapter 18.

Thandi Matthews, for scrutinizing Colin's story so carefully, all the way from South Africa.

Kakul Gautam, for giving me Urdu words in between swimming with dolphins, and for always inspiring.

Aanchal Malhotra, for all our chats on writing, for being the first person to listen to the plot from start to finish, for allowing me to reference your book *Remnants of a Separation* in chapter 16, and for reading this novel and giving me swoon-worthy praise.

Avni Doshi, for reading the manuscript so swiftly during such an important time for yourself, and for saying the things you have about it.

Prayaag Akbar, for reading this twice, once while shifting cities with a baby and two cats, and still finding the time to send me such detailed, thoughtful comments, notes and now a blurb! Bless.

Nilanjana Roy, for appearing as an angel at the very last moment and giving me your blessings. Your kindness will not be forgotten.

Lisa Ray. My guiding sister, thank you for being the immensely warm, real, vital human you are, and for making time for this book, and for me, always. So very grateful our paths crossed.

To Sunita Misra whose tears reminded me words have the power to move, and Mushtaq Salim whose love for Gyan and Asha gave me faith in their story.

Diya Katyal, my bae, for reading the manuscript in two

days flat, and for investing in it so deeply and with such joy.

Anirudh Nair, for reading everything I have ever sent you over the last twenty years, and for your precise feedback on this novel. You will see that I heeded most of it!

Ela Jhaveri, whose faith in reading and in human equality are key components of this book, and who introduced me to the wonderful Ann Patchett.

Ann, your generosity is astounding – thank you for letting your name grace this book.

Saba Azad, my love, for being the reason Daya is a dancer and for checking my Punjabi on the day your niece was born and you had far more exciting things to do!

Neha Kaul Mehra, for every conversation on imposter syndrome, for laying down hard truths when I needed them, and balle balles when I deserved them. Thank you, Enkayemm, yaara.

Mihika Tewari, thank you for everything, always, my top bird, but also for Between The Covers, the little book club that could, and its precious permanent members. Becky, Shivi, Mihi, thank you for doing me the honour of making this book one of ours.

To everyone who learnt of my work through the noisy world of social media, thank you for following, 'hearting', sharing, and for staying patiently on this journey with me.

Shilo Shiv Suleman and Haitenlo Semy for creating the jacket for the book's original hardcover edition, and Rhea Gupte for taking on so gracefully the challenge of reinventing it. Your art and your life are reminders of what is precious in this world. Thank you, Rhea.

Haitenlo Semy, for your seamless sense of design and eye for perfection.

Dipika Dasgupta, your praise for this book reached me on a very hard day, and brightened it considerably. Thank you for your edits.

R. Ajith Kumar, 'typeset' seems almost too simple a word for the alchemy of turning a manuscript finally into a work of art. Thank you for doing so repeatedly with every new version I sent.

Bharti Taneja, Ditsha Gupta and all those I haven't had the pleasure of meeting but who I know worked behind the scenes at Pan Macmillan India – thank you for giving this book a home after it had wandered the world without one for so many years.

Teesta Guha Sarkar, writers dream of having an editor like you. It could not have been anyone but you. Thank you for having faith, for treading these pages so gently, and for cutting a path through the thick woods of words, when necessary. It's been such a great pleasure and immense joy to create this with you.

Nayantara and Danika Parikh, thank you for being excited even on days I wasn't, and turning excitement to empathy, the way only sisters can. I love you so much – you are my heroes. The real reason I wrote this book is to finally be worthy of you both.

My parents, a dedication is not enough. Ma, especially you, for the eagle-eye edits. Thank you, both, sincerely, for the wings and ten thousand other things.

And finally, Amitesh Ray, for reminding me that wings are made of feathers and feathers can be turned into quills. I always had a love of language, but it is you who gave me the language of love, and urged me to create a space for myself in this world. Thus, I was finally able to tell the story I wanted to. Thank you, jaan. There is no exaggeration when I say that without you, this book, this story, and most of all, Aaftab, would not exist.

Notes

The Markova School of Dance is entirely imagined but was named so in the book as a tribute to the dancer Alicia Markova.

The poem, 'At the Place of Execution' (Sar-e-Maqtal), on the cover in Urdu and in English in chapter 3, is from *Poems by Faiz*, Faiz Ahmed Faiz, translated, with an Introduction and Notes by V. G. Kiernan, Oxford University Press, 1971. The translation that appears in the book has been adapted from Kiernan as well.

All collective nouns and the legend of the Book of St Albans were sourced from *An Exaltation of Larks*, James Lipton, Penguin Books, 1993.

I Only Have To Close My Eyes, which Gyan adapts in chapter 8, is the most wonderful children's book by Kenneth Williams, now sadly out of print but originally published by J. M. Dent & Sons Ltd, 1986.

The story about Manto in Chapter 10 I owe to Shashank 'Sunny' Arora who traced the original through the wonderful Nandita Das. It appears in Manto's sketch about his friendship with the actor Shyam, 'Murli Ki Dhun', as well as in the short story, 'Sahay'. Das aptly calls the incident 'the straw that broke the camel's back'.

The details of the interview between Oriana Fallaci and Ayatollah Khomeini were sourced from Margaret Talbot's piece, 'The Agitator', published in the *New Yorker*, 5 June 2006.

The line Aaftab quotes to Daya – 'To thine own self be true' – is Polonius in William Shakespeare's *Hamlet*.

The spoof advertisement for an imam in chapter 17 first appeared in 1997 in the Muslim youth magazine *Trends*, and I learnt about it in ex-editor Inayat Bungalwala's article about it, which appeared in the *Guardian* on 5 June 2007.

The title of the book is inspired by the opening line of a poem Emily Dickinson wrote in 1924, which was borrowed in 1993 by the composer Michael Nyman for what is arguably the most celebrated track in his soundtrack for the Oscar-winning Jane Campion film, *The Piano*.